1978

On the Prehistory of Marriage

Classics in Anthropology
Rodney Needham, Editor

Josef Köhler

Josef Kohler

On the Prehistory of Marriage

Totemism, Group Marriage, Mother Right

Translated from the German by
R. H. Barnes and Ruth Barnes

Edited and with an Introduction by R. H. Barnes

University of Chicago Press
Chicago and London

R. H. Barnes has taught at the University of Southern
California and the University of Edinburgh. His publications include Kédang: A Study of Collective Thought
of an Eastern Indonesian People.

The University of Chicago Press, Chicago 60637

The University of Chicago Press, Ltd., London

© 1975 by The University of Chicago

All rights reserved. Published 1975

Printed in the United States of America

Library of Congress Cataloging in Publication Data

Kohler, Josef, 1849-1919.
    On the prehistory of marriage.

    (Classics in anthropology)
    Translation of Zur Urgeschichte der Ehe.
    Bibliography: p.
    Includes index.
    1. Marriage--History. 2. Kinship. 3. Society,
Primitive. I. Title.
HQ504.K64   301.42   74-11626
ISBN 0-226-45024-4

Contents

Editor's Preface

The English version of Kohler's book on the antecedents of
marriage offered here deviates in several ways from the
German original. Kohler's prolix sentences, for example,
have been broken down and his paragraphs altered. But we
have tried to keep as close as possible to the literal
sense of the original, while making those tacit concessions
to good style and readability which were absolutely necessary; and we hope it conveys as clearly as possible
Kohler's actual meaning.

Kohler's use of the words Totem and Stamm provides a
particular difficulty. Reflecting the uncertain use of
the terms in the ethnological writings of the time,
Kohler's employment of them confuses a variety of ideas
which we should today keep separate. With the word Totem,
Kohler sometimes intends the totem animal, sometimes the
totem group or even the institution of totemism. Stamm
may refer to tribe, clan, family, or even, in Australia, a
class in a section system. We have tried to render the
terms in the sense intended, but they reflect an analytic
confusion, not entirely to be resolved through correct

translation; and the reader is advised to refer to the original when in doubt.

    Kohler's genealogical diagrams in chapter 3 required
recasting to make them accord with modern conventions.
The essential changes are these: Kohler employs a solid dot
to represent a man, a wedge or reclining right triangle to
represent a woman, vertical or slanting lines to represent
descent, and a horizontal line to represent marriage. In
keeping with present practice, a triangle is used for a
man, a circle for a woman; descent is indicated by a vertical line, marriage by an equals sign, and a sibling relation by a bracket above the pair. These differences may be
seen by comparing these two versions of one of Kohler's
diagrams taken from page 113 of the original. The first
is as Kohler drew it; the second shows the form it is
given in this translation.

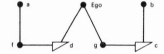 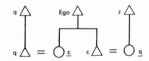

    As can be seen, in some of the diagrams we have also
altered the letters used to indicate the various relatives.
It seemed almost necessary to standardize their employment
during much of the first part of the chapter. Later,
Kohler changes to another topic and style of presentation,
and it no longer seemed necessary or convenient to continue
to change them. Other than one or two modifications of
little consequence, the diagrams in all other respects are
as Kohler published them.

For this edition a bibliography and index have been
provided. The entries in the bibliography are, insofar as
they could be determined, the editions used by Kohler. In
the interest of economy, footnotes have, where possible,
been incorporated into the text. Tribal names have been
given their modern forms; for the North American Indians,
G. P. Murdock's Ethnographic Bibliography of North America
(1960) has been taken as the standard; elsewhere reference
has been to the original ethnography. Quotations have been
checked with the original, but otherwise page references
and the general accuracy of Kohler's reading of his sources
have been examined only when they have been locally available.

I should like to express my gratitude to Dr. Rodney
Needham, who minutely examined an early draft of the first
chapter and then read the Introduction and complete final
translation, and to Dr. James J. Fox, who gave both the
translation and the Introduction a careful reading. Their
suggestions and corrections have resulted in many material
improvements. Thanks are also due my father for his as-
sistance in translating the quotation in ancient Spanish
from Venegas.

R. H. B.

Editor's Introduction

For over three-quarters of a century, since the publication
in 1897 of Josef Kohler's Zur Urgeschichte der Ehe, a
topic which has come to be known as "the Crow-Omaha problem" has received the most persistent comparative and
theoretical attention by anthropologists, resulting in a
burgeoning literature and several ambitious attempts at its
solution. With hardly an exception, the leading figures of
each subsequent period have had something to contribute to
the question, and several would regard their efforts in
this direction as among their central achievements.

By all indications, the care and attention lavished on
this subject should have brought us to a point of advanced
understanding. Here, if anywhere, social anthropology
should be able to point to a secure store of analytic and
theoretical accomplishments, comparable perhaps only to
those in the literature of prescriptive alliance, dual
symbolic organization, or complementary governance. Yet,
perplexingly, the successful issue from all this labor
appears to have remained in abeyance. The plans for what
we might have expected to be a major book on the subject by

one of the most eminent of present-day social anthropologists have been abandoned, and we have been assured that
the difficulties entailed in the analysis of Crow-Omaha
systems "are in the province, not of the social anthropologist, but of the mathematician."[1] Another authority
has concluded variously that "there exists no general explication of Crow-Omaha terminologies," that an intensive
comparative survey of such terminologies and their social
contexts is "surely one of the most pressing and important
tasks in this field of social anthropology," that "nothing
of any real elucidatory value" has resulted from all the
attention given them, and more radically that "there exists no useful generalization about this factitious class
of Omaha terminologies."[2]

It can be argued that the only solid analytic advance in this area was given prominence jointly by Kohler
in his book and by Durkheim in his review of it in 1897,[3]
to wit, that the Omaha distribution of terms accords with a
patrilineal rule of descent, the Crow (or as Kohler called
it the Choctaw) distribution with a matrilineal rule.
This was indeed a fundamental advance and a permanent
achievement which has been continually cited since its
discovery,[4] and if it were the only virtue of Kohler's
book--which it is not--it alone would be sufficient reason
to make this work at last available to an English-reading
public.

There are, however, additional points justifying the
interest of a modern public, and these will be set out more

fully later. Kohler presents for the first time detailed
and diagrammatic studies of relationship systems approach-
ing the scope which scholars have come to regard as essential to modern investigations. Secondly, we may expect
that the time has finally come for the sort of intensive
comparative survey of Crow-Omaha systems mentioned above,
and any such survey must begin with the work which initiated this line of speculative interest, demonstrated its
only undisputed analytic achievement, and even gave it a
name. Finally, Kohler was a leading jurist with an international following who made great and continuous contributions to topics in social anthropology throughout his
lifetime, and did so from an original and by now (for most
anthropologists) unfamiliar philosophical position. On
the Prehistory of Marriage may allow us to make a re-
acquaintance with this most interesting side of our
intellectual antecedents.

I

Josef Kohler was professor of law at the University of
Berlin from 1888 until his death in 1919. He had held a
previous chair at the University of Würzburg from 1878.
He has been described as the only universal jurist of his
time and the foremost of (then) living jurists.[5] He was
known particularly for his research into universal legal
history and the philosophy of law, about which he wrote a
standard text that went through many editions and was
translated into English.[6] His efforts, however, extended
into all branches of the field, and he made particularly

notable contributions to the law of immaterial rights, the
law of patents, copyright, and trademarks, as well as
criminal law[7] and--of special interest here--to the comparative study of legal systems with particular reference
to ancient civilizations and to simple societies of the
present era.

Leonhard Adam remarked that it was plainly impossible
for a single individual to make an accurate estimation of
all of Kohler's contributions, and difficult to acquire a
general view of them. In order to master his complete
scholarship in the area of jurisprudence, one would have
to be a jurist with knowledge of all its special areas; to
assess his legal philosophy, one would have to be a phil-
osopher; to understand his rich contributions to universal
legal history, one would have to be an expert cultural
historian, orientalist, or ethnologist.[8]

Kohler's total literary productions themselves seem
to exceed human capacities. His final bibliography of
over 2,500 titles took his son ten years to collect and
includes 104 titles appearing in book form. Eighty-six
percent of the entries pertain to jurisprudence and legal
history (including ethnology); the rest touch on the major
world religions and Asian and European philosophy, history,
sociology, art, music, aesthetics, and literature (including publications on Dante, Petrarch, Shakespeare, Cer-
vantes, Camões, Goethe, Schiller, and Richard Wagner).
There are many publications containing personal opinion,
reminiscence, and travel accounts plus fictional and

poetic works and humorous sketches, including a free
translation of the <u>Divine</u> <u>Comedy</u>, translations from Petrarch, Lao-tzu, and Shakespeare's <u>King</u> <u>Richard</u> <u>II</u>, a novel
(<u>Eine</u> <u>Faustnatur</u>) and two novella. He also published
twenty-five songs, influenced of course by Wagner.

Kohler was a robust and inexhaustible man; and the
breadth of his productions brought the reputation of a
"universal genius" and inevitable comparison to Goethe,
Hegel, Wagner, Nietzsche, and other Promethean figures of
nineteenth-century German life. He attracted an international following through his publications and courses at
Berlin, his influence being greatest apparently in Japan,
Italy, and Greece. Enthusiastic Japanese students bought
his library after his death, transported it to Tokyo, and
reestablished it as the "Josef Kohler Library," only to
see it destroyed by the earthquake of 1 September 1933.[9]
Full recognition of his importance seems to have come in
Germany only after he was awarded an honorary doctorate by
the University of Chicago (1904) and given honorary membership by a number of foreign scholarly societies.[10] He is
said never to have founded a school of followers,[11] as
certain other jurists did, but a great many subsequently
influential persons attended his courses, including the
social anthropologists Max Schmidt and Richard Thurnwald.
In 1930 an American nominee to the World Court was compared
by American colleagues to the late Josef Kohler "in fecun-
dity and range of creation."[12]

His fertility in scholarship was matched by his

linguistic accomplishments; and indeed his work is stamped
by the realization that no people can be really understood
without a knowledge of their language, and that, especially, comparative jurisprudence demands an allegiance with
the linguistic sciences. Kohler is said to have mastered
all Germanic and Romance languages, to have had a good
knowledge of Hebrew and Sanskrit, and to have made himself
familiar with the structure and fundamentals of several
other European languages.[13]

How Kohler could have mustered the energy to accom-
plish so much may be explained by what Leonhard Adam calls
Kohler's spartan simplicity. In youth and in the prime of
his life he made only the most measured use of alcohol, and
during his last twenty years was completely abstinent. He
never smoked during his whole life. He employed a strict
division and use of his time; for many years he worked
every night until four in the morning, slept very little,
and usually appeared for lectures by 8:00 A.M. From the
winter semester of 1878/79 until the summer semester of
1919 he held lectures and seminars on all aspects of jurisprudence for as many as twenty-seven hours a week, a far
heavier load than that of any of his colleagues at the University in Berlin.[14]

His prolificacy extended to professional journals
as well. He was founder, editor or publisher, and usually
principle contributor, of seven periodicals,[15] including
the leading journal for the philosophy of law (Archiv für
Rechts- und Wirtschaftsphilosophie) and that for compara-

tive law (<u>Zeitschrift</u> <u>für</u> <u>vergleichende</u> <u>Rechtswissenschaft</u>).
What is more, he managed to keep abreast of current publi-
cations in all languages in each of these areas, as is
shown by extensive series of book reviews published under
his name in the journals with which he was associated. He
was member or honorary fellow of at least eleven professional societies in six countries, ranging as far afield
as the Greek Philological Society at Constantinople, the
Genootschap van Kunsten en Wetenschappen of Batavia, the
Koninklijk Instituut voor Taal-, Land- en Volkenkunde van
Nederlandsch-Indië, and the Société Académique Indo-
Chinoise in Paris.[16]

II

Josef Kohler's seventieth birthday on 9 March 1919 was the
occasion for two **Festschriften**, the third and fourth of his
career.[17] Close friends and admirers who celebrated the
occasion in his home[18] retained the impression of a man
with many fruitful years of scholarly activity remaining
to him. This seems to have been his own opinion, for he
wrote at the time that he felt the full strength of his
powers and planned more work. His death five months later,
3 August 1919, was quite unexpected.[19]

Contemporaries associated his death with the ter-
rible disruption Germany suffered after its defeat in
World War I and with his remorse over the shattering of
his pronounced internationalism.[20] Kohler too was caught
up in the general war enthusiasm that seized Germany in
1914, which even turned pacifists into nationalists over-

night, professors and artists into propagandists.[21] Like
other prominent Germans (Gerhart Hauptmann, Thomas Mann),
he published a number of angry writings in support of the
German cause, in which he believed implicitly until the
end, though he regretted much of this after the war. But
his shattered expectations, according to Osterrieth, may
well have removed his will to live.[22]

Josef Kohler was born on 9 March 1849 in the
southern German town of Offenburg--just across the Rhine
from Strasbourg--in the Grand Duchy of Baden. His father,
named Josef before him, was a teacher in the local elementary school and found his modest circumstances endangered
by his having taken part in a revolutionary meeting in
the same year of his son's birth--at a time when Offenburg,
which had absorbed much of the spirit of the French revolution, was one of the centers of Baden's own revolution.
Josef Kohler, the younger, was the last of three children
and was born when his mother, Amalie Schmider from nearby
Zell am Harmersbach, was forty years of age.

From his mother he acquired a Celtic heritage to
which he attributed traits of serenity, cheerfulness, a
sense of the beauty of life, and adaptability. From his
father he felt he had inherited a certain mystical bent, a
strong sensuality, his philosophical talent, a certain
nervous haste in choosing his life's goals, and whatever
acquisitiveness he had.[23]

Despite his parents' limited means, he attended the
humanistic Gymnasium (high school) in Offenburg and (in

his last year) the Gymnasium in Rastatt. The intellectual
limits and mechanical methods of these schools left him
with a painful memory of these times. His family also
provided limited cultural sustenance, though his father
taught him to play the piano and violin and instructed him
in the elements of counterpoint.[24]

At seventeen he left school and went to spend
several months with his mother's brother in Pruntrut,
Switzerland, a French-speaking town near Berne. His uncle
was a wealthy merchant with lively cultural interests, and
during his stay Kohler learned to translate Plato and
Tacitus into French. He was introduced for the first time
to a sense of social grace and culture after a French
style. Here he became acquainted with Shakespeare, Dante,
and Chopin, who remained important figures for him for
the rest of his life.[25]

Forced to choose a profession in which he could
support himself (ein Brotstudium), he took up law, which
he then pursued with enthusiasm. None of his teachers at
Freiburg, where he spent his first four semesters, or at
Heidelberg, where he finished, seems to have left a strong
impression on him. The most famous of them, K. A. Vangerow
at Heidelberg, apparently disappointed him. Kohler later
spoke of Vangerow as displaying "a certain fanaticism for
a tightly closed circle of ideas." Kohler was too slight
in build to be drafted for the Franco-Prussian War of
1870-71, which occurred while he was at the university. He
passed his first and second examinations in 1871 and 1873

with a distinction that was remembered by his teachers for
many years.[26]

After completing his university studies, Kohler became a clerk to a lawyer in Mannheim. He was soon given a
position on the military court in Mannheim, and in this
position he was quickly drawn into the commercial life of
this large industrial city.

> I was thrust into the midst of a great com-
> mercial traffic. For hours I watched the Rhine
> from its bridge, following in spirit the water on
> its way to the mighty ocean and its proud ships.
> The Rhine steamers arrived and departed majestical-
> ly, cargo was loaded and unloaded. Questions of an
> entirely new nature swarmed before my eyes, ques-
> tions of which Vangerow and his Pandects had heard
> nothing. Fortunes of thousands of marks hung by a
> thread. The struggle between honesty and sneaking
> imposture, intellect versus the blind but cunning
> vampyrism in trade, work versus base idleness--all
> of this suddenly assaulted me, and at night I
> struggled with legal questions in my dreams... A
> modern life absorbed me; I greeted each question
> which grew out of this life almost with jubilation.[27]

Kohler began publishing scholarly contributions in
response to his practical experiences in the city almost
as soon as he arrived in Mannheim. A question from a
client drew him into the controversy surrounding patent
law, which was then in an underdeveloped state in Germany
and the cause for an intellectual and political struggle
of considerable consequence. Kohler published his important Deutsches Patentrecht in 1877 and 1878 and was re-
warded with a teaching position at the University of
Würzburg in October 1878, during his thirtieth year.[28]

Here he earnestly set about his new teaching and
scholarly duties, expanding the horizons of his legal
researches well beyond those of any predecessor, while at

the same time producing numerous essays and discussions on
art, literature, and music. Some of the latter, such as
his <u>Shakespeare</u> <u>vor</u> <u>dem</u> <u>Forum</u> <u>der</u> <u>Jurisprudenz</u> (1883),[29]
combined his legal with his literary interests. During
this period Kohler also greatly extended his reading of
literature, especially Russian and French; Goethe's complete works, Zola, Flaubert, Daudet, Gogol, Dostoevski,
Turgenev, and Ibsen occupied him in Würzburg. Nevertheless,
he came to feel restricted in Würzburg, whose rich baroque
art did not appeal to him,[30] and was pleased when he was
called to Berlin in 1888.

The Berlin appointment he called the "greatest event
in my life." Kohler was especially impressed by the
library of the Humboldt University and by the faculty which
contained so many leading figures of the various branches
of knowledge.[31] From them he learned much, but according
to Osterrieth his inner development was completed by the
time he arrived in Berlin.[32]

Kohler's first courses in Berlin were in civil litigation, French civil law, and comparative jurisprudence.
He later added lectures in criminal law, civil law in its
various branches, criminal litigation, commercial law,
introduction to law, legal philosophy in conjunction with
comparative jurisprudence, and finally international law.
The courses were well attended; in some as many as five
hundred students enrolled.[33]

His schedules left little time for entertainment.
Though he visited the concert and theater, he withdrew from

social life soon after moving to Berlin. But he used all
his vacations, four each year, for travel. These trips,
through much of Europe, to Egypt, Algiers, and the United
States, were frequently described in travel accounts for
Berlin newspapers.[34]

Despite his many successes, Kohler was for many years
bitter that he had not received sufficient recognition.[35]
Though this eventually changed, he never felt quite at
home in Prussia. In South Germany he was accustomed to
unrestricted self-expression, in which imagination and a
vivid emotional life were highly valued. He was offended
by the cool reserve and sober factuality of the northern
Germans and by the strictness and formality of social life
in the circles of the academics and higher civil servants.
But he also gave offense by his unrestrained expression of
opinions and feelings and by his utter lack of respect for
persons, especially representatives of older schools of
jurisprudence to which he was opposed. He could be willful
and would stand no contradiction. Osterrieth says of him
that he lacked any knowledge of human nature and was un-
practiced in the art of handling men.[36]

It was often charged that he did not give adequate
acknowledgment to other men's ideas of which he made
use.[37] Rabel even suggests that Kohler held an inflated
idea of his own originality. In any case, Kohler had
vehement opponents, as well as many admirers--including,
according to Rabel, a sort of Byzantine court of insipid
flatterers.[38]

His family were good Catholics, but Kohler was never himself a strict follower of any church. His personal be-
liefs and philosophical position tended more toward a form
of pantheism, though his Catholic background can be dis-
cerned in the course taken by his work. Adam, at least,
attributes his leaning toward the political center to
this influence. Kohler was for the most part unpolitical
and contributed to journals of various political allegian-
ces, but he always showed a tendency toward liberalism.
After the revolution of 1919, he joined the German Demo-
cratic Party (Deutsche Demokratische Partei)--a party of
liberal parliamentarians.[39]

III

To capture Kohler's central philosophy, we may turn to two
resounding declarations from the preface to his Philosophy
of Law. "A unity of spirit rules mankind, and evolution
forces its way out of universal substance." "Materialism
is dead; the philosophy of spirit still lives."[40]

    Josef Kohler was the leading figure of a school of
legal philosophy which dubbed itself Neo-Hegelian. In
essence he followed Hegel in his rejection of the Kantian
dualism between subject and object, regarding it as the
chief error of Kant's philosophy, exaggerated into a
monstrosity. Kant's whole system of thought, Kohler asserted, is a maze, "a mental gymnastic exercise with the
most monstrous movements and distortions in which the
straight is bent crooked and the crooked straight." Its
principal error bears the unmistakable mark of its ante-

cedents in the skepticism of Hume and Berkeley. According-
ly, Kohler recommends the abandonment of Kantian dualism
and the free profession of monism.[41]

Hegel, in Kohler's view, demolished Kant's dualism
in his Philosophy of Identity, where he showed that there
is only a relative difference between subject and object
and that there is no confrontation between the ego and the
external world. "Essentially the activity in the external
world and the activity of our own ego are the same, and
each of us is 'a breath of eternity.'"[42]

This monism rests on a form of pantheism which
recognizes behind human history an Idea, the universal
spirit (Allseele), which expresses itself in historical
development. To monism, Kohler adds the Hegelian idea of
evolution, "the scientific principle of all mental science,
of our whole history, and of everything that lives and
moves in our human culture."[43] Evolution works itself out
through human culture, which is the "totality of humanity's
achievements," "the highest possible development of human
knowledge and . . . the highest possible development of
human control of nature."[44] Knowledge and power, the
highest cultural goods, are the divine aspect of humanity.
The ultimate end of cultural evolution is the progressive
revelation of the divine. In a pun on the word Erlösung
(salvation, literally "release"), Kohler declares that it
is not God who redeems humanity, but mankind who releases
divinity.[45]

Accepting from Hegel's philosophy its monism and its

evolutionary doctrine, Kohler rejects Hegel's famous logical dialectic. He follows the criticism of Schopenhauer
and Nietzsche, taking the view that "the logic of the
world's history is mixed with much that is illogical." Not
everything develops in accordance with a definite logical
spirit. "Side by side with reason, stands its opposite,"
but in the final development of world history, reason
triumphs.[46]

Kohler may be said to subscribe to a theory of uni-
linear evolution, but in his case it is far from being as
rigid as similar nineteenth-century evolutionary theories.
Indeed, he speaks of the "unmeasured multifariousness" of
evolution, and the charming, often tragic diversity of history. "Even if progress appears certain, yet the way is
altogether uncertain." The magnificent sometimes perishes
never to return; there are sometimes pathological periods
of strong decline, directly opposed to the course of human
development; "reason and brutality operate side by side
with wisdom and stability," and therefore it is possible
for thought to advance beyond the current pace of human
progress.[47] He argues that evolution within one people
may proceed unequally, so that one aspect of their culture
may advance while another stagnates; and it is even possible
for a culture to regress.[48] "Without question, not everything in history develops according to a particular cycle
and in keeping with the law of a predetermined series;
rather, everything moves in accordance with endless con-
tingencies, so that at best a certain wave-like rhythm can

be observed only in large segments of time." He quotes
approvingly Goethe's comment that God does not draw up the
week's reckoning every day of the week.[49]

Kohler parts with Hegel in this regard and gives full
recognition to the individuality of historical events.
"History must be studied in its detail."[50] But how are we
to estimate the importance or value of the individual
historical event? This is the point at which science
knocks at the gates of metaphysics. The higher value of
an event can only be measured by its influence on subsequent history. When a royal speech impediment leads to the
use of le carrosse instead of la carrosse in the French language, it is obviously a strong intervention in the course
of events, but the question remains whether the result has
any importance beyond the mere fact itself? This however is
a teleological question which can only be answered with the
help of metaphysics, for it requires measuring the
favorable or unfavorable consequences of the event on the
progress of culture.[51]

The individual event is not thereby unrelated to
higher historical purposes; it is part of both a narrower
and a wider sphere of occurrences. It is in any case an
expression of the universal spirit; despite itself, it is in
the service of the higher power. The purely contingent in
history is eventually to be seen as a function of the universal spirit. Expectably, Kohler rejects nominalism, and
declares his allegiance to the realism of mediaeval scholas-
ticism. He refers to the authority of Anselm of Canterbury

to the effect that concepts are not merely the product of
human abstraction but are archetypes with an existence
quite different from the reality of mere phenomena, though
the reality of these phenomena is not to be doubted.
Kohler's realism leads to the view that the teleological
connection of historical events is a reality standing in
the same relation to individual happenings as archetypal
concepts stand to individual objects.[52]

The methods of legal philosophy must be those of cultural history, ethnic psychology, sociology, philosophy of
history, and finally metaphysics. An institution must be
examined from all sides. Kohler opposed the nonhistorical
Natural Law theories of Kant, and for him one of the principal tasks of Neo-Hegelianism was to combat the Neo-
Kantian school of Stammler and others, which he regarded as
unhistorical and worthless.[53]

At the same time Kohler avoided the limits of a purely
historical approach; and though he rejected positivism, he
was sympathetic to sociology and considered it an essential
part of jurisprudence. In fact, he translated Kant's categorical imperative into the social voice (soziale Stimme),
the reminder to the individual of the unity of society. The
social instincts belong to the mightiest drives of humanity.[54] In contrast to cultural history, sociology is not
only historical, it also is a subject which searches for the
laws of social development (Vergesellschaftung). But sociology cannot encompass all of history, for it is limited to
the factors of socialization and the formation of groups;

hence it does not even include all of the more or less
regular influences on culture, such as those of ecology
and geography. History is only partly free of contingency,
and sociology concerns itself with only one of the regular
factors of culture.[55]

Implied in his many-pronged approach is a strong
element of relativism. Culture is nothing fixed but is in
constant motion, constantly changing. There is also no
static ideal behind it. Each culture and each period
develops according to its own ideal of progress.[56] Law
provides the appropriate order to culture. It has a co-
ercive influence on the individual because it is a rational
influence suited to contemporary culture and therefore
corresponds with an inner (social) human drive.[57] This
formulation leads Kohler to speak of the tremendous relativity of law. "Law cannot remain unaltered. It must
adapt itself to a constantly advancing culture." There is
no eternal law. "The law that is suitable for one period
is not so for another." This view corresponds with the
rejection of any Natural Law theory. But Kohler also rejects the positivists' view of law, for he acknowledges
that existing law may for one reason or another not always
be the law best suited to existing culture.[58]

Since, like other aspects of culture, law works itself
out through the human soul, legal philosophy must resort to
ethnic psychology to see what effect the collective soul of
a people may have on the expression of its law. The constant struggle between the individual and society is one of

the most important factors in the progress of law, and for
this reason sociological methods are indispensable. Legal
evolution is a historical process, requiring the attention
of cultural history. Since history has a pantheistic background, metaphysics must be brought to the interpretation
of law. Finally, the function of law is to secure and in-
crease the progress of culture.[59]

One of the most original contributions made by Kohler
was to help widen German legal scholarship to include the
comparative study of the institutions of simple societies
and ancient civilizations. Kohler was one of the founders
and the leading German practitioner of comparative law or
ethnological jurisprudence. The latter term was first
coined by Albert Hermann Post, who published the first book
on the subject in 1872,[60] before Kohler's own work; but
according to Leonhard Adam, this book was of little scholarly depth, and Kohler is not to be regarded as a follower
of Post.[61] The leading journal in the subject, Zeitschrift
für vergleichende Rechtswissenschaft, was founded in 1880
by Franz Bernhöft and Georg Cohn. Kohler did not join it
as associate editor until its third volume in 1882, but he
was the leading spirit of the journal from then until his
death. In recognition of this fact, his name was placed on
the cover of the journal as cofounder, beginning in 1920
with volume 38.[62]

The principal purpose of comparative jurisprudence was
to provide an evolutionary history of legal institutions.[63]
This goal was in keeping with the historical and cultural

relativism of the Neo-Hegelians and with their ambitions
to establish a universal history. The comparative method
was regarded as an alternative where historical material
failed, adequate to reveal the prehistory of modern legal
institutions. Kohler's views in this area show the strong
influence of nineteenth-century anthropologists, Bachofen
(with whom he had personal contact), McLennan, and especially Morgan, particularly in their adherence to the idea that
human society has passed through universal stages of evolution, beginning with matriarchy, totemism, and group
marriage.

Kohler's massive output did not escape considerable
criticism. One charge was that his views were vitiated by
an excessive relativity.[64] Another perennial complaint was
that he never gave a proper definition of culture;[65] and
indeed his view of culture as the greatest possible development of human knowledge and control over nature, (even
though faithful to the etymology of the word "culture")
must seem strange to modern readers, as does his teleological philosophy of history, his pantheism, his evolutionary theory and its attendant realism. An associate and
follower admits that he never achieved a closed philosophical system. The heterogeneous sources of his intellectual
inspiration, including the Vedanta philosophers, Lao-tzu,
Persian Sufis, Averroës, Eckhart, Thomas Aquinas, Duns
Scotus, Hobbes, Fichte, Hegel, and Nietzsche were never
fully brought into reconciliation.[66]

His comparative monographs were greeted by some as the

products of a merely private interest in exotic cultures
and without relevance to modern jurisprudence. His methods
were criticized as superficial, and his series of monographs
were looked upon as little more than collections of curiosities. His manifold productions brought him in some
quarters the reputation of a Vielschreiber; and Adam acknowledges that it would have been better if he had left
some of his works unwritten.[67] In any case, for a man with
an artistic and literary bent, he could be surprisingly
careless about the form in which he presented his argument,
disregarding the niceties of expression and clarity, excessive in his use of verbal short cuts, inexact in his
attribution of sources, and showing signs of haste in
exposition.

It is enough to acknowledge these points. It should
be recalled, though, that Kohler brought about a tremendous
expansion in the intellectual horizons of German legal
studies, performed the humane service of extending the
bounds of serious legal scholarship to include simpler
societies, exhibited in practice the imaginative comprehension of their cultures through the methodical study of (at
least aspects of) their languages, and cast his researches
in terms of an original and sophisticated philosophical
attitude, worthy of the interest and respect of present-day
students of anthropology.

IV

The leading argument of Kohler's Prehistory of Marriage concerns what he asserts to be the intimate historical connec-

tion among the institutions of totemism, mother right,
group marriage and exogamy. The term totemism has been
applied to a constellation of customs from various groups
in different parts of the world, all having in common, at
best, only some sort of relationship that is claimed to
exist between men (individuals or social groups) and animals, plants, or other natural objects.

The topic requires no lengthy review;[68] the word
itself derives from the language of the Ojibwa Indians and
was first used--in the form totam--by John Long in 1791 in
a description of certain customs found among Algonkian
tribes.[69] In 1836, Albert Gallatin reported a system of
exogamous clans among several American Indian groups and
demonstrated an association between these clans and a belief in common descent from an animal.[70] A similar system
had already been described for Australia by Scott Nind in
1831 and later by Sir George Grey in 1841.[71] A great mass
of similar material from all over the world was gathered by
John F. McLennan and published in 1869 and 1870.[72]

McLennan originated the doctrine that totemism was
linked with matriliny, clans and exogamy; and this doctrine
came to have great influence, especially after it was adopted and propagated by W. Robertson Smith in his Kinship and
Marriage in Early Arabia.(1885). Totemism grew into one of
the most prominent scholarly topics of the last century,
giving rise to works such as Sir James Frazer's four-volume
Totem and Exogamy (1910) and Arnold van Gennep's L'État
actuel du problème totémique (1920). In the same year as

the book by Frazer, Alexander Goldenweiser, influenced by
Tylor and Boas, published an important study which did
much to divert attention from the by now traditional topic.
Goldenweiser showed, for example, that exogamy and a number
of other institutions which had come to be regarded as part
of the totemic complex--such as taboo and religious regard
for the totem--all failed to be invariable characteristics
of totemism. Each trait manifested "more or less striking
independence in its distribution, and most of them can be
shown to be widely-spread ethnic phenomena, diverse in origin, not necessarily coordinated in development, and displaying a rich variability of psychological make-up."[73]
"If totemism includes, roughly speaking, everything," he
went on, "is totemism itself anything in particular?" The
suspicion was near that the word was applied to one set of
features in one area, to another set in a second area, and
in a third area possibly to both sets. In a general view,
it was possible to conclude that, "while almost anything
may be included, no feature is necessary or characteristic."[74] The topic was finally demolished by Claude
Lévi-Strauss, who, in a book published in 1962 and taking a
cue from a remark by Tylor, redirected scholarly attention
from the supposed institution of totemism to the general
question of classification.[75]

     If much of Kohler's thesis was taken from McLennan,
his book was conceived as a direct defense of Lewis Henry
Morgan. Having encountered, during his researches among
the Iroquois, a relationship system entirely different from

the European, Morgan subsequently discovered the same system
among other American Indian tribes. With the aid of the
United States government, Morgan sent questionnaires to
missionaries and government officials in contact with simple
societies all over the world, inquiring into their relationship terminologies. The results of these researches
were eventually published in a huge comparative monograph
entitled Systems of Consanguinity and Affinity of the Human
Family (1870).

On the basis of these terminologies, Morgan distinguished between two broad systems of relationship: (1)
the descriptive, of which our own is a close approximation,
in which each recognized (genealogical) relationship is
called by a primary term (e.g., father) or by the appropriate combination of primary terms (father's brother); and
(2) the classificatory system, of which there were several
versions, in which many different genealogical relations
may be called by the same term (e.g., the same term might
be used for both father and father's brother and other
relatives as well).

In addition to this distinction, Morgan set up a
hypothetical evolutionary series of some fifteen stages,
beginning with the brutish stage of promiscuous intercourse
and proceeding through communal marriage of brothers and
sisters to the formation of the communal family. The latter
could, through the addition of outsiders, result in either
polygamy or polyandry or a combination of both--this last
possibility representing a stage called by Morgan the

Hawaiian custom and giving rise to the Malayan (cognatic)
relationship terminology. The next phase, tribal organization, produced the Turanian (Asian) and Ganowánian
(American) relationship terminologies. And so Morgan's
scheme advances until the appearance of the civilized family and the overthrow of classificatory terminologies and
their consequent replacement by descriptive systems.[76]

Morgan's program rested on the assumption that
relationship systems or "kinship terminologies" reflected
past conditions of society, in particular consanguineous
ties produced by specific types of group marriage. The
Malay or cognatic type, in which brothers and sisters and
cousins are called by the same term, is the product of a
stage in which all brothers and all sisters marry each
other communally. The American and Asian classificatory
systems originated after marriage between brother and sister
had been prohibited, but marriage of cousins was still allowed.[77] This doctrine rested on two notions of great importance for subsequent discussions of kinship. The first
is that "marriage forms the basis of relationships"; and
the second is that the relationships created by these marriages are consanguineous.[78]

Morgan's theories inevitably came under attack. The
first and one of the most important objections was made by
McLennan, who claimed that the terms Morgan had collected
had nothing at all to do with ties of blood. "What duties
or rights are affected by the 'relationships' comprised in
the classificatory system? Absolutely none. They are bar-

ren of consequences except indeed as comprising a code of
courtesies and ceremonial addresses in social intercourse."[79]

McLennan greatly exaggerated, but he made an important discovery which was subsequently taken up by Starcke,
Lubbock, and Westermarck. Starcke commented that the value
of McLennan's suggestions "consists in his emphatic assertion that nomenclature is in no way founded on the facts of
procreation, and that its development is due to the altogether formal principle of reciprocity." McLennan did not
justly estimate these points, but "he is right with respect
to this formal principle." "The nomenclature was in every
respect the faithful reflection of the juridical relations."[80]

Westermarck adopted McLennan's position in an
endeavor to prove that Morgan's inference of a stage of
promiscuous intercourse was untenable. "All depends on the
point whether the 'classificatory system' is a system of
blood-ties . . . Mr. Morgan assumes this, instead of proving it." And he asserts further that "in the terms themselves there is, generally, nothing which indicates that
they imply an idea of consanguinity." "The terms for
relationships were originally mere terms of address, given
chiefly with reference to sex and age, as also to the external, or social, relationship in which the speaker stood
to the person whom he or she addressed."[81]

These were substantial objections, and they were
joined by others. Perhaps most importantly the notion of

group marriage came under devastating attack. The existence of marriage classes in Australia seems first to have
been described in 1831 by Nind, who writes, "The whole body
of the natives are divided into two classes, <u>Erniung</u> and
<u>Tem</u> or <u>Táǎman</u>; and the chief regulation is, that these
classes must intermarry, that is, an <u>Erniung</u> with a
<u>Táǎman</u>."[82] Subsequent descriptions were presented by Grey
in 1841, C. P. Hodgson in his <u>Reminiscences of Australia</u>
(1846), Daniel Bunce in <u>Language of the Aborigines of Vic-</u>
<u>toria</u> (1865), and William Ridley in <u>Kamilaroi and other</u>
<u>Australian Languages</u> (1875). Finally, Fison and Howitt,
strongly influenced by Morgan, published <u>Kamilaroi and</u>
<u>Kurnai</u> (1880).

>   Fison writes of Australian systems that

>> marriage is theoretically communal. In other words
>> it is based upon the marriage of all the males in
>> one division of a tribe to all the females of the
>> same generation in another division. Hence, rela-
>> tionship is not merely that of one individual to
>> another, but of group to group.[83]
>> The idea of marriage under the classificatory
>> system of kinship is founded on the rights of the
>> tribe or rather of the classes into which the tribe
>> is divided. Class marriage is not a contract enter-
>> ed into by two parties. <u>It is</u> <u>a natural state into</u>
>> <u>which both parties are born.</u>[84]

However, Fison had to make the concession that his
formulation represented not present usage, but ancient
rule.[85] "Although strong evidence seems to point . . . to
a more ancient undivided commune this has never yet been
found; and I know of no record of which we can positively
affirm that it describes such a commune, and that the
writer of it was a fully qualified witness in the case."[86]

>   Fison's work brought strong contradiction from Curr,

who asserted that "amongst the Australians there is no community of women. The husband is the absolute owner of his
wife (or wives)."[87] Curr points to Fison's admission that
an Aborigine, asked to define a particular relation, "frequently takes into consideration matter other than [genea-
logical] relationship, and so gives words which are not
specific terms of kinship," and that Fison was, after many
years of inquiry into the matter, hopelessly puzzled.[88]
This confession, it seemed to Curr, was sufficiently damn-
ing of Fison's claim to deduce the former existence of
group marriage from relationship terms.[89] Curr concludes
that "there is not within our knowledge a single fact or
linguistic expression which requires us to have recourse to
the theory of group-marriage to explain it, but that there
are several, as we have seen, directly at variance with
that theory."[90] Among these contrary facts is the absence
of any evidence that among the Aborigines "several men may
be seen living in a state of promiscuous cohabitation with
several women."[91]

        Another Australian observer, John Mathew, wrote in
1889 that he failed to see that group marriage "has been
proven to exist in the past, and it certainly does not occur in Australia now."[92] Finally, Westermarck reviewed
these and many other items of evidence and came to similar
conclusions. He asserted the untenability of Morgan's inference of a stage of promiscuous intercourse,[93] denied that
any inference concerning early marriage customs can be drawn
from terms of relationship,[94] and concluded that there is

no proof of the hypothesis of promiscuity or communal marriage.[95]

Another author, in a work apparently unknown to these men and to Kohler, concluded from Fison's evidence that "Group-marriage is not promiscuity," and further that there is no real evidence of the former existence of the undivided commune nor for a stage of sexual promiscuity.[96] Finally, Paul and Fritz Sarasin, in a work which Kohler subjects to an extended polemic,[97] tried to infer from the condition of the present Vedda of Ceylon to the prehistoric state of mankind in order to establish that the original humans were monogamous.

Whatever value may be attributed to this last work, it is clear that by the time Kohler wrote his essay on the prehistory of marriage, support for Morgan's evolutionary scheme was crumbling. Indeed, the elements were available for a far more sophisticated understanding of such institutions as relationship terminologies and marriage arrangements like the Australian class systems.

Among these elements, the following have already been mentioned. Australian class marriage is not a contract between two parties, but a state into which the parties are born, based on the rights of the classes, not of individuals (Fison). The Australian class system does not necessarily imply promiscuous cohabitation or communal marriage of several men with several women (Curr, Mathew, Westermarck, Wake). There is no evidence for Morgan's initial stage of the undivided commune, nor a stage of sexual promiscuity

(Wake). Relationship terminologies do not provide evidence
of group marriage, nor are classificatory terminologies
based on consanguinity (McLennan, Starcke, Westermarck,
etc.).

These analytic discoveries are not sufficient to
provide an explanation of relationship terminologies or of
marriage systems; yet they were important and indispensable
advances. Other such achievements were the discovery of
the relations of endogamy and exogamy by McLennan,[98] and
the proper explanation of these ideas by Morgan,[99] Fison's
observation that certain relatives in Australian section
systems are affines rather than cognates,[100] and Wake's
that marital groups are not so large in practice as in
theory.[101]

Another line of debate touching on Kohler's argument
has to do with the primacy of the rule of descent. In pre-
supposing an initial stage of matriarchy, Kohler followed
Bachofen and McLennan. This view was in contradiction to
the received opinion, represented most prominently by
Maine,[102] that the original primitive society was patri-
archal. The obvious question was whether we must suppose
primitive societies to have all begun with the same principle. Wake, at least, answered negatively.[103] Starcke's
position was similar. "We only assert that the conditions
which exist among Australians do not entitle us to regard
the female line of descent as the primitive one."[104] For
the American tribes, "there is not a single witness which
would entitle us to infer that there was originally a fe-

male line of descent."[105] Elsewhere he claims that "the
choice between the two possible lines is decided by the
economic organization of the community and by the local
grouping of individuals."[106] He denies however that it may
have anything to do with sexual relations or with the
organization of the family.[107] Wake had made another crucial distinction between tracing line of descent and the
attribution of authority. Tracing kinship through the
female line "is very different from the establishment of
the supremacy of women."[108] Mother right was "based, not
so much on maternity, as on certain social ideas with which
woman herself had only a secondary concern."[109]

In a work published much later, but one which Kohler
read and responded to, Thomas argued that patrilineal descent may not always have been preceded by matrilineal
descent, and, further, that the problem of the alleged
priority of matrilineal descent "is probably insoluble."
He observed, contrary to Starcke, that "customs of residence
are no guide to the principles on which descent is regulated." "No proof of the existence of paternal authority
in the family throws any light on the question of whether
the children belong to the kin of the father rather than of
the mother." "No general rule can be laid down as to the
relations between matrilineal descent and other cultural
conditions." And "no questions of potestas seem to have
exercised any influence in bringing about the transition
from matrilineal to patrilineal descent."[110]

V

Before embarking on a more detailed estimation of Kohler's
argument, we must give consideration to one aspect of his
position which was common to most nineteenth-century
theorists. Like McLennan and Morgan, Kohler was concerned
with reconstructing past stages of human development, and
he conceived comparative jurisprudence as a branch of
scholarship which should provide an evolutionary history
of legal institutions. Other figures, such as Starcke and
Wake, revealed a more sociological cast of mind, antici-
pating an era of analysis opened up by Durkheim.[111] A
contemporary such as Ernst Grosse, for example, published
a study with the avowed intention of describing the various
forms of the family through direct observation, relating
them to the concomitant conditions but making no attempt to
arrange them in a chronological or causal series. He argued
that the veritable causes of institutions are found much
less in the past--that is, in similar institutions which
precede them--than in the present, in the social milieu of
which they are a part and upon which they depend.[112]

The latter position is much closer to modern social
anthropology, especially the version which affirms that
"science deals with relations, not with origins and essen-
ces."[113] But though we may not subscribe to Kohler's
hypotheses, we cannot rightly reject his interests in the
historical antecedents of institutions. Historical conjectures of this sort fall fully within the truth of
Darwin's conviction that "without speculation there is no

good and original observation."[114] In any case, Kohler's
evolutionary doctrine was far from rigid, as is shown by
his comments in chapter 1 of the present work.

Kohler rejects the idea that a simple economic or
intellectual level of a people presupposes that their legal
system is identical with that of an original stage of
humanity. It is quite possible for a people who have only
a rudimentary economic system to have developed complicated
marriage arrangements or a structurally sophisticated language capable of making the most delicate distinctions in
the relations of place, time or causation, whereas great
civilizations may have remained behind them in one or
another respect. Change is not always the same thing as
cultural progress.[115]

Even the very rudimentary conditions found among the
Vedda of Ceylon cannot be taken as evidence that our ancestors were monogamous. The social condition of humanity is
the feature most conducive to progress. In modern times,
a repletion of social contrivances and influences binds us
together, so that our monogamous customs may be no dis-
advantage, but in primordial times the continuous communication and exchange of ideas upon which progress depended was produced primarily by the communal marriage institutions. In Kohler's view, the apparent lack of cultural
development among the Vedda may be explained by a deter-
ioration of their social instinct through the isolation of
the family and the practice of endogamy.[116]

Kohler then sets up a list of six principles which

may nevertheless allow some inferences concerning the
historical connections between institutions. These principles, in part at least, represent the application of the
method of concomitant variation to historical matters and
reflect the influence of Tylor.[117]

VI

Though we may sympathize with Kohler's rejection of the
Sarasin brothers' argument that the Vedda display the prehistoric conditions of our own ancestors, modern anthropologists are not likely to show much enthusiasm for
Kohler's own hypothesis of an intimate connection among
totemism, mother right, group marriage and exogamy. There
is no necessary logical or empirical tie between a rule of
exogamy and any particular mode of tracing descent, nor is
there a necessary connection between exogamy and the existence of clans. Not only are totemic clans not necessarily exogamous;[118] but we now know of many instances where
marriage may be allowed or even required within the clan,
and this can occur where clans are identified by totemic
attachment. Clans are not the only groups which may possess a rule of marrying out, and such a rule may occur in
societies without unilineal descent groups of any sort, in
connection with different kinds of social groups; for
example there may be village or band exogamy.

Totemic institutions of one sort or another occur in
societies with and in those without unilineal descent systems, and they occur in conjunction with both patrilineal
and matrilineal institutions. Furthermore, substantialist

terms such as "totemism," "mother right" and "group marriage" have lost favor with modern anthropologists, who
turn increasingly to the recovery of more abstract and more
easily employed principles and sociological correlations.[119]
The presence of a matrilineal rule of descent tells us
nothing in advance about the distribution of authority nor
about the organization of the family. It is by now a com-
monplace that even in matrilineal societies, authority is
characteristically vested in the hands of men, but even
this way of putting the matter is generally too clumsy a
phrasing to tell us much about the nature of authority in a
given community. We know, for instance, that "jural authority is not a single thing";[120] and even if jural offices
and responsibilities are preponderantly vested in one sex,
this does not necessarily mean that the other sex is excluded from these or other jural responsibilities.

          Kohler is quite wrong in asserting that the two
principles of descent may not occur within the same
group.[121] He contradicts himself on this, in fact, when he
speaks of a mixed system among the Eskimo, and when, in
another context, he suggests the possibility of a combination within one tribe, where one family is ordered by
father right and the other by mother right.[122] In any
case, it is not clear what implications for this assertion
are to be found in his opinion that survivals of mother
right occur in societies like the Omaha which are based
on a patrilineal rule.[123] Had he referred to Starcke, he
would have encountered a description of an African society

with institutions based on both agnation and descent through

females. Since the publication of descriptions by Forde and

van Wouden, we have a good idea of how such societies may

work.[124]

Furthermore, his assertion that it is more natural

to trace descent through the mother would not be accepted

today. It repeats McLennan's misconception that the blood

tie to the mother is more obvious than that to the

father.[125] But this view had already been thrown into

question by Starcke, in his observation that "blood-rela-

tionship is not the ground for the legal connection between

father and son."[126] Van Gennep later argued that the rule

of descent is not determined by the certainty of parentage

from the mother, or uncertainty from the father.[127] The

modern view is stated by Murdock: "There is nothing in-

herently obvious or 'natural' about any rule of

descent."[128]

VII

After making his way through the above lengthy review, the

reader may be surprised to find that the principal value

of Kohler's study lies not in his evolutionary arguments but

in another area entirely. Kohler begins his work by com-

menting upon the great value of the information on relation-

ship systems which Morgan presented in the lengthy tables

of his monograph on systems of consanguinity and affinity.

These Kohler thinks should have immediately become the ob-

ject of intensive scholarship; and after their appearance,

anyone who would wish to speak on the topic of descent

should first demonstrate a mastery of Morgan's data.

Indeed, Morgan's information did attract considerable attention and became the vehicle for much debate during the twenty-seven years that intervened between their appearance and the publication of Kohler's analyses in the present work. Subsequently, anthropological opinion has varied between two poles; the one, perhaps initiated by McLennan, is that kinship terminologies are largely irrelevant. Their study was depreciated by Malinowski as "kinship algebra." On the other hand, considerable serious attention has been given them over the years, and many unquestionable achievements have resulted.

One of the two poles of thought is represented by Edmund Leach, who (perhaps revealing a trace of Malinowski's influence) has asserted that, "the utility of the study of kin-term systems as sets . . . is pretty well worked out."[129] If, however, as Needham has argued elsewhere, social anthropology "is primarily the empirical investigation of human understanding by means of the comparative study of cultural categories," then the social classification represented in terminologies are a central interest, and their constancy as compared with the extreme variety of institutions makes them especially amenable to concentrated investigations and more likely to support comparative propositions.[130]

It is as systems of social classifications that Kohler treats the terminologies he reviews, and it is in the discovery of principles through the analysis of their

structure that his main achievement lies. Though many
scholars made use of Morgan's tables, and some of Kohler's
arguments are anticipated in various quarters, Kohler was
the first to subject them to such detailed and diagrammati-
cal analysis.

The logic of Kohler's argument proceeds in a slightly
different sequence than the order of his exposition, and it
is well to set it out here. Kohler argues that group marriage is found in America in three forms. The first of
these, also found in Australia and among the Dravidians,
is the version in which the men of one section marry the
women of the second and vice versa. In other words, it is
what today is called a two section system of prescribed
marriage, in which there is a reciprocal or symmetric
exchange of spouses. According to Kohler, this rule of
marriage gives rise to what he calls the "general type of
classificatory kinship terminology." This is an important
assertion to which we will return. The second form of
group marriage is that in which a man marries a woman, her
aunt (her father's sister), and her niece (her brother's
daughter). This is the system of the Omaha tribe and, as
he later remarks,[131] derives from father right (patrilineal
descent) and produces a terminological system in accordance
with it. The third version is that of the Choctaw; it derives from matrilineal descent and in it a woman marries a
man, his uncle (mother's brother) and his nephew (sister's
son). The Omaha type is placed second here only because it
is well described in the monograph by Dorsey, whereas there
is only scant information about the Choctaw. But in the

logic of Kohler's evolutionary scheme, the Choctaw version
should be second, the Omaha version third. Kohler also
briefly discusses a fourth type, the Hawaiian system based
on the marriage of brothers and sisters;[132] but, in distinction to Morgan, he regards the existence of such a
system as merely a possibility and its analysis is not a
major part of his argument.

Kohler has most frequently been cited because of his
analyses of the Omaha and Choctaw systems, but his study of
the Dravidian and Australian systems are an important part
of his argument and essential to understanding the rest of
it, and it is to this part that we will turn first.

VIII

Morgan had already remarked on the apparent resemblance between the relationship system of the Iroquois and that of
the Dravidians;[133] and the similarity between the latter
and the Australian and various Polynesian systems (particularly the Fijian) was subsequently recognized in several quarters. Fison made an essential discovery when he
observed that in Australian systems certain categories of
relation are not uncles and aunts, nephews and nieces
(i.e., cognatic relatives) but fathers-in-law, mothers-in-
law, sons-in-law, and daughters-in-law (i.e., affines).
This is the germ of the true explanation of such systems,
which was finally set out by Louis Dumont in 1953 in his
demonstration that these systems are based on the formal
relation of an inherited alliance through marriage.[134]

There has subsequently been an immense amount of

work done in this area; and I want to review merely a few
points bearing on the relevance of Kohler's exposition. Two
section systems, such as those of the Dravidians, the Fiji-
ans, and the Australian groups are a version of what have
come to be known as systems of prescriptive marriage alliance. They are based on obligatory marriage into a single
social category including the bilateral cross-cousin, the
children of the mother's brother and the father's sister
(though certain Australian systems restrict marriage to
second cousins and remove the first cousins from the mar-
riageable category).

The above systems are all symmetric and imply the
direct exchange of marriage partners. There is a second
major type of prescriptive system, which involves the asymmetric exchange of spouses among descent lines and marriage
into a social category including (for a man) the mother's
brother's daughter and excluding the father's sister's
daughter. Kohler does not deal with this second type, and
it need not detain us.

What we need to know about symmetric prescriptive
systems is that they are based on an obligatory rule of
marriage into a single and predetermined social category.
This rule of marriage can be read off through certain
terminological equations. Such terminologies are necessarily lineal, but they do not necessarily imply the existence of lineal descent groups. They are compatible with
either a patrilineal or matrilineal rule of descent, but,
with rare exceptions, most such terminologies give no indication whether descent is traced through males or females.

The significance of this will be explained later, but for the moment it should be noted that these are apparently the only kinds of lineal terminology which do not give some indication of the rule of descent. The two-line terminology is logically the simplest form of social classification, based on an obligatory marriage rule and lineal descent. In common with other prescriptive systems this type is a total classification encompassing the whole social field. Nonprescriptive terminologies may not have this latter feature, and they certainly lack the feature of being ordered by a rule of marriage.

Formally, relationship terminologies can be divided into those which are lineal and those which are not (cognatic). Lineal terminologies can be further divided into those which are prescriptive and those which are not. And prescriptive terminologies can be divided basically into those which are symmetric and those which are asymmetric, though certain minor additional qualifications could be made. The implication of all this is that there is good reason to begin the formal analysis of classificatory systems of relation with just those that Kohler chose, the Dravidian and the Australian, the most simple known.[135]

What then did Kohler make of these systems? He began on a good footing in assuming that the Australian and the Dravidian nomenclature represent the general type of classificatory kinship terminology. In fact, not all Australian terminologies are so simple as the Dravidian,[136] but there is nevertheless a formal similarity. He also was

correct in recognizing that certain features of this general form will also be found in his second and third types;
so it is not so surprising as it might seem that he em-
barks on his analysis by taking these general features, not,
as one would expect, from the Dravidians or Australians,
but from the Omaha.

He extracts the following genealogical equations:[137]

```
F = FB, FFBS, etc.
M = MZ, MMZD, etc.
FF = FFB, etc.
FM = FMZ, etc.
S = BS, FBSS, MZSS
D = BD, FBSD, MZSD
SS = BSS, etc.
B = FBS, MZS, etc.
Z = FBD, MZD, etc.
```

He further observes the following distinctions:

```
BS ≠ ZS
FB ≠ MB
MZ ≠ FZ
FZS ≠ FBS, MZS
MBS ≠ FBS, MZS
```

The equations and distinctions reviewed in chapter
3, section II, paragraphs XV ff, should be discussed in a
different context and we will return to them later.

The equations and distinctions which Kohler has out-
lined here,[138] under the rubric of the general classificatory system, are essentially those which would be found in
most lineal terminologies. When we take the equations together with the distinctions, we have formal criteria for
concluding that the terminology is lineal and not cognatic.
But beyond this we cannot yet go. They do not reflect a

particular rule of descent, nor do they tell us whether
there is an obligatory rule of marriage.

Having established these indications of a lineal
terminology, Kohler's next step is to look at the affinal
terms, and we must skip ahead in his exposition to the
point (chap. 3, sec. V) where he again takes up the general
classificatory system. Here he reveals the following
equations:

$$
\begin{array}{ll}
\text{FBW} = \text{M} & \text{FBSW} = \text{BW} \\
\text{MZH} = \text{F} & \text{MZSW} = \text{BW} \\
\text{BSW} = \text{SW} & \text{MBW} = \text{FZ} \\
\text{BDH} = \text{DH} & \text{FZH} = \text{MB}
\end{array}
$$

The first six of these are common in lineal terminologies, and Kohler explains them in terms of the lineal
equations already established. The latter two, however,
are consistent with a prescribed rule of marriage, and
when taken together with the others, they would suggest
the presence of a symmetric system. This is indeed how
Kohler explains them. In addition, he lists the following
equations which are also indicative of such a system:

$$
\begin{array}{ll}
\text{WZ} = \text{BW (m.s.)} & \text{HZ} = \text{BW (f.s.)} \\
\text{HB} = \text{ZH (f.s.)} & \text{WB} = \text{ZH (m.s.)}
\end{array}
$$

Further along (sec. X), his analysis of the Dravidian system becomes even more decisive. Here he argues that
group marriage, by which he means in this case the reciprocal exchange of spouses between two lines, leads directly
to cousin marriage, if marriage is restricted to the same
generation. If men and women of the two lines marry in the

first generation, then--given the nature of the classificatory systems--the men and women of the second generation of
opposite lines will be related as cousins. The two lines
are related by the formula, brother's son marries sister's
daughter, brother's daughter marries sister's son--in other
words by a formula of marriage between bilateral cross-
cousins. Dravidian kinship terminology, he argues, is
based on this rule of cousin marriage, and it produces the
following equations.

WF = MB	FZSS (m.s.) = ZS (m.s.)
HF = MB	FZDS (f.s.) = BS (f.s.)
WM = FZ	MBSS (m.s.) = ZS (m.s.)
HM = FZ	MBDS (f.s.) = BS (f.s.)
DH = ZS (m.s.), BS (f.s.)	S = MBDS (m.s.), MBSS (f.s.)
SW = ZD (m.s.), BD (f.s.)	WB, HB = MBS, FZS
D = ZSW (m.s.), BSW (f.s.)	WZ, HZ = MBD, FZD
S = ZDH (m.s.), BDH (f.s.)	WBW = Z
FBSW, MZSW = MBD, FZD	HBW = Z
FBDH, MZDH = MBS, FZS	ZH = MBS, FZS
Z = FZSW, MBSW	BW = MBD, FZD
B = FZDH, MBDH	
S = FZDS (m.s.), FZSS (f.s.)	

Two of the equations he lists, WZH = MBS, FZS, and
HZH = MBS, FZS, are not in fact consistent with a two-sec-
tion system, as Kohler himself notes. WZH and HZH should
logically be equated with brother; but this is not an important deviation.

We may now see that Kohler's discussion (chap. 3,
sec. II) concerning the classification of the children of
cousins in the Dravidian system is reflected in the above
list of equations, and the rationale (that it too results
from the rule of cousin marriage) is repeated in section
IX of chapter 3 in the discussion of Kohler's equation XI.

IX

Having reviewed Kohler's examination of the Dravidian and
the Australian versions, we may now look at his second and
third forms, what he designated the Omaha and the Choctaw
types. It is in his analysis of these latter systems that
the particular fame of his study rests. As is well known,
the Omaha are a society with patrilineal descent, while the
Choctaw are, or were, a society with matrilineal descent.
Kohler draws attention at one point (chap. 1, sec. IV) "to
the basically different nomenclature for the cousins in
Omaha and Choctaw relationship, and to the unbelievable
consistency with which the subtlest conclusions are drawn."
Elsewhere he remarks that "the two systems are distinguished
in that the Choctaw system derives from mother right and
the Omaha system from father right" (chap. 3, sec. VIII).

Émile Durkheim, in a review of Kohler's work which
is almost as famous as the book itself and which was largely
responsible for making its chief contribution known, says
that the greatest interest of Kohler's study lies in its
comparison of the Omaha and Choctaw systems.[139] Kohler's
analysis had shown that the two systems are everywhere the
same except for a certain inversion in the distribution of
terms, which, Durkheim argued, is "the logical consequence
of the inversion indicated in the system of filiation."[140]
Since the distribution of terms "varies with the kinship
organization, it is clear that it depends on it and that it
expresses it."[141]

This was a great analytic advance made jointly by

Kohler, his predecessor Bernhöft, and Durkheim. Although,
following Bernhöft, Kohler made the observation and in
effect demonstrated it in his examination, he actually was
concerned to put forward a somewhat different explanation,
and it was left to Durkheim to state the issue clearly and
to draw the important conclusions from it.

Kohler of course argued that each system derived
from a special type of group marriage, though he also argued that each type was the only one possible given the
specific rule of descent (chap. 3, sec. VIII). But the
question remained whether group marriage really had anything to do with the Omaha and Choctaw terminologies.
Durkheim thought not. "The hypothesis of a collective marriage has never been anything other than an _ultima_ _ratio_,
useful as an aid for imagining strange customs; but it is
impossible to overlook all the problems it presents."
Examples of polygyny and polyandry do occur, but they have
nothing to do with promiscuity nor with those forms of
group marriage presupposed by Morgan and Kohler, in which
"a confused and enormous group of men [marry] an equally
indeterminate group of women."[142]

Durkheim's critique here is decisive. He begins
by showing that Kohler never properly dealt with the objections to Morgan's notion that the kinship terms reflect
ties of blood. If several women are called by the same
term as is the mother, the relation it designates has nothing to do with a tie of blood. And if the terms have
nothing to do with blood ties, they cannot be explained by

the nature of the marriage, nor can they demonstrate the
marriage form.[143] Kohler's explication of the Omaha system begins with the term for mother, inaha (chap. 3, sec.
III). Dorsey had reported of the Omaha that if a man wan-
ted to take a second wife, he might take his first wife's
sister, her brother's daughter, or her father's sister.
This Kohler took to be the specific rule of group marriage
for the Omaha. If a man married any one of these women,
then his child would regard her as his mother; and by
logical progression all the other equations characteristic
of the Omaha terminology would result.

Here Durkheim stops to ask, what does this word
inaha "actually mean?" The information given by Kohler and
Morgan shows that the word is applied indifferently to "all
women in the family (or clan?) into which my father has
contracted marriage." It is certain then that it expresses
something quite different than ties of consanguinity.[144]

With these two reservations made, perhaps we can
look again to see what Kohler did with the Omaha nomenclature. We have already seen that in section II of chapter 3 Kohler extracts those aspects of the Omaha terminology which he regards as typical of the general classificatory system; and we have seen that this information demonstrates that it is in fact a lineal terminology. In section
III Kohler reveals another series of equations (numbered
I-VI). The first of these demonstrates what Durkheim was
referring to above: all the women in the line into which
father marries are called by the same term. Actually,

Durkheim speaks of family or clan, but we now know that
lineal terminologies need not imply the existence of descent groups and it is best to restrict ourselves to the
more formal and more accurate term "line." In any case,
inaha is also applied to relatives who may not even be in
mother's clan. Formally, this series of equations actually
indicate a patrilineal rule of descent, as they cut across
several genealogical (generation) levels and are linked
through males related as father and son. Kohler's diagram
shows this quite clearly.

Kohler's series II through IV are in keeping with
the first, although it should be recognized that not all
these equations actually occur among the Omaha, and they
accord with the rule of patrilineal descent. Series V
(MB = MBS = MBSS) is often taken as defining an Omaha system, and it too is confirmation of a patrilineal rule.
Other patrilineal equations among the many which might be
extracted by independent inspection from the Omaha terminology are the following.

$$MFBS = MFBSS = MFBSSS \qquad MMB = MMBS = MMBSS$$
$$WB = WBS = WBSS \qquad\qquad FMB = FMBS = FMBSS$$
$$WBD = WBSD$$

Two aspects of this terminology are easily established then, that it is lineal and that it is obviously
patrilineal, no equations suggestive of a matrilineal rule
being present.

The next step would be to see if there is any marriage rule indicated. We now know that a marriage rule is

indicated in a terminology only when there is a marriage
prescription into a single category. This would imply that
we should look for eouations and distinctions characteristic of such systems. There are a few suggestive of such a
rule: MB = FZH, ZH = WB, FZ = MBW. The preponderance of
evidence, however, shows that there is no marriage prescription of any kind:

FZH ≠ WF	MBD ≠ FZD
MB ≠ WF	FZS ≠ ZH
FZ ≠ WM	WBS ≠ ZS
MBS ≠ FZS	ZS ≠ DH
MBS ≠ WB	SW ≠ ZD
MBD ≠ BW	

Since there is no marriage prescription implying the
continued inheritance of marriage ties between lines, it is
not surprising that the Omaha terminology actually recognizes a great number of distinct affinal lines. In a prescriptive terminology these would be consolidated into a
small number, depending in part upon the nature of the ·
prescription. Here, though, the presumption is that marriage ties will not be repeated and so there are distinct
affinal lines at each genealogical level.

Now if we look at the words used to name the various
social categories in the Omaha language, we observe first
that, unlike many other systems, a strict distinction is
kept between male and female relatives; that is, no category includes both males and females. Secondly, the terms
are distributed among the various descent lines by rank
order. If we look at the terms Kohler transcribes as
itiga (including FF, MF) and ika (including FM, MM), we

may see that, whatever principles of application are used,
these two terms are always at the head of any series in
which they appear. An assessment of their meaning should
take us beyond the range of interest narrowly called
"kinship," but for our present purposes we can conclude
that, whenever they are used, the terms imply one or another kind of superiority. These terms not only appear at
the head of the series denoting one's own lineal relatives;
they also appear at the head of several patrilines which
have given women to one's own (the lines of FMF, MF, WF,
SWF) or lines which have done so at second remove (MMF, WMF).
However, neither of these terms appear to be applied to
relatives in any patriline (those of FZH, ZH, DH, SDH) which
have taken wives from Ego's own. This feature suggests a
possible status superiority of wife-giving lines over wife-
taking lines.

In any case, the feature is in keeping with a general diagonal distribution often found among the terms in
patrilineal systems, in which characteristically more re-
spectful terms are applied to relatives traced through
women who have married into the line than are applied to
relatives traced through women born into one's own line and
hence marrying out. One indication of this feature is
found in the contrast between the equations MBD = M and
FZD = ZD, and in that between MBS = MB and FZS = ZS. These
equations reveal another aspect of the terminology which was
noted by Kohler. Relationships are often reciprocal; if the
same term is employed for MBS and MB, then both FZS and ZS

will be called by the reciprocal of this first term.

If we look now at the Choctaw system, we will see
that it too displays indications of a lineal terminology.
Furthermore, it indicates its matrilineal character.

$$FMB = F = FZS = FZDS \qquad MBC = C$$
$$MB \ = B = ZS \qquad\qquad\quad MBW = BW = ZSW$$

It could be shown further that there is no prescribed rule
of marriage, that diverse affinal matrilines are recognized,
that the terms are distributed by rank order, that there is
a diagonal distribution, but in the opposite direction from
the Omaha system, and that relationships are reciprocal.
Furthermore, "cousin" terms are the inverse of those found
among the Omaha. Here MBD = D and FZD = FZ (or FM), while
MBS = S and FZS = F.

X

At this point we may pause to consider some of the historical consequences of Kohler and Durkheim's comparison of the
two forms of nomenclature. The analytic advance derived
from it was not entirely unanticipated. Morgan himself
broached the question whether rule of descent has effect on
terminology, only to reject the idea.[145] Fison had suggested that the difference between the American and the Asian
systems lay in rule of descent, matrilineal in the former
case, patrilineal in the latter. But this was an incorrect
ethnographic generalization, as both rules are to be found
on the two continents.[146]

The clearest predecessors, seemingly, were Bernhöft,

who has been mentioned, and Starcke. Starcke wrote,
"Tribes which have only a single designation for the mother's
brother and all his descendants follow the male line, but
those tribes which call the father's sister 'mother' and
'grandmother' observe the female line."[147] He recognized
then what has usually been taken as the minimal defining
feature of the Omaha type (the equation MBS = MB). The
corresponding feature for what Kohler called the Choctaw
type is the equation FZD = FZ.[148]

Before taking up the vagaries of debate occasioned
by these two supposed types, a note about their names would
be in order. Kohler can be said to have initiated the
Crow-Omaha problem and to have given it a name; in his terms
it would be the Choctaw-Omaha problem. The reader will observe that Kohler's arguments are not confined to the Omaha
and Choctaw themselves, but that his analysis concerns a
number of tribes simultaneously. Often a given equation
which is taken up in part of his argument will not be found
in all the tribes of the given group, but will appear in
one or more of them. So Kohler already adopts the dubious
habit of thinking in types, and his argument proceeds at a
certain remove from ethnographic fact. What Kohler designates the "Omaha group" includes a series of Siouan and Algonkian peoples, all possessing the common feature of
patrilineal descent. The second set he calls the "Choctaw
group," and it includes another series of Siouan tribes,
plus Pawnee and Arickara and one Algonkian group, the Cree--
all of which are matrilineal.

In 1917, Robert Lowie recognized two variants of
what he called the Dakota principle--which we can see is,
in effect, the principle of lineal descent.[149]   The first
of these he called the "Hidatsa variant," to which, he
wrote, the Crow scheme is almost identical. The second he
called the Omaha variant. The Hidatsa variant is associated with matrilineal descent, the Omaha with patrilineal
descent.[150]   Though Lowie argued against thinking in terms
of types of kinship systems and said we should "speak rather of kinship categories, features, or principles of
classification,"[151] Leslie Spier, in 1925, set up a classification of kinship systems including what he designated
the Omaha and Crow types.[152]   These he explained were merely empirical categories, serving to indicate the distribution of terms for cousins; but they remained permanently
embedded in the vocabulary of the profession, providing
strong and repeated temptation to false generalization.

Kohler's designation for the Omaha group has survived unchanged into modern jargon, but his "Choctaw
group" has eventually come to be called the Crow type. A
reason for this shift is found in a peculiarity of the
Choctaw terminology, overlooked by Kohler, but which prevents it from being, as is the Crow nomenclature, the strict
matrilineal analogue for the Omaha system. Morgan reports
the equations of FZS = FZSS = FZSSS, etc.[153]   This is, in
fact, a series of patrilineal equations in what is otherwise a terminology ordered by a matrilineal rule of descent.
Eggan gives evidence that this is a change introduced in

historical times in response to pressure from missionaries.[154] It makes the Choctaw in any case less suited
than are the Crow to represent matrilineal societies.

If--as was already shown by Lowie in 1917--there are
no Crow and Omaha types, then the massive body of attempts,
which has grown up since then, to account for them by
causal explanations of one sort or another, exemplifies,
once again, the tendency for prominent errors to become
social institutions. Other than a frequent association with
exogamous social groups--matrilineal ones in the case of
Crow terminologies, patrilineal for Omaha terminologies--no
other sociological feature has ever been shown to have a
necessary (or even usual) correspondence to the cousin
terms which have come to be taken as definitive for Crow
and Omaha systems. Indeed, Needham has shown that a variety of terminologies may possess the supposedly definitive
feature for one or the other type (MB = MBS for the Omaha,
FZ = FZD for the Crow) and yet still "differ from each
other in practically everything else."[155]

Another dubious point in anthropological tradition
surrounding the Crow-Omaha systems is the focus on cousin
terms. The above equations are only a selection from among
a large number of lineal equations in each of the two
terminologies, and there is little evident reason for
giving them special attention. This matter provides the
opportunity to take up yet another point in need of some
clarification. Anthropologists speak of lineal equations
of one or another kind. To say that an equation is patri-

lineal or matrilineal is a purely formal designation. We have seen, as in the case of the Choctaw, that both matrilineal and patrilineal equations may sometimes occur in the same terminology. Usually, such equations are found in conjunction with lineal institutions of the appropriate mode, or an anomaly such as that of the Choctaw may be satisfactorily related to specific historical or sociological conditions. However, terminological features do not necessarily imply anything at all about the institutions in the societies in which they are found, and a particular lineal equation may have little or nothing to do with the lineal institutions in a given society.[156] A formal inspection of a terminology is an appropriate preliminary, but the explanation of its features can only be obtained through a total analysis, not only of the terminology (hence the futility of focusing on a few limited equations or distinctions out of the multitude to be found in a social classification) but of all the institutions within the society.

Another landmark of sorts in the history of anthropological reactions to Kohler and Durkheim's insight was established when Radcliffe-Brown transformed the lineal principles they had isolated into his "principle of the unity of the lineage group."[157] Radcliffe-Brown did not do something more, but actually something less than his predecessors, including Lowie and Kroeber. The descent lines which others had displayed in these terminologies, Radcliffe-Brown explained as resulting from a unity of their members as perceived by Ego. Insofar as Radcliffe-Brown implied

that all the relatives called by the same term within a
given descent line--and only those relatives--feel a sense
of solidarity, his explanation was wrong and demonstrably
illogical. Insofar as it was "an immediate abstraction from
observed facts," his new principle merely disguised in his
own words an analytic precept which since Durkheim had become a part of the anthropological public domain. This
supposed new principle has enjoyed a good deal of populari-
ty, but not universally. It led Louis Dumont, for example,
to remark that it is nothing more "than a kind of tauto-
logical blinkers, preventing any view beyond that of the
lineage as a thing-in-itself. Together with the 'principle
of the unity of the sibling group,' this principle's function is to reduce complementarity to 'unity,' structure to
substance."[158]

        Another feature of Kohler's exposition, which to
this point has been given only passing attention, also had
considerable influence on subsequent anthropological speculation. The attempt to explain relationship terminologies
by marriage rules, which was begun by Morgan and continued
by Fison, Kohler, and others, has since then taken many
forms and had many practitioners. Kohler, for example,
quite correctly argues that the form of the Dravidian
terminology is related to a particular rule of marriage, and
his consideration of this and the Australian systems would
form an entry in a historical register of studies of prescriptive alliance. It is only prescriptive terminologies
which have been shown to embody any marriage rule at all.

Kohler, however, also argued that the Choctaw and the Omaha terminologies were structured as a result of certain marriages which followed upon an initial one, thus certain kinds of secondary marriages. Rivers (who later drew attention in the English-speaking world to Kohler's work) and Gifford made similar claims.[159] The possibility that some terminological features reflect special sociological institutions continues to exert an influence on some scholars,[160] and conceivably a particular case might sustain such an explanation. But as for accounting for a general range of terminologies, the prevalent anthropological opinion seems to follow Kroeber who argued that parallel features of classification and sociology should be regarded as expressions of the same thing.[161] Radcliffe-Brown, for example, took over Kroeber's position, without thanks to its author; and both Murdock and Lévi-Strauss have followed in rejecting the idea that secondary marriages are likely to have great effects on the structure of a terminology.[162]

It has been argued by others that Crow-Omaha systems may arise as a consequence of asymmetric cross-cousin marriage preferences or prescriptions.[163] This proposition suffers from a number of defects; for example it confuses preference with prescription, genealogy with category. Both Needham and Lévi-Strauss have pointed out that Crow and Omaha terminologies are not to be assimilated to asymmetric prescriptive systems on the coincidence of lineal equations involving cross-cousins.[164] Furthermore, this

hypothesis requires a past quite at variance with the
present circumstances of most such societies; so that even
if it were correct, which is possible, that in a former
period they did have such preferences, the present character of their institutions would still be left unexplained.
We may recall that there is no indication of prescribed
marriage among the Omaha themselves, for whom, in fact,
marriage with either cross-cousin is forbidden.

One other hypothesis relating these terminologies to
marriage rules remains. It is based on an idea which
McKinley, characterizing an argument by Lévi-Strauss, has
called "dispersed affinal alliance."[165] It is Lévi-
Strauss's view that Crow-Omaha systems locate themselves
between elementary structures--societies with marriage
prescriptions or preferences--and complex structures in
which the relationship (kinship) system has little or nothing to do with determining or limiting the choice of
spouse.

Lévi-Strauss suggests that the most suitable manner
of defining a Crow-Omaha system may be "to say that each
time Ego chooses a line from which to obtain a wife, all
its members are automatically excluded for several generations from among the spouses available to Ego's line."[166]
This of course is just the reverse of the situation found
in societies with marriage prescriptions. But we may ask
whether this formula fairly characterizes particular Crow-
Omaha societies?

Formally, in a prescriptive system all the men of

one line (at least those of the same generation) marry women
of the same category and are prohibited women of the
remaining categories. This fact may be altered by subsidiary considerations of generation or genealogy. In principle, however, a new alliance has similar implications for
the marriage possibilities of the men of the same line.
Now if we look at the Omaha, we find that Dorsey reports
marriage is forbidden with women of mother's clan, and with
women of the subclans of mother's mother, mother's mother's
mother, father's mother, and father's mother's mother. So
in this case, we know that Omaha marriage prohibitions apply to a class of women, designated by the terms *ika* and
inaha; and that the prohibitions are limited by subsidiary
considerations of descent group membership. What we do not
know, because the ethnographer does not make it explicit,
is whether the marriages of collateral relatives within
Ego's own clan have any implications for his marriage prohibitions. This is a question to be determined by ethnographic investigation in each case, and since there is no
genuine class of Crow-Omaha societies, there is no reason
to expect any uniformity of answer.

     If all males of a clan and of the same generation
share the same prohibitions, which is doubtful, then this
might indeed conduce to a severe limitation of possible
mates. But it is not likely that, as Lévi-Strauss suggests,
a "system of unconscious prescriptions" could appear, or
that it would "return on itself periodically in such a way
that, taking any initial state whatsoever, after a few

generations a structure of a certain type must necessarily emerge."[167] In a society such as the Omaha, with ten clans and a limited number of subclans, the consequence of the rule Lévi-Strauss suggests would be that—if in addition to the subclans prohibited him through his direct genealogical relations, Ego had to consider the subclans of the relevant relatives of his lineage mates—the small store of open subclans would soon be reduced until there would be no possible marriage partners left. This result would be even more drastically certain, if we took Lévi-Strauss at his word and assumed that the marriages of lineage mates of Ego's own generation limited his choice of spouse. It is rather more likely that Crow-Omaha marriage prohibitions do not have the extensive implications which are characteristic of marriage prescriptions.

In McKinley's hands the idea of dispersed alliance becomes an explanation of the existence of Crow-Omaha terminologies. Before even considering his explanation, it must be observed that it can at best have validity for only some societies with the Omaha or Crow distribution of cousin terms. Dispersed alliance cannot account for societies with prescriptive marriage systems, for example; and it cannot directly explain Crow-Omaha terminologies in societies lacking the features by which McKinley characterizes dispersed affinal alliance.

Assuming though, which might still be possible, that there is a specific class of society for which his hypothesis would apply, we may look to its features. McKinley suggests

that this form of kinship terminology may have the effect
of resolving certain contradictions in the social system.
The contradiction in this case is that between "a desire to
retain old marriage alliances while at the same time creat-
ing as many new ones as possible."[168] It may not be merely
quibbling to point out that, as a practical matter, the same
result can be achieved perfectly easily in a prescriptive
alliance system without any violation of its principles, and
that in some such societies overt steps in this direction
are actually taken.

In any case, it remains a question whether there
really is any contradiction of this sort in connection with
dispersed alliance. McKinley argues that the lineal equations often found in the wife-giving lines in Crow-Omaha
terminologies serve to freeze the time dimension. "This is
important since in a system of dispersed alliance it is the
passing of time, in generations, which weakens the importance of an original alliance and which tends to draw the
clans of one's father and mother apart from each other."[169]
By ignoring the passing of generations with respect to important interlineage ties,[170] Crow-Omaha systems hold on to
a relationship which is generationally ephemeral.

It could be argued that what these features indicate,
if anything, is that the nature of alliances changes with
the passing of generations. By suggesting that such terminologies provide a "convenient fiction" for maintaining
old relationships,[171] McKinley seems to suggest the pre-
tense will be maintained that the alliance contracted by

father's father will continue to have the same implications
in Ego's generation. On the contrary, however, it would
seem the terminology recognizes that the character of such
alliances must change with the passing of generations. Why
else recognize distinct affinal lines?

We may put the case in this way. Like jural authority, alliance is no single thing. If a society in fact
values the establishment by means of marriage of alliances
between descent groups or families, but prohibits the repe-
tition of such alliances in succeeding generations, it may
be perfectly in keeping with its own notion of alliance that
the ties be kept up in other ways through the generations
and that the sociological expression of the alliance change
through time. Even in prescriptive systems, the idea of
alliance will involve a heterogenous collection of obliga-
tions and expectations; and what the constellation will be
may vary in particulars from society to society. The notion
of alliance may, for example, have strongly marked political
implications in one society and none at all in another. In
other words, alliance is a formal term which may have a particular correspondence in a given society and overt recognition in idiom and ideology; but the definition of alliance
in a given case will depend upon ethnographic examination.

Consequently, the first test of McKinley's hypothesis
of the contradiction inherent in dispersed alliance would
be an examination of the ideas about alliance in the societies to which it is supposed to apply. Perhaps, in one or
another of these an inherent or explicitly recognized

contradiction may exist between the cultural definition of
alliance and the institutions of the society. But until a
detailed and comparative investigation is made of the collective representations of Crow-Omaha societies, we have no
real reason to suppose that the form of their kinship terminologies is the consequence of (reflects?) any supposed
contradictions in their marriage institutions.[172]

McKinley suggests that the Omaha pattern of marriage
might serve to enhance social solidarity by bringing about
a condition in which all the members of the tribe were relatives. But the same argument has been used in connection
with prescriptive societies, in which all members are relatives by definition. This argument could have, then, no
distinctive application for the Omaha.

McKinley thinks that exogamous unilineal descent
groups are an essential precondition to Crow-Omaha terminologies because they are the units which would be involved
in a system of dispersed alliance.[173] By the same reasoning, exogamous unilineal descent groups would be essential
to prescriptive alliance systems, but examples such as the
Sinhalese of Ceylon or the Sirionó of Bolivia have shown
that this is certainly not the case. We have known for a
long time that not all Crow-Omaha societies have unilineal
descent groups,[174] and by McKinley's own showing some 10
percent of Crow-Omaha groups in his sample must lack them.[175]

A final question is whether the Crow-Omaha distribution of cousin terms requires any general explanation such
as has presumably been provided for cousin terms in prescrip-

tive systems. Here the answer is clear. One of the major
analytic advances in the study of prescriptive alliance was
the realization that the relevant relationship categories
were not primarily defined by genealogical ties like those
of cousins. What integral explanations of these systems
were finally arrived at were extrinsic to the cousin relationships, and though the explanations could in fact account
for the differential distribution of cousins among the categories, they depended not at all on considerations of
genealogy. Furthermore, the distribution of cousin relationships is not always entirely uniform among prescriptive
systems of similar kind; but these variations relate to
factors which are quite secondary.

        We obviously will get nowhere by puzzling why cousins
are raised or lowered a generation. Of course, nothing of
the kind is done to them. This formulation is the consequence of the illusion that generation has primacy over line
and of the even more elementary mistake of assuming that
classificatory terms take their definition from certain primary genealogical relations (like mother's brother) and are
then extended to cover more remote relatives (such as mother's brother's son). The answers are to be sought in a
structural investigation of the whole terminology; and the
real problems may be found in certain formal characteristics.
An explanation is needed not for cousin terms but for the
problem why some lineal terminologies are largely symmetric,
whereas others display an asymmetric skew. Once we know why
a rank order series of terms comes to be given a diagonal

distribution across the social field, then the explanation
for particular lineal equations will be given.

XI

There remains one other approach to Crow-Omaha terminologies that needs brief attention. This version is a formal
approach which styles itself transformational analysis. It
avers that kinship is based on genealogy, that the relations
of kinship derive from the primary relations within the
nuclear family, and it holds to the extensionist hypothesis
whereby the terms for primary relatives are extended to
cover other relations. "The _real_ 'father' is F, the _real_
'mother' is M. These are _basic_ meanings; others are _exten-_
sions. _Real_ 'uncles' and 'aunts' are (unmerged) siblings
of parents, etc."[176]

The results of this form of analysis are not going
to be regarded of any consequence by those who hold that the
premises themselves are wrong. There have been such since
long before Kohler published his work, and modern social
anthropological opinion generally regards the premises as
elementary mistakes. Nevertheless, these assumptions resemble Kohler's own; and it may be worth while to look into
the originality of the analysis based on them.

In this regard, Coult has demonstrated that the
transformation rules Lounsbury established for "predicting"
the Omaha-type kinship terminology of the Fox Indians are
identical with the rules of succession given by Tax in his
original account of the Fox terminology. In other words,
Tax had priority; he "developed in a most explicit fashion

the technique of transformational analysis." Furthermore,
his technique accounts for the Fox nomenclature more completely, and it is less redundant. Coult also implies that
Tax has the advantage of directness and clarity of expression.[177]

If we want to compare the virtues of transformational analysis with those of Kohler's work, then, it is to Tax
that we should turn. Tax presents six rules of succession
which when accompanied by two additional principles account
for the entire Fox system. These six rules, however, are
identical with, though somewhat more complete than, Lounsbury's skewing, merging, half-sibling rules, and attendant
corollaries. The latter were intended to predict back the
data at hand, thereby providing an exact replica of the Fox
system.[178]

It can be shown though that even Tax's six rules were
already to be found in Kohler's work. Rule 1 states that
"the offspring of persons called 'father' or 'mother's
sister' are always 'siblings.'" The same fact is found
below (chapter 3, section II, series VIII and XI) in the
equations of brother or sister with the child of the FB or
his equivalent and of MZ or her equivalent. Rule 2 states,
"the offspring of a sibling of the same sex are always
'son' and 'daughter,' and of a sibling of the opposite sex
always 'nephew' and 'niece.'" This is quite explicitly set
out by Kohler in chapter 3. Rule 3 records, "the offspring
of a son, daughter, niece, or nephew are always 'grandchildren.'" This is recognized by Kohler, when he reports

the equation grandson = brother's grandson, father's brother's great-grandson, and when he remarks that the children of nephews and nieces are equivalent to grandchildren.
According to rule 4, "offspring of grandchildren are always
'grandchildren' again." Kohler reports that there are no
terms for descendants below grandchildren; by which he apparently means there are no separate terms. Rule 5 reads,
"the offspring of a 'mother's brother' are always 'mother's
brother' and 'mother's sister,'" This states the two famous "Omaha-type" equations: $M = MBD = MBSD$ and $MB = MBS =
MBSS$. These are found in chapter 3, section III, equations I
and V, respectively. The last rule, 6, reads, "the offspring of a father's sister are always the same as the offspring of one's own sister."[179] This fact is demonstrated
in chapter 3, section III, equation VI, and in the subsequent discussion.

It says nothing against Tax's particular analysis of
the Fox to show that it was anticipated by Kohler's analysis
of the Omaha; but if there is any special value in Tax's
demonstration, then it must be found in Kohler's as well.
The parallels in Kohler's analysis extend beyond the rules
of succession. For example, his demonstrations often depend upon the assumption that relations are reciprocal; if
a given relative is regarded as "mother's brother," then Ego
will be regarded by him as a "sister's son." This common
feature of terminologies became in Tax's hands the principle
of "constant reciprocals." Elsewhere Kohler's examination
comes to resemble Tax's two rules of uniform descent and

uniform ascent. If a given relative is called "nephew,"
then Ego will use the same term for his son as he uses for
nephew's son.

Kohler's procedures differ from transformational
analysis only in that he took an assumed sociological feature, a rule of marriage, as his starting point. From
there he proceeded to develop the system by the logic of
accumulated genealogical equations. These he did not ele-
vate into imposing rules, formulae, and technical apparatus;
but he forestalled anything later to be developed by transformational analysis. In the process he provided a rather
good formal analysis of the features of terminologies of
several different types, and usefully displayed the structural contrasts among them. It has been held against formal analyses of the sort Lounsbury practices that they
"habitually move so far away from the original ethnography
that the whole exercise becomes worthless."[180] Kohler sins
to some degree in this way, but on the whole the interest
of his work lies in his direct confrontation of the ethnographic facts and in his imaginative attempts to come to
understand them in their own terms. It is this quality
which allowed him to arrive, at the end of his long and
painstaking examination of the Omaha and Choctaw terms, at
the only analytic result of any consequence to come from all
this formal concern with Crow and Omaha systems.

XII

A few comments about Kohler's style may be of some final
use to the reader.

Albert Kocourek remarked that Kohler's capacities required a virile disposition, which he often displayed in his
treatment of opponents. Referring to the "elemental savage-
ry of German criticism," Kocourek observed that Kohler, as
an antagonist, "fights with deadly weapons."[181]

The nineteenth century was a time in which basic issues in anthropology were being sorted out through the clash
of vigorous minds. In a superficial reading of the works of
the era, we may be impressed only by a few lurid fallacies
and thus carry away the comforting view that it was left to
the twentieth century to set scholarship on a right footing.
A closer look, however, shows that we are heirs to a rich
body of hard analytic criticism in many essential issues,
and it is this collective product of the inspired contro-
versies of the nineteenth century which may be taken as the
true foundation of modern anthropology.

As a controversialist, Kohler is usually devastating
and sometimes entertaining; but his bluntness makes few
distinctions concerning the quality of his opponents.
Mucke, apparently, deserves everything he gets--although,
taken at its most abstract, his idea that relationship systems might be related in some respect to spatial considerations would be given a better hearing today than it got
from Kohler.

However, when Kohler turns to attack a very much
stronger argument by Westermarck (chap. 1, sec. IV), he
traduces Westermarck's actual position and thereby mis-
understands a point that has the greatest implications for

his own book.

Similarly, on very inappropriate grounds he summari-
ly dismisses Karl Schmidt's investigation of the jus primae
noctis. Starcke, on the contrary, speaks of it as "a tho-
rough and intelligent study of the subject";[182] and, indeed,
it is a standard work to which anyone interested in the
question today should turn. It did much the same service
with regard to the so-called "first night privilege" as
Goldenweiser provided in connection with totemism. After
Schmidt, there were no longer any grounds to think that the
heterogeneous customs from around the world which had been
labeled by this term had anything in common.

On the Prehistory of Marriage

To Professor E. B. Tylor, of Oxford University,
in profound respect

1
Critique

I

Morgan assured himself a permanent place in history with his
Systems of Consanguinity and Affinity of the Human Family
(1870). It contains a wealth of information, presented,
despite some inaccuracies, with great care; and with it he
has provided comparative jurisprudence the most fruitful
material for years of study and assimilation. This service
is so much the greater in that he has collected material
which would otherwise have permanently disappeared along
with the peoples and social conditions from which it was
drawn.

It should have been expected that science would take
immediate possession of this material in order to discover
the general impetus behind the data given in the many tables
and to discern the guiding law of human development which is
revealed by them. The study is difficult, the profit however immeasurable, for it is a question of coming closer to
the prehistory of our species and fathoming the conditions
of periods of which we have no knowledge and can in no other
way acquire any.

Unfortunately, a series of criticisms of Morgan's
studies were raised which attempted to contradict the clear
conclusions he drew from the tables. These criticisms might
be acceptable. But there are quite a few students of comparative jurisprudence who wish to enter the arena without
even having worked through Morgan's tables or who have merely spotted something while skipping through the works of
this or that author. In answer to them, it must be emphatic-
ally stressed that comparative jurisprudence, just like comparative linguistics, is an independent and important science,
requiring intensive study. Though the classical philologist
may be a good Hellenist, he is not thereby entitled to form
a judgment about the universal development of the verbal
suffix and the importance of the passive and middle voices
in the history of language, or about the transition from
the ideogram to the phonetic alphabet. In the same way,
someone who may be very experienced in modern law is not
yet, for that reason, necessarily in the position to give
an authoritative judgment about legal development among
aborigines or about the initial stages in the evolution of
marriage.   ;

This point should be, and is, self-evident. Therefore, I will ignore the comments of those who have occasionally tried, in passing, to touch upon problems of universal
history even when the assurance of their judgment stands, as
so often, in inverse relation to its importance and its
grounding in the sources. It is self-evident that science
need only be discussed in its own circles, and whoever talks

about descent without knowledge of Morgan's tables is like
a man who would speak about Roman law and its importance
without having minutely examined the Corpus juris civilis.

Other authors have entered the lists with much ma-
ial and have also included the basic sources of compara-
ive jurisprudence in their studies; these may be taken into
consideration. However, there are some scholars who, despite an abundance of detailed material, lack the right
method and have therefore been unable to come to any correct
results or to establish any principles, but have rather
been in the position of straying on wrong trails into a
dense and pathless thicket or into a defile from which there
is no way out.

It is method that distinguishes the true scholar from
the learned dilettante. But method above all is very
seriously lacking in Westermarck's work, History of Human
Marriage (1891). This work has been extolled as a paragon
of erudition. And, in fact, the author disposes of an immense range of subjects, the compilation of the literature
is exemplary; but the preparation lacks all proper method,
and the work can claim importance only as a rich collection
of material. In this, it is like Karl Schmidt's Jus Primae
Noctis (1881), which is completely wanting not only in
method but also in an essential scientific attitude.

Even more grievous are the errors in the book by
Mucke (1895), which will be discussed below. And if the
Sarasin brothers believed that they had gotten at the "rid-
dles lying in the phylogeny of man" by the path they

traveled in their otherwise quite appreciable work on the
Vedda, then this was a serious mistake.

II

In so young a science, certainly, there is as yet no generally recognized method, and for every scholar mistakes
are unavoidable.

In any case, I have already made some suggestions
about method which I think might lead to agreement (1895a,
193 ff.)

If we regard comparative jurisprudence as a historical science which should provide an evolutionary history of
legal institutions, then it is essentially a question of
determining what precedes and what follows (the _prius_ and
the _posterius_) in the individual development of each
institution.

An error has arisen here which has had the strangest
flowering in the writings of Hildebrand (1894), but which
has also sprouted luxuriant foliage in the works of some
authors who dabble every once in a while in comparative law.

It is believed that the simpler a people's material
or intellectual culture, the more original its law must be,
and that the law of the Hottentots or the Bushmen is the
prototype of primitive law. The Sarasin brothers are completely prepossessed with this notion, and even a scholar
like the late Lothar Dargun is subject to it. In response,
I must persist in pointing out that the simple economic and
intellectual level of a people offers no proof that its
present system of law is the original one. Such a conclu-

sion would be like inferring from their economic level that
the language of the Bushmen was the original language of humanity or that the language of the Hottentots was merely an
ape-like babble. But even if these people have not made
more progress in material and intellectual culture, their
language already has a very complicated and widely developed
structure and demonstrates that they have long stages of
development behind them.

Some peoples for one reason or another have not
developed agriculture or even the domestication of animals.
In this case, individualization and the drive for acquisi-
tion generally have also remained limited, and of course,
along with the acquisitive drive, property law and economy.
It is equally understandable that such peoples should not
have learned to count, for one first learns to count when a
need for it is present, and the need generally comes first
with money.

That such peoples are in the highest degree unecono-
mical, living from day to day without, so far as they could,
caring for the future, is also very understandable because
care for the future comes first when the economic concept,
that is the regulated concern with property, begins to awake.

Naturally, the development of their thought is not
thereby interrupted, it has merely had narrow limits set for
it. They may possess very complicated marriage arrangements,
in which regard they may have gone through great revolutions;
the same could be true too for their language, which may
already allow the relations of place, time, causation, and

so on to be expressed with great refinement.

Whether a development of artistic talent is possible
at their stage depends upon many circumstances; it is not
impossible, provided that they succeed in procuring the
necessary tools. Music and crafts can arise among men at
lower stages, and artistic, dramatic dances are frequent.

I have already displayed elsewhere (1895a, 197) the
methodological error of drawing from a people's so-called
general culture level the conclusion that their institutions
are the original ones. This point of view can give us some
information about the initial circumstances of their property law, but none at all concerning their marriage and
family law.

A people that has remained behind in the first stages
of material culture, and therefore also in those of intellectual culture, can in a short time have changed from its
original legal condition to another; whereas other peoples
with a more progressive culture have with the greatest
tenacity retained earlier conditions. Would anyone dispute,
for instance, that the Etruscans had mother right on the
basis of the fact that some peoples at the lowest cultural
level have father right? The Romans wrested themselves with
difficulty from the agnatic family to cognation; on the other
hand there are Negro peoples and Malayan tribes who have
already developed the cognatic family. Elsewhere (1895a,
197) I have shown that it is possible for a people of a high
level of culture to retain an uninflected language: the
culture of the Chinese was certainly higher than that of the

American Indians, and still they did not achieve an agglutinative language, which assuredly represents a much higher stage of linguistic development.

Other scholars put special store in the events of animal life. Because it is assumed that certain animal species, especially anthropoid apes, lived in monogamous marriage, it cannot be supposed that the genus Homo began with promiscuous or group marriage.

Arguments of this sort must be immediately rejected. The mating patterns of different animals are notably various; for example, two species which in other respects are closely related often are fundamentally different with regard to their sex lives; so that from the one species one may conclude nothing at all about the other. And the further inference to human marriage customs is a fortiori completely incorrect; for the mental level of animals does not at all depend upon their sexual propriety. Furthermore, it is precisely social life which has always been especially characteristic of man and conducive to his development, so that it would be easier to conclude that a unifying element holding society so firmly together as does group marriage may have been a primary agent for development in the first prehistoric culture.

How little there is to arguments from animal species is shown by the circumstance that the same reasoning has been used in the attempt to dispute both the fact of human omnivorousness and, in particular, that of cannibalism. The case for cannibalism is certain;[1] the human species has

committed atrocities from which almost every animal would
shrink--and still the human species has bypassed all the
animals and has become the undisputed lord of the earth. It
is not tenderness and a delicate reserve which have been
given priority in animal nature; most significant are the
social drives and the organized unity of the masses, and it
has been emphasized with justice that the anthropoid apes
were surpassed by (otherwise) lower animals in just this respect (Rauber 1884, 2: 306 ff.).

Regarding the earlier or later appearance of a legal
institution, and the development from one to another, from
the point of view of critical method the following principles alone are correct:

1. When in the life of nations it can be demonstrated that an institution a has evolved into institution b,
and if a reverse development is nowhere to be found (or at
least only under very exceptional circumstances), then the
conclusion is methodologically permissible that institution
a is the earlier.

2. This conclusion can be further strengthened if
the elements which have brought the development about can be
identified; if it can be shown that these elements recur
among the most diverse peoples; and if in particular it can
be shown in human nature and from the character of the evolution of material or ideal culture that peoples strive more
after institution b than a.

3. This would still not prove that institution b has
developed from institution a everywhere it is found, because

it is conceivable that a people began with institution b or
that this institution emerged from another institution (for
example, x). Here various considerations may come to our
aid in order to free us from uncertainty and to supply us a
firm foundation: among these are analogy and historical re-
collection, and above all the residual forms which appear to
be relics of a particular original institution.

4. Observations of these residual forms is therefore
of special importance. The following principle holds here:
where we find only the residual form among one people, while
among another the institution is in full flower, the latter
people should be given special consideration to reveal the
institution's character and its original constitution. We
should not object on the ground that the latter people may
otherwise belong to a higher cultural level and that one
would actually expect a fading of its original structure.
One may best study totemism among American Indians--better,
for example, than among Negro tribes--while on the other hand
the Africans (and the Australians) provide the most instructive examples of adolescent initiation.

5. The question of what is to be regarded as a residual form is to be solved in particular through observation
of peoples among whom it may be historically demonstrated
that the institution has deteriorated into a mere formality.
The assumption that the forms are residual would naturally
be supported if there are a number of similar ones apparently bearing this character. And the assumption would be
significantly strengthened if it proved impossible or in-

conceivable to trace the form back to a different set of
structural elements, and especially if there are particular
external signs which recur regularly. Thus the avunculate
will gain credibility as a sign of former mother right if
it is proved that it is constantly the mother's brother
rather than the father's brother who exercises the special
rights, and that the rights which are due the uncle are
those which are otherwise invested in the father and guar-
dian--those then which indicate familial authority.

6. Finally, the link between two institutions is an
important point. The inference of an internal connection
between institutions will seem more probable when we constantly encounter a link between them, especially if this is
found in different stages of cultural development. This inference will be valuable because it will make it possible
for us to deduce with probability that the one institution
exists or was formerly present where we find the other. This
deduction will acquire certainty if we succeed in making
evident the psychological and sociological connections of
the two institutions; so that the intuitive assumption of
probability is confirmed by the internal comprehension of
the phenomena.

I refer here, by way of example, to the connection
among totemism, group marriage, and mother right, which will
be clarified below.

With these criteria it will be possible to secure a
firm basis, especially with respect to family organization
and its history. To proceed on any other course leads to

deviations and will-o'-the-wisps. And if, on top of this, a
scholar, out of pure reverence for the human species, even
shrinks from accepting certain historical facts because they
are unworthy of the human race (in the same way perhaps as
the jus primae noctis has been combated because it was taken as impossible that such a stain could rest on humanity),
then scientific objectivity is completely lacking and research may by chance bring something fruitful to light, but
its method offers no assurance of a correct foundation and
there can be no talk of a sufficiently scientific evaluation
of the proffered material.

III

In recent times great weight has been given to the Sarasin
brothers' account of the Vedda, which indeed claims to be
an attempt to advance the prehistory of humanity; and a number of serious scholars have allowed themselves to be per-
suaded by the nature of the Vedda into thinking prehistoric
man lived in very orderly monogamous or quasi-monogamous
relationships, and thus into regarding the doctrine of
sexual communism as refuted.

Here again is the persistent error of imagining that
tribes at a low economic or intellectual level also represent the legal prehistory of humanity. It is on the contrary just those deteriorating, miserable human remnants,
fallen into the greatest poverty, who have necessarily fallen away from the original legal conditions. They have perhaps suffered the greatest social defects, so that one social
trait after the other has disappeared and a pitiable indi-

vidual existence is left. This does not mean to say that
the Vedda formerly had a civilization, but that the original
humans were more socially inclined than appears to be the
case among the Vedda, just as one also acquires from the
historical data the impression of a formerly more intensive
activity among this people, even if these data leave much
room for doubt.[2]

So when the Sarasin brothers infer from the Vedda's
inferior state that they represent humanity's primal condition, they are just as wrong as they would be if they
supposed the Vedda spoke the original human language. In
fact the Vedda language has changed so much that it seems
to have almost completely merged with Sinhalese. What
grounds then do we have to infer a static immutability of
their law from prehistoric times? Their simple material and
intellectual culture? But is simple culture then equivalent
to persistence in original conditions? Such tribes might
have gone through the greatest revolutions in social structure, though these may not have led to civilization. Is
every transformation tantamount to cultural progress?
Changes in social structure would probably have arisen in
just such difficult subsistence conditions as occurred
among less developed peoples. And the whole hypothesis that
the Vedda represent original human conditions certainly
hangs as much in the air as the Sarasin brothers' remarkable
phantasm (Sarasin 1895, 595) of searching for the prototype
of Adam and Eve among the Vedda and seeing the origin of the
paradise myth in the narrative traditions from the time when

they populated India. We could equally well conclude that
their physical appearance still displays the pure original
human form and that we should conceive Adam and Eve as Ved-
doid types. But human build and physique may have changed
very much in the course of time, even among people without
any civilization to speak of, and the same holds for their
social and legal organization. Change is just not the same
thing as cultural progress; this tenet has been overlooked
innumerable times.

The Sarasins' report offers a pleasing confirmation
of what is already known, but despite their personal observation and learned apparatus, in view of what is presented
in the Rechtsvergleichenden Studien (Kohler 1889a, 213), it
offers little that is new.[3] We learn (Sarasin 1895, 482)
that the mountain Vedda live in individual families, where
the family head possibly occupies a preponderent position
de facto (thus without a legally established and fixed
chieftainship and without a more detailed legal organization
of the family united in a clan, varga); we learn (p. 475)
that the individual family jealously reserves individual
hunting areas for itself, and (460 ff.) that marriage occurs without much ceremony (either completely without ceremony or with the simple offering of gifts or girding with
the waistband). Especially confirmed (pp. 465 ff.) is the
proposition, unjustly doubted by others, that they marry
their sisters (even their daughters).

On the other hand, Gillings's report, on the basis
of which I inferred a right for the husband to repudiate his

wife and a certain mother right, is contested, inasmuch as
Gillings is supposed not only to have confused mountain and
village Vedda, but doubtless also other (Sinhalese) tribes.
It is explained rather that marriage is strictly monogamous
until death[4] and that father right exists at least to the
extent that weapons are inherited by sons from their
fathers.[5] Furthermore, the report of compensation for
murder based on Gillings is also to be contested; rather
murder or adultery simply call for blood revenge. Still,
even according to the Sarasins we have in one case a kind
of compensation. Namely, the varga owns the cliff honey in
its region. Collecting it is dangerous, and while a man of
the varga gathers it, another person must secure his rope.
If the first meets with an accident, the second must answer
for him (Sarasin 1895, 490).

I will leave the contested points in Gillings open
and will assume complete, lifelong monogamy. The Sarasins
have not proved the existence of father right; for they seem
not to have considered that if marriage is sibling marriage,
the mother's brother is necessarily none other than the
father, and if the son inherits the weapons from the father,
then one does not know if the father is to be taken here as
father or as mother's brother. And should this form of inheritance also take place in those exceptional cases where
the marriage was not sibling marriage, then it is conceivable that precisely the rule according to which the uncle
is equivalent to the father has in such cases simply led to
analogy.

In general, all this only proves that while in-breed-
ing prevailed, an isolation and exclusiveness set in through
which the human social impulse became stunted. It is the
more understandable that one man had relations with only one
woman, since polygamy and the communal possession were pro-
moted only by the taking of the wife from outside, on the
one hand, and by lively intercourse among different families,
on the other. The Vedda offer the example of a people who,
through isolation of the family and endogamy, largely lost
their social instinct and therefore became incapable of
rising to a more developed cultural form. There can be no
talk here of a primal picture of the earliest times of our
race; humanity would be pitiable if it had had this origin.
Rough, wild, dissolute man may have been, but he had in himself a wealth of creative energy and a wealth of social ties
which enabled him to unfold the rich kernel after stripping
off the rough shell. The people that originally lived in
strictly isolated pairs is not the people destined to rule
the world. And even though the picture of a lifelong,
faithful monogamy among the Vedda may be more attractive
to us than the communal possession of women, one must consider that in cultivated times, alongside of the monogamous
isolation of the family, a repletion of social contrivances
and influences binds us together, whereas in primordial
times it was precisely the communistic conditions in marriage relations which had to lead to continual communication
and continual exchange of ideas. For world history, we must
take into consideration, not what appears attractive or re-

pulsive when isolated from the whole, but what has been ad-
vantageous in the development of the races.

IV

The work by Westermarck which has already been mentioned
stands under a different sign. It does not rely upon a
single people, but searches all over the earth for the
material to solve the question of the original family.
However, the diligent collection of material does not make
the scholar, and it is only a methodical assimilation and
not just any array of the material that helps. In this regard Westermarck fails from beginning to end, and his work
is therefore of importance only as a collection of material.

Morgan's conclusions about the classificatory form
of relationship are dispatched by the fact that relationship expressions depend not on consanguinity but on other
ties, especially on the elder or younger series of the persons united in a clan. It is thereby stressed, with the
greatest misunderstanding (Westermarck 1891, 89), that only
the uncertainty of paternity could have led to designating
several men as father, but that this does not hold true of
a multiplicity of women as mothers--as though the classificatory relationship could have arisen from the uncertainty of descent from the father rather than from the idea of
group marriage, that is, marriage between groups instead of
individuals. A series of peoples are therewith unmethodi-
cally jumbled together, among some of whom relationship is
reckoned in one way, and among others in a different way.

In fact, however, a methodical study of Morgan's

tables and a study of the evidence for the Omaha given by
Dorsey shows most clearly that all of these relationship
forms could have sprung only from the concept of group marriage. We have the clearest proof for this in the Omaha and
Choctaw forms, because here the special nature of group
marriage has led to a system of relationship nomenclature
which is as complicated as it is strictly logical, and
whose standards were set not by age and youth but by the
relations occasioned by this special mode of conjugal tie.
Perusal of this material shows in addition that the same
thing is also strictly observed in affinity. I refer only
to the basically different nomenclature for the cousins in
Omaha and Choctaw relationship, and to the unbelievable
consistency with which the subtlest conclusions are drawn.
Proof of this will be given below (chap. 3); to say more
here would anticipate our later presentation.[6]

     The allegation that a savage unable to count the
fingers of his own hand would certainly not be in a position to keep such complicated kinship forms straight (Westermarck 1891, 89) likewise lacks any scientific basis.
Counting is a completely different function from distinguishing relationship, and some tribes who cannot count to five
retain the most complicated relationship systems in their
heads. After all, such peoples do have a fairly large stock
of words in their language; they do have their particles
and suffixes which they make use of flawlessly and with
great certainty. And they do have the subtlest rules of
assimilation, combination and dissociation. In fact they

also have a rich treasury of myths and fables. Insofar as
they need to, they distinguish very exactly among plants
and animals. That they do not count is a consequence of the
fact that they have no need to, in the absence of money, and
therefore have not learned to; counting presupposes a kind
of abstraction with which their life can dispense. If however these tribes live in accord with the idea of group marriage, they will use the concepts of uncle, nephew, brother-
in-law, son-in-law, following group marriage just as correctly as they would following individual marriage if that
were their marriage type. If the savage knows that a man
forms his family with his wife, her sister, niece and aunt,
then he will automatically understand that a cousin will
sometimes also be a brother, sometimes a nephew, uncle or
son. This will appear complicated only to us, who must remove ourselves from the grip of kinship ideas based on
individual marriage and think our way into a completely
different world of kinship. It is just as if we were to
find ourselves in a region where the three dimensions were
displaced and where we would have to rethink our concept of
space. This would cause us great difficulty, whereas a
people who were native there would find their way about just
as easily as do our savages in our three dimensions. If we
were suddenly to be reduced to the size of ants, it would
take us a long time to find our way about in this small
spatial dimension as well as the ants do which we trample
when we go for a walk.

        Westermarck's treatment of mother right suffers from

the same faults. What does it mean when (pp. 98 ff.) he
brings together in the same place a multitude of peoples
having both father right and mother right? This treatment
advances us not one iota in regard to the question of prius
and posterius. It is far more important to study the development of single tribes to see whether father right developed later (which indeed has been shown to be the case among
a number of tribes).

In addition, father right is often connected with
the special character of the marriage form, as becomes immediately evident among the Malays and the African Negroes.
Without a consideration of all these circumstances no
scientific solution of the question is possible, and the
compilation of this sort of data has no value beyond that
of a compilation.

Nevertheless, Westermarck's whole work is cast after
this fashion, and no explanation is required if we value it
only as a collection of material.

V

Mucke has traveled a new path in the reconstruction of prehistory in his work on the horde and the family (1895). To
be sure, we must be astonished by the wealth of new illumi-
nation which it provides—if it were only halfway right!
In view of this work, the efforts of ethnological jurisprudence should stand completely aside as befits monstrous
aberrations, for we have all traveled the wrong path. Morgan, Bachofen, Post, and finally I myself have all worked
by false methods and have unscientifically manufactured wild

and speculative inventions based on incompletely analyzed
observations.

Let us see what the author has to offer. Penetrating
into the depths of gray antiquity, this scholar informs us
that the family was preceded by the horde, which was a
strictly ordered and regulated unit, not a legal but a natural order like perhaps a beehive--a natural order before
knowledge and hence a sort of paradise without sin. The
horde camped in the form of a ship in accordance with the
principle "like seeks like." The women located themselves
on one side, the men on the other. Similarly, there were
assigned locations for each of the different age groups;
after being weaned, the boys lived in one room, the men in
a second, and the old men in a third; and the women were
analogously distributed by age.

Why should men and women need to live together? Sexual union occurred only at certain periods of the year, for
example in the spring and, indeed, in public.

Upon reaching a certain age level the boys advanced
to the men's chamber, while the men moved on to that of the
old men, and this transfer would have been associated with
certain ceremonies. This produced in particular youth initiation, frequently accompanied by circumcision (which no
doubt automatically led to fasts, to temporary withdrawal
from the community, and to obligatory beatings when the
recalcitrant did not submit).

These conditions naturally make completely self-ex-
planatory the classificatory system of kinship, according

to which Ego calls all the men of one room father, the children of the other rooms son or daughter; and everything
which has been inferred since Morgan concerning the possibility of group marriage means no more than a fantastic
speculation.

On the contrary, everything follows very simply from
spatial considerations, including the feeling of sympathy
among the members of the horde, which increases and decreas-
es according to distance (Mucke 1895, 55). In fact, we
have all failed to understand the importance of space.

Marriage came about automatically. Due to certain
psychological laws marriage had to be monogamous and,
indeed, it had to be sibling marriage. It was a predetermined arrangement of nature that the brother automatically
marry the sister. This doubtlessly requires us to assume
that boys and girls were born in regular alternation.

This pleasant order of things was disrupted by kid-
napping. A woman was abducted, but for use as slave labor
and by no means for sexual purposes. Once in a while, however, things went awry, and the abductor himself was cap-
tured and taken prisoner into the horde which he had intended to harm. Such slaves, which the author designates as
"famels" in his new terminology, were given a special settlement (round, not in the form of a ship) near the horde. They
served the horde as a source of labor; and things would again
have been in order if sexual irregularities had not gradually
set in. Not that the wife abductor had actually had relations with the wife from the beginning; but gradually such

things did occur (as these things happen), and thus arose
a special community in which the abducted woman and her
children lived together. And since she had a rather stren-
uous life and carried her children on her back while she
worked, Mucke conjectures, quite tentatively but very ingen-
iously, that by this means the children developed into
brachycephals (pp. 113 ff., 191).

The author describes how the family was formed by
such famels living near the horde and how under the pressure of the family the horde gradually disintegrated. Unfortunately, he has not given a detailed representation of
this evolution, and the history of clanship up to the present family is more intimated than detailed.

The author succeeds in demonstrating this grandiose
process of development through a series of illuminating
linguistic derivations which we recommend to the consideration of our philologists; for in these things the philologist must assist the ethnologist.

"Relationship" (Verwandschaft) is connected with
"wall" (Wand); and "relatives" (Verwandte) are the "locally
inwalled" (Umwandeten). In the same way Geburt ("birth,
origin") is connected with bûr ("farmer") and Anglo-Saxon
bûr in the meaning of "dwelling, room" (p. 18); and "horde,"
orta, orda, with Latin ordo and German ort ("place," etc.).[7]

In fact, the same word appears also in the expression
Ordal ("ordeal"); Ordal (Urtel, Urtheil) was originally the
horde oracle. The connection with the ordeal depends on a
later Christian view, and thus the original meaning was lost,

so that even a Jacob Grimm erroneously derived the expression from Anglo-Saxon (pp. 104, 105).

We have then a connection of "horde," "place" (Ort), "earth" (Erde), "ordeal" (Ordal)--all in accordance with a local encampment and ordering of the human community.

The author finds proof for his opinion in the words of other languages as well. In Hawaiian ka-na means "my husband" and ma-ku-a-hu-na-hai "my father-in-law." Why these elongated names? They are "verbal allusions to the proximity or distance in living space from the standpoint of the speaker" (p. 25), just like when a savage shouts "ah-ah-a-a-a-a-a" when he wants to say that someone lives quite far away (p. 26).

And this is not even the end of the etymological list. For example, the eteri (ceteri), from e and ter (ter in pater, mater, terra), stand in opposition to clan (from which comes clandestine). Furthermore, though we may previously have interpreted Indian varna, "caste," as color, we are now instructed that varna, verna comes from ves-na: ves or vas means "to dwell" (hence vester). Purus derives from pur, "inwalling," and castus from cast, "encampment" (pp. 243-45). The word Geschlecht (slahta, meaning "descent," "family," "race") likewise originally had a spatial significance; it comes from Schlag ("stroke") in the sense of Verschlag ("partition," "compartment," p. 199). The same is true, too, for Schlacht ("battle"), for just as a Scharmutzel ("skirmish") is a fight among several Scharen ("bands," "troops"), so is a Slacht a battle among several slahtas (p. 199).

No less important psychological explanations lend
support to these convincing linguistic proofs. Sexual relations were formerly monogamous, and a man's wife was originally strictly predetermined, for how could prehistoric
man have had any impulse for variation? For that a combinatorial imagination is required, and this he lacked (p. 57).
It is very improbable "that prehistoric man could through
contemplative imagination have arrived at the conviction
that a second and third woman would provide today the same
delight which a first woman had provoked yesterday" (p. 59).
No, he must have felt the need to mate with the woman with
whom he had previously united; and consequently conjugal relations were permanently monogamous. These arguments completely confirm our conviction of the rich combinatorial
imagination of Tom Cat, who searches for variety on the
roofs, or of the hunting dog who is capable of grasping the
analogy between one game animal and another ...

Thus by means of psychological analysis, Mucke dis-
proves that the horde developed on consanguineous principles.
We were wrong to believe until now that primitives have always associated the child with the mother who bore it, carried it, and what is more, nursed it for perhaps two or
three years; and naturally we were also wrong when we explained on this basis the mother cult and the cult of the
umbilical cord. For "there is all the difference in the
world between the perception that a child comes from the
corporal mother's womb and the recognition that one owes

one's existence to a particular mother" (p. 167).

We have all overlooked the fact that descent from the actual mother cannot be established through our own observation but only through those of a third person. As for the physiological connection to the mother, how could prehistoric man have solved such scientific problems? And on the other hand, if the tie to the mother is obvious at first glance, why is the mother cult, mysticism, coupled with so simple a fact (p. 167)?

Of course, blood is in general such a mysterious fluid that a blood tie could never have been the basis of the first organizations (p. 21); from which inference one automatically arrives at the author's opinion that the first relationships were spatial ones. Once this is recognized, the most complicated problems may be solved with the greatest simplicity (p. 21).

Mucke uses psychology to refute the notion that violence was a decisive factor in prehistoric times, for violence "depends on desire for power, which is no elementary desire and already presupposes a conception of the future" (p. 299). Prehistoric man, however, did not yet have a conception of the future, which developed only later (p. 110).

To this we must modestly add that an intelligent house dog which fears his master, or a trained animal which can be brought to act through just this awareness of impending pleasure or pain, stands a gigantic step above prehistoric man. The latter is supposed to have known no fear. He was the youth who could learn no fear, because, as the author adds, children learn fear relatively late. When they experience "fright" this is something else (p. 299).

We are also convincingly shown that abduction of women could originally have had no sexual purpose. Originally the subduer even kept away from the slave: "The sensual soul was not yet ripe and ready for sexual desire because that requires a feeling of equality, which between two originally unequal beings can only be gained by an abstraction in which the superior represses his superiority" (p. 118). Naturally! Wicked abstraction! It has all those sexual irregularities on its conscience.

Mucke also draws upon psychological reports concerning the experience of pleasure and pain among primitives to conclude that sexuality must have been quite limited, so that the periodic sexual festivals were completely sufficient (p. 111). And should anyone remind us of the terribly sensuous power in the dances of the so-called primitive peoples, then we must doubtless recall that it was only in later stages that our humanity became tainted with this sensuality.

Furthermore, though Westermarck set forth the idea that circumcision, like tattooing, originally had a decorative character, Mucke refutes this notion by means of the following psychological arguments. Such an ornamental embellishment would of course have had meaning only if one or another individual had adopted it. However, if they all did so, where then lay the attractiveness that ornamentation was supposed to afford (p. 78)? This is a very conclusive de-

duction, which might still today have a very civilizing
influence on the foppish endeavors of men and the fashion
rage of women.

Also, by philosophically deductive means, Mucke
demonstrates various things which to our downfall we have
overlooked. Simple observation can naturally lead to nothing if it is not analyzed, and when it is incorrectly
analyzed, then it is just our own sort of wild hypotheses
which are produced.

Order, not disorder, must have reigned in the beginning, for how could order arise from disorder? Prehistoric man could certainly construct nothing he did not
perceive. Hence, he must have seen order, and that could
only have been the sensually perceivable order of the orda.
If humanity had lived in group marriage, it would have
grown wild and could not have struggled upward to cultural
maturity (p. 35). And should we have the reply on the tip
of our tongue that the unregulated could indeed become
regulated through modification in continuous stages and
that, in view of humanity's inexhaustible potential, the
wildness and sensuousness of youth did not cut it off from
the possibility of a future achievement of culture, then we
must supress our speculative error in order not to become
even more involved in disaster. We should add that the
author explains that group marriage is impossible, for how
could man arrive at individual marriage from group marriage?
From what source of knowledge could humanity draw the experience in order to mount to the former? From external

experience? This was lacking because the object of sensory
intuition was lacking. From internal experience? But this
must have been preceded by external experience. If group
marriage had existed, it would have had to endure eternally
(pp. 63, 64). Probatum est.

We find further on that it was an error when we supposed that the infant betrothal which occurs among some
peoples is the result of a later development. This of
course contradicts the evolutionary law which advances from
the unconscious to the conscious, from necessity to freedom
(p. 58).

Naturally, all the prisons of mankind are original,
the forest is now freer than ever, and the law regulating
mushroom and berry picking comes from primordial times.

Since the author erects his structure on such a
clear basis, he is satisfied with a relatively small stock
of observations; and how can we regard it as an error that
he somewhat wildly mixes them up? He does, after all, succeed by his method in correcting the observations of his
sources and in proving that, on very important points, errors of observation must be present.

Of course, at first sight the author's theory is in
danger of suffering shipwreck on a single fact, the fact of
the thoroughgoing prohibition on marriage within the totem.
Among American Indians and Australian Aborigines, nothing
seems more certainly attested than this prohibition. But
here errors of observation must be present, or these must
be secondary phenomena, resulting from the fact that the

regular alternation in the series of brothers and sisters
got out of order (p. 102). Thus Howitt's report is cor-
rected, when he expressly declares of one Australian tribe
that marriage within the totem is forbidden because the
members of the totem spring from the same blood. The whole
context is said to show on the contrary that the so called
noa marriage which is described there is horde marriage, and
thus a marriage between relatives (p. 146). In the same way
Kubary's description of the Mortlock Islands is amended.
Kubary says as certainly as can be that sexual promiscuity
within the same clan is treated as incest and is immediately
avenged. By vengeance he naturally means punishment from
the people because incest is reckoned by such peoples as a
sinful abomination. From this the following tenet has developed on the Mortlock and Pelau Islands: women marry not
in their own clan but into a strange one; they can also
surrender themselves temporarily to a strange clan as armengols (servants).

The author corrects Kubary first of all in that no
vengeance is possible within the group, for on these islands where the horde condition exists such a deviation from
the horde principle is undoubtedly not to be considered.
Armengols must be "famels," that is stolen or bought women.
One should read for oneself the author's critique (pp 283
ff.), which finds obscure points in Kubary's report even
though he has used only the abstract of it from volume 53
of Das Ausland.

I also have it from Buch's reports on the Votiak

that the unmarried maidens there live in a form of communism
and that it seems a blessing to them to have quite a few il-
legitimate children.   I have been so much the more confident
that this was true because Buch was not, after all, a passing
traveler but lived three years as a doctor among the Votiak
and says expressly on page 45 of his work, "Maidens and boys
have sexual relations with one another completely without
restraint, and so-called chastity sets no limits to their
love." In this connection he mentions a proverb: "If the
peasant doesn't love, neither will God love." He also mentions that he received reports from Russian peasants in Votiak villages and that an informant told him of a marriage
game among maidens and youths in which the pairs give themselves up to sexual wantoness. He mentions a case in which
a Votiak maiden had a child by a Russian officer and was
thereafter courted by many suitors and adds to this, "I
could tell of many such examples." However, when I deduce
from this a sort of premarital communism, I am sternly re-
proved by Mucke. If a maiden bears a child before marriage,
this does not necessarily mean that she has had traffic with
more than one man, and especially with other than the future
husband. It is only a question of a bit of boasting which
one allows oneself in an animated mood. How can a traveler
follow a maiden around on her heels for months and years on
end? "Neither a jurist nor a statistician should regard
such traveler's conjectures as fact (p. 142)!"

       With this I can close the critique. It requires no
justification if I leave this work out of further consider-

ation, as it lacks all method (whether historical, juristic, psychological, or philosophical), as it adopts such an attitude toward the evidence of observation, and as it leads in this manner to insupportable fantasies and cannot even claim the value of an instructive error.

2
Totemism and Mother Right

I

The totem belief is one of humanity's most civilizing and
vigorous religious impulses, for it contains the seed of the
future structure of the family and state.

We may therefore derive uncommon instruction concerning the history of humanity from the American Indians, among
whom this belief has most vividly persisted. Nowhere else
has this universal institution been so plastically implemented as it has been among the Indians, including those of the
far North (cf. Parkman 1884: LI; Schoolcraft 1851-57: 2:
49; Frazer 1887: 2 ff.). It is only among the Indians in
the West that the institution has fallen into decay.[1]

The Indian tribes are divided into distinct totems,
claiming descent from an animal, for which reason they may
not kill the totem animal or even touch it. Their cosmo-
logical legends record this descent, and the Indians believe
that after death they turn back into the animal. Even the
personal names used within the totem are frequently borrowed
from the characteristics and activities of the animal.

Similarly, they often copy their hairstyle and decoration from the totem animal, and it is used in tattooing

as a sort of family arms. The Indians mimic the animal in
dances, they masquerade as the animal, and they design their
face masks and costumes in imitation of it. Animal paint-
ings, which are the oldest art form, and mimicry of animals,
which is the oldest form of drama, originate in this ancient
and hallowed totemism (cf. Kohler 1895b, 37 ff.).

The custom of marriage to plants also derives from
it, as I have demonstrated several times in my studies of
Indian law (1891, 331; 1892, 119). I regarded the institution then as an artificial arrangement intended to achieve
specific aims. This is doubtless what it became later, but
the investigations of the Melusin myth convinced me that
these practices are based on a naive belief, and this belief is that man may unite with the spirit contained in a
plant, an animal , or even in an implement. The same belief
is therefore also found in America in the Huron custom of
marrying virgins to the spirit of a fishnet laid among the
brides (Parkman 1884, lxix).

II

The great variety which totemism may display in its development is best seen in the practical form it is given among
individual tribes, from which we give the following selection (see also Waitz 1862, 3: 120; Morgan 1877, 151 ff.;
and Frazer 1887, 3 ff., 11 ff., 25 ff.).

The Wyandot have eleven totems: deer, bear, hawk,
beaver, wolf, sea snake, porcupine, and four species of
turtle.[2] Each totem clan has its distinctive manner of face
painting and decoration (Powell 1881, 64) and a distinct

cult of the totem animal (p. 65). Several totem clans are
joined in special friendship associations or phratries (p.
60); so that these eleven totem clans are distributed among
four phratries, which have importance in worship and at
festivals (pp. 60, 65). Personal names are derived from
the characteristics, habits, and activities of the totem
animal (p. 60); and each year the clan bestows the names on
the children born in the previous year (p. 64).

The six Iroquois tribes (the Mohawk, Seneca, Onondaga, Cayuga, Oneida, and Tuscarora) have nine totems: wolf,
bear, turtle, beaver, deer, snipe, heron, eel, and hawk,[3]
some of which however have been split into subtotems. Not
all of these totems are now found among each of the tribes;
the Seneca, Cayuga, and Onondaga each have eight. The Tuscarora apparently also have eight, but among them wolf has
divided into gray and yellow wolf, and turtle into large
and small turtle. On the other hand, only three totems are
present among the Oneida and Mohawk.[4]   Among the Iroquois,
too, the clans sometimes are closely confederated with one
another as brother totems. These are clans which appear
to have arisen through branching off from an original clan.
For example, among the Seneca the wolf, bear, beaver and
turtle clans are in one association, while the deer, snipe
and heron and hawk clans are in the other (Morgan 1870, 10;
1851, 79).

Among the descendants of the Mohawk, the St. Regis
Indians on the Canadian border, there are today still the
wolf, bear, turtle, and plover totems (Dept. of the Inter-

ior 1894, 475).

The Delaware (Heckewelder 1821, 434) and the Mohegans had the totems: turtle, turkey and wolf. The Potawatomi had fifteen and the Ojibwa even as many as twenty-three totems (Morgan 1877, 166, 167).

Among the Iroquois and the Delaware, face painting and animal dances were connected with totemism (Loskiel 1789, 64; Heckewelder, p. 429 ff.). The Iroquois bear dance was mentioned as early as 1676 in a Jesuit report: "The third feast was a masquerade by people dressed as bears and who danced in a most surprising manner" (Anon. 1854). Loskiel reports of the Delaware and Iroquois that they had festivals where old men and women covered themselves in deerskins (p. 55). They also avoided killing the totem animal and believed themselves to have descended from it (Heckewelder, p. 429 ff.; Dwight 1821: 4: 196).

The same is true of the Attiguatan, whose dances were already described by Champlain (1830, 1: 387): "When dancing, they each have a bear or some other animal's skin on their heads, though bearskin is most common."

Dorsey's excellent work (1884a, 211 ff.) gives us exceptionally detailed evidence concerning the totemic arrangement among the Omaha. The actual Omaha comprise ten totem clans, which split into subclans. Their ten clans are Elk, Black Shoulder Buffalo, Hanga Buffalo, Catada (consisting of Black Bear, Small Bird, Eagle, and Turtle), Green Clay, Wolf, Buffalo Tail, Dear Head, Buffalo Calf, and Reptile. The first five clans form one group (called Hangacenu),

while the second five form another group (_Ictasanda_). When
they camp together, they make a circle with a path in the
middle and with five clans on the right of the path and five
on the left.

The nature of totemism, that is, the doctrine of descent from and the worship of a totem animal, is especially
clearly shown among the Omaha. The Elk clan may not eat
(male) elk or deer or they will break out in boils (Dorsey
1884_a_, 225). The Black Shoulder Buffalo clan has several
sections which have different prohibitions; for example, one
section may not eat buffalo tongue and may not touch a
buffalo head (p. 231). _Hanga_ clan descends from buffalo and
splits into several sub-clans with corresponding food prohibitions; some of these may not eat buffalo tongue or may
eat nothing from the side of the buffalo (p. 235). There
are also several different prohibitions among the subclans
of the _Catada._ Some of them may not eat black bear nor touch
its skin, while others may not eat small birds and others no
turtles (pp. 236 ff.). The Green Clay clan may touch no
verdigris (p. 241). The Buffalo Tail clan may not eat calves
of cattle or buffalo while they are still red (p. 244). Members of Dear Head clan may not eat deerskin or fat (p. 245);
Buffalo Calf members may eat no buffalo calves (p. 248); and
reptiles are forbidden to members of Reptile clan (p. 248;
Morgan's report, 1877, differs somewhat).

An interesting example of the tie to a totem is shown
when at his death a member of a buffalo clan is dressed in
a buffalo robe and told, "You come from the buffalo, return

to it" (Dorsey 1884a, 229, 233; cf. Kohler 1895b, 39). Another such tie reveals itself in a clan's special hairstyle,
designed to resemble the totem animal. The best example is
provided by the Turtle subclan, who shave the head leaving
two locks on each side, as well as one over the forehead and
one at back, representing feet, head and tail (Dorsey,
1884a, p. 240).

The first names (individual names) commonly used
within a clan frequently refer to its totem animal. Among
the Elk totem there are names like the Soft Horn, the Yellow
Horn, the Branching Horns, the Four Horns, the Dark Horn,
Young Elk, White Elk, Big Elk and so on (Dorsey 1884a, 227);
and in the Black Bear subclan there are names like the
Young Black Bear, the Four Eyes (two spots over the eyes),
Gray Foot and so on (p. 237). But the personal name is not
always totemic, and there is in addition the reasonable pro-
vision that two members of the same totem may not have the
same name, which automatically leads to the adoption of
other naming systems (p. 227, n. 3).

There are also dances referring to a totem animal
where the dancer imitates a bear, eagle or something of the
sort (pp. 349, 280).

The Osage, who are related to the Omaha, also have
two moieties, the peace moiety, which formerly could kill
no animal, and the war moiety which is divided again into
two sections. Formerly these groupings comprised, respectively, seven plus seven plus seven clans; later, since the
clans of the war moiety fused, only seven plus seven, equal-

ing fourteen clans, among them Buffalo Face, Red Eagle, and
Thunder (Dorsey 1884b, 113).

The clans of the Ottawa (also related to the Omaha)
descend from rabbit, carp, and bear and have their corresponding creation story (Dorman 1881, 233). The Kansa possessed a wolf and panther totem (Hunter 1823, 310). The
Iowa had the totems eagle, dove, wolf, bear, elk, beaver,
buffalo, snake; and each of these had its own special hairstyle (Schoolcraft 1851-57, 3:269; cf. Morgan 1877, 156).
Among the Mandan there were the totems buffalo, beaver, elk,
and bear (Catlin 1857, 1:136, 145; Morgan [1877, 158] differs) and doubtless also eagle, raven, and ermine; and the
braves wore eagle or raven feathers, ermine or buffalo horns
on their heads (Catlin 1857, 1:127). Of course they could
hardly avoid eating buffalo, their main food source, just as
little as could the other buffalo clans; but perhaps they
abstained from buffalo tongue or other parts of the animal.

The Crow Indians and the Assiniboin spliced extra
lengths to their hair in order to give themselves the appearance of crows (Catlin, 1:50, 55). The Cheyenne had
hunting dances in which some dancers represented buffalo and
antelope and other game while others represented hunters
(Kate 1885a, 363). The Dakota had the bear totem and performed dances in which they imitated bears (Catlin 1:245);
they also had snake, turtle, wolf, and buffalo totems (Carver, in Morgan 1877, 154). The buffalo totem occurs among
the related Blackfoot where the bravest wore buffalo horns
on their heads (Catlin, 1:34). They also had a bear totem

and the medicine man dressed up like a bear (Catlin, 1:40.
Morgan [1877, 171] lists further totems). The Sauk have a
trout totem (Long 1824, 1:231).[5]

The Caddo (related to the Pawnee) have the totems wolf,
panther, bear, buffalo, beaver, raccoon and crow (Kate
1885a, 375. Morgan [1877, 165] gives a similar list for the
Pawnee). Among the Creek there are seventeen to eighteen
totems, including bear, wolf, beaver, eagle, raccoon, otter,
alligator, maize, and potato (Kate, p. 411; cf. Morgan 1877,
161).[6] The Cherokee have seven totems including wolf and
bird, while formerly there were eight or even ten totems
(Kate, p. 424; Morgan 1877, p. 164).

The Choctaw had among others a crab totem, for which
a legend relates that the members of this clan once lived
under the earth and crawled on all fours, until they were
caught by the Choctaw, who taught them to speak and took
them into the tribe (Catlin 1857, 2:128; cf. below sec. IV
of this chapter). All of these Gulf tribes abstain from
eating their totem animal, which Adair (1775, 130 ff.) erroneously ascribes to fear of impurity.

The Hopi and Zuni and the other Pueblo peoples have
totems like corn, frog, parrot, eagle, sun, bear, butterfly,
and rattlesnake; and they carry these totems on their
shields (Bourke 1890, 116). The Comanche have six totems
(Morgan 1877, 177).

Totemism has pretty much disappeared among the
western tribes in Oregon Territory (Gibbs 1877, 184) and in
California. The same is true for the Navajo and the Apache
(Bourke, p. 111, and Matthews 1890, 103 ff.). On the other

hand, the peoples of British Columbia are totemic; they have
the totems whale, eagle, raven, wolf, and frog and put pic-
tures of the animals on beams which support the roofs, on
the front of houses, on oars and boats, and on graves (R.
C. Mayne, pp. 257, 258, 271; Macfie 1865, 444). Totems on
graves are also found elsewhere (cf. Schoolcraft 1851-57,
1:356). The idea that the deceased changes into his clan
animal is shown by the fact that on graves of the Raven and
Eagle clans the bird is represented in flight, signifying
the deceased who flies away (Mayne, pp. 271-72). Obviously
the Indians would not themselves hurt the totem animal; but
they also regard it as a grave insult if someone else does
so in their presence--a horror before which they cover the
head in shame (R. C. Mayne, p. 258). The cosmology of the
British Columbia tribes is also totemic. Legends relate
how in the beginning birds came from heaven, laid aside their
feather clothing and became men and the ancestral fathers
of the clan (Boas 1887a, 423). The way they think the subclans originated is very interesting. The legends of the
British Columbia tribes relate that men went to sea or up
the mountains and copulated with animals, becoming in this
way the ancestral fathers of the subclans (Boas 1887a, 423).[7]

The northern Indians have retained their totemism in
an especially strong form, particularly the Tlingit, who
have the totems whale, raven, wolf, and eagle (Dall 1870,
413, 414; Badlam 1890, 75 ff.; Ritter 1862, 256: see below, sec. VI of this chapter). More exactly, they have two
main totems, raven and wolf, and the first is split further
into raven, frog, goose, sea lion, eagle-owl, salmon, while

the second is divided into wolf, bear, eagle, whale, and
auk (Holmberg 1855-63, 293; Krause 1885, 112; cf. Bancroft
1883, 1:109; Jackson 1879, 105; Pinart 1872, 792 ff.). They
carve the totems on their utensils (Dall 1870, 414; Holmberg, pp. 293 ff.) and erect totem images next to their
houses--these represent the inhabitants and their ancestors
and often reach a considerable height (Dall 1870, 414;
Krause, pp. 131 ff.). On festive occasions they wear clothing reminiscent of the totem (Holmberg, p. 328; Dall 1870,
414), and they put the totem figure on the wooden helmets
worn in single combat (Holmberg p. 323). A chief will appear, especially at memorial feasts for the ancestors, with
the family totem and is greeted with a cry from a member
imitating the totem animal (Dall 1870, 419). This cry also
determines whether one or more slaves should be sacrificed
at the festival (Holmberg, p. 328). Food prohibition occurs
to the extent that, for example, members of the Whale clan
may eat no whale oil (Dall 1870, 413); and the main totem
animal, the bear, is seldom killed because he is regarded as
a man in disguise (Holmberg, p. 310).

    The world of legend similarly inclines to totemic
representations. One legend relates how the bringer of
light turned himself into a raven, which procured for humanity the water that the wolf (the evil spirit) guarded (Dall
1870, 422).[8] The two main totems, that of the good and that
of the bad spirit, derive from these figures, and each is
joined by its related spirits.

    The Haida also have totems and build totem poles in

front of their houses (Krause, p. 308), and totemic tattooing is common among them (James G. Swan 1874, 5 ff.). Their
totems are eagle, wolf, hawk, black bear, and killer whale.
The Kutchin have three totems: deer, bird, and land animal
(Dall 1870, 197).[9] The Kenai, like the Tlingit, have two
main totems, which are further divided into six and five
subtotems. At the creation, the raven is supposed to have
formed two ancestral women out of different material, and
from them originated the six and five lineages (Wrangell
1839, 1:104, 111). The Northern Chippewa derive from a dog
and therefore treat the dog with a sort of religious reserve
(Bancroft 1883, 1:118). On the other hand the totem system
has expired among the Innuit (Eskimo), where only its branches,
family totemism, and the Manitu cult (sec. IV, this chapter)
are still to be found.

III
The following points naturally result from the concept of
the totem.

        1. No one may belong to more than one totem clan.
Membership in more than one would result in a mixed animal,
which would be a monstrous being of the sort which is indeed to be found in legend, but only exceptionally and not
as ordinary figures.

        Consequently, the clan must be based on either father
or mother right; that is, membership must be determined
through either relation to the mother or to the father; a
double membership is impossible. This inference leads directly to the question of mother right, which will be dis-

cussed below (sec. IV, this chapter).

2. Totemism depends upon a blood tie. The totem animal descends from animals; conseauently, blood tie is the basis of human unity. The family develops from totemism, as does the clan-based state. This latter forms through an aggregation of totem clans, for which at least two are neces-sary. In time these clans branch into subclans, and in this way it comes about that perhaps eight, ten, twelve, or fourteen clans form a tribe.

The placing of the tents of the clans is also totem-ic; so that the totem clans split into two sections, group-ing themselves into riaht and left. The Indians camp in a horseshoe, where each totem has its assicned place. This is true among the Wyandot (Powell 1881: 64); and, as has al-ready been mentioned, among the Omaha five clans were located on the right, five on the left, and a street led throuah the middle (Dorsey 1884a, 219-20; cf. above sec. II, this chap-ter). Among the Osage there were seven totems on the left, seven on the right (Dorsey 1884b, 113 ff.); among the Chey-enne, there were three on one side, one at the end, and four on the other side (Kate 1885a, 361).

3. The totem clan is necessarily exogamous. No ani-mal may marry itself; self-besmirchment would be considered an outrageous abomination. Incest in this sense, if it oc-curs at all, usually has death as its conseauence.

Therefore totemic exogamy is universal. It is found among the Wyandot (Powell, pp. 61, 63), the Iroauois (Schoolcraft 1847, 128; Morgan 1851, 84; 1870, 139, 165;

1881, 5, 66), the Omaha (Dorsey 1884a, 255), among the Caddo and Pawnee (Kate 1885a, 375), the southern tribes (Jones
1873, 66) and among the peoples of British Columbia (R. C.
Mayne, p. 258). It is also decided law among the northern
Indians, especially among the Tlingit (Holmberg, p. 313;
Dall 1870, 414; Krause, p. 220), the Kenai (Wrangell, 1:
104), the Haida (Krause, p. 312), and among the Kutchin, although here violation of the prohibition does not produce
such severe consequences (only public derision--Dall 1870,
197).

The rule of exogamy may extend beyond the tribe, so
that if someone marries outside his own tribe he may not
marry into the corresponding clan of the other tribe; as was
the case in Iroquois law (Schoolcraft 1847, 130; Morgan
1851, 81; 1881, 33) and in the law of the British Columbia
tribes (R. C. Mayne, pp. 257-58; Macfie 1865, 444-45). But
the corresponding clans of the two tribes may also regard
each other as being different animals, therefore permitting
marriage, as is the case in Omaha law (Dorsey 1884a, 257).

IV

Like every historical institution, totemism carries within
itself the element of decay; but when it disintegrates, the
institution leaves behind the viable germs of further development.

One element of decay consists in the fact that the
expanding clans split into subclans until finally the original unity of the clan is forgotten and marriage between
subclans of the same clan becomes possible. In this way

the clan gradually changes into the tribe or subtribe. The
subclans, however, no longer bear the totemic characteristics with the same strength; and consequently the end is
near for the institution. What remains of totemism is a
general tribal totemism, which, however, in the end has only
mythological and cosmic interest.[10]

Thus the Crane Indians (of the Ojibwa) believe that
they descended from the crane and became men (Dorman 1881,
232 ff.); other Ojibwa worship the rattlesnake, call it
their grandfather, and dread killing it (Dorman, p. 264 ff.).
The Beaver tribe of the Algonkin believe themselves descended from the beaver (Parkman, p. lxviii). The Pomo of
California regard the Coyote as their ancestral father, although one division is named after a snake (Powers 1877,
147). The Yokuts also worship the rattlesnake and the coyote, which they regard as the ancestral father of the whole
world (Powers, p. 379). Also to be found among the Californians is, for example, the legend that the wolf created
the first man and woman (Wrangell, 1:93). Similarly for
the Innuit (Eskimo), the Kaniagmut believe that they are
descended from a dog (Dall 1870, 404 ff.); and these tribes
still have their special ways of styling their hair and
tattooing (Klutschak 1881, 228).

In this way, the splitting of clans into subclans led
to the expansion of totemism into a tribal totemism. As has
been mentioned, the splitting of clans occurs among the
Omaha (Dorsey 1884a, 236 ff., 239-40) and also the Chickasaw
and the Choctaw, who split into two divisions, of which each

has four brother clans. The Ojibwa, Delaware, and Mohegan
have or had several subclans (Morgan 1877, 162-63, 166, 171
ff.).

The way in which the subclans acquired their new ancestral animal is easily comprehended. Either this was
brought about through the intrusion of father right, where
the subclan was named after the man from whom it descends
and to whom the ancestral mother of the subclan was married;
or else the subclan is named after the Manitu, the individual
guardian spirit, of one of its prominent members.

Another way in which the disintegration of totemism
could take place is that the whole community of clans could
split into several groups, each containing representatives
of all the clans. For some time afterward the idea of clan
unity may have been effective and clan exogamy may have extended beyond the border of the tribe, as above in the case
of the Iroquois. With time, however, the equivalence of
clans will have disappeared in the face of the difference of
tribes, and it will have been replaced by the tenet that a
member of one tribe may marry a member of another without
consideration of their respective clan membership. Tribal
exogamy, then, develops in place of clan exogamy.

Another strong enemy of totemism is the growth of
the individual totem, the Manitu, to which we will now turn.
The Manitu belief is already found in totemism's prime
period. It is the belief that each individual has a protective animal, which may be more or less freely chosen.[11]

Reference to the Manitu was made above in relation to

the Omaha. In the Buffalo clan, a youth may not only be
named the Last Runner, the Thick Shouldered, the Black-tongued
(i.e., Buffalo), but he may acquire as well the name Hawk,
Rabbit, Turkey, Crow, Swan, or Bear (Dorsey 1884a, 232-33,
236).

Marquette, in 1673, already remarked in this regard,
"Each of them has his lord [namely God], which they call
their manitou; this is a snake or a bird or a stone or something similar, which they have received in their sleep and
in which they put their complete confidence for the success
of their warfare, their fishing, and their hunting" (Marquette 1852, 57).

Either in early youth, or during youth initiation, a
person has the Manitu he worships revealed to him in dreams;
so that he never kills the animal representing it.[12] If he
kills it by mistake, he asks forgiveness of it and puts the
skin in his medicine sack (Dorman, p. 229).

He carries objects (bones, feathers, skin, and so on)
in his medicine sack which relate to the guardian spirit or
were formerly revealed to him in dreams as signs of the Manitu.[13] Remarkable natural appearances, for example, specially
formed rocks, are also regarded as emanations of a Manitu;
and they often place Manitu images in the form of rough
representations of animals or men near them (Bradbury 1817,
24 ff.; cf. Anonymous 1861, 34).

It is also very common to call an individual by the
name of his Manitu. This is done especially in the West; it
is not uncommon among the Californians, for example, the

Nisenan, to give an individual an animal name (Powers, p.
316) or to name him after a plant, tree, or other object
(Wrangell, 1:87). Related to this is the widespread custom
of avoiding someone else's name because this would awaken,
attract, and offend the guardian spirit. We frequently find
this idea among Indians. It occurs among the Comanche (Kate
1885a, 393) and the British Columbian tribes (R. C. Mayne,
p. 279). It is also prohibited among Californian tribes,
particularly the Nisenan, to call someone, especially a
woman, by name (Powers, pp. 315 ff.).

We also find individual guardian spirits among the
northern tribes, particularly among the Tlingit (Dall 1870,
422-23), where the guardian spirit is called kinajek
(Krause, p. 292). Among the Coyukon on the Yukon actual
totemism has foundered under the guardian spirit system
(Dall 1870, 196). The same has occurred among the Innuit
(Eskimo); here a person at puberty (or his parents may have
done so during his childhood) selects an animal as guardian
spirit. If this one does not take, then another is selected; nevertheless this no longer prevents the killing of the
animal (Dall 1870, 145).

V

I have documented the totemism of the Australians elsewhere
(Kohler 1887b, 334 ff.; 1895b, 38). To this I add the
following.

The Thargominda in Central Australia have the totems
emu, snake, opossum, and so on (Curr 1886-87, 2:37). On
the Nogoa River the totems opossum, dog, emu, kangaroo,

eaglehawk, bee, and scrub turkey are represented (Curr, 3:91). The tribes around Mount Gambier number ten totems: crow, fish-hawk, pelican, black cockatoo, snake, ti-tree, turkey, white cockatoo, as well as two others that were not named. Each totem group avoids killing the totem animal except in cases of extreme need and then only with attestations of sorrow as if one had killed a relative (Curr, 3:461-62). The Dieri have eleven totems: corn, rain, mouse, emu, kangaroo, rat, marten, fish, iguana, dog, and crow. They believe that they originated from animals, but do not abstain from eating the totem animal (Gason 1895, 167 ff.).

The nature of totem divisions acquires a special dimension here as some Australian tribes draw connections between their totems and the universe and subsume the most varied things under the totem. Thus, at Mount Gambier the crow has rain, thunder, lightening, hail, clouds; and the black cockatoo has the stars and the moon; while the white cockatoo has the kangaroo, the summer season and so on under it (Curr, 3:461).

Totem group exogamy is also the rule among the Australian Aborigines (Kohler 1887b, 334 ff.). Among the Thargominda in Central Australia violation of the rule of exogamy would result in death (Curr 2:37); and the same is true, with equal severity, for the Dieri (Gason 1895, 168-69).

Among some tribes, for example at Mount Gambier, the importance of exogamy for the totem group has been lost (Curr 3:462). Here totemic exogamy has changed into class

exogamy. This process has occurred among most Australians.
Of course it subsequently became necessary to divide the
classes again into subclasses, but these have nothing to do
with totemism, for the subclasses represent the various
generation levels of the tribe.

Typical here is the division of the Kamilaroi, where
the tribe divides into two classes and each class into two
subclasses: a man of a particular subclass within one of
the classes must marry a woman of a specific subgroup of the
other class, and their children will belong to yet other
subclasses (Kohler 1887b, 330 ff.). All of this leads to
the following results (the classes are designated as A and
B and the subclasses as A^1, A^2, B^1, and B^2):

given mother right,

A^1 marries B^1,

and the child is B^2,

B^2 marries A^2,

and the child is A^1;

given father right,

A^1 marries B^1,

and the child is A^2,

A^2 marries B^2

and the child is A^1.

The classes and subclasses of other tribes are ar-
ranged in a similar way, sometimes with more and sometimes
with less complication.

The Ngurla tribe (on the De Gray River coast) have
four classes:

Poorungnoo marries Parrijari, and the children are Kiamoona;

Kiamoona marries Banakoo, and the children are Poorungnoo;

Parrijari marries Poorungnoo, and the children are Banakoo;

Banakoo marries Kiamoona, and the children are Parrijari.

Since the children belong to the father's group, it
works out as follows:

Class I, if the first generation is Poorungnoo,

the second is Kiaroona;

Class II, if the first generation is Parrijari,

the second is Banakoo.

It is self-evident then that a Poorungnoo marries a
Parrijari, a Kiamoona a Banakoo, and vice versa (Curr,
1:290-91).

There is a very similar situation, even regarding
the names, among the neighboring tribes of the Nickol Bay:

Booroongoo marries a Panaka, and the children are Kymurra;

Kymurra marries a Palyeery, and the children are Booroongoo;

Panaka marries a Booroongoo, and the children are Palyeery;

Palyeery marries a Kymurra, and the children are Panaka.

Therefore,

Class I, if the first generation is Booroongoo, the second

is Kymurra;

Class II, if the first generation is Panaka, the second

is Palyeera;

from which the above results automatically (Curr 1:298).

Similarly, among the tribes on the Halifax Bay the
system of classes and subclasses is composed as follows
(Curr 2:425):

A Korkoro marries a Wongarungan,

   and the son is Wotero, the daughter a Woterungan;

A Wotero marries a Korkeelingan,

   and the son is a Korkeen, the daughter a Korkorungan;

A Wongo marries a Korkorungan,

   and the son is Korkeen, the daughter a Korkeelingan;

A Korkeen marries a Woterungan,

   and the son is a Wongo, the daughter a Wongarungan.

   If we assume that mother right obtains here, which, however, is not certain, then the division is as follows:

   Class I, if the first generation is Korkoro,

   the second is Korkeen;

   Class II, if the first generation is Wongo,

   the second is Wotero.

   It should be remarked that this cycle is also observed when the man marries outside his tribe, if the neighboring tribes have a similar division.

   The people of Port Mackay (Curr, 3:45) are likewise divided into two classes, Yungaroo and Wootaroo, of which the first divides further into Gurgela and Bunbai, the second into Koobaroo and Woongo.

   Gurgela marries a Koobarooan,

   and the children are Woongo and Woongoan;

   Woongo marries a Bunbaian,

   and the children are Gurgela and Gurgelan;

   Koobaroo marries a Gurgelan,

   and the children are Bunbai and Bunbaian;

   Bunbai marries a Woongoan,

and the children are Koobaroo and Koobarooan.

Therefore, given mother right, marriage and descent
follow this scheme:

A^1 marries B^1, B^1 marries A^1,

the child is B^2,   the child is A^2,

B^2 marries A^2, A^2 marries B^2,

the child is A^1.   the child is B^1.

The same pattern is followed, with similar names, in
Peak Downs District (Curr, 3:64) and on the Nogoa River
(Curr, 3:91).

Among the Mary River tribes (Curr, 3:163) the class
arrangement seems to have disintegrated somewhat. The
classes are: I, Baran and Balkun; II, Dherwen and Bonda.
Formerly,

Baran married Dherwen, and the child was a Bonda;

Bonda married a Balkun, and the child was a Baran;

Dherwen married a Baran, and the child was a Balkun;

Balkun married a Bonda, and the child was a Dherwen.

Now, however, a Baran is allowed to marry a Dherwen
or a Bonda; and a Dherwen may marry a Baran or Balkun, while
the children belong to the class of their mother, but always to the other subclass.

A remarkable variation is found among the tribes in
New Norcia, which have six classes Mondorop, Tirarop,
Tondorop, Noiognok, Jiragiok, and Palarop (Curr, 1:320).
No one may marry into his own class and,

Mondorop is forbidden Tirarop;

Tirarop is forbidden Mondorop and Tondorop;

Tondorop is forbidden Tirarop;

Noiognok is forbidden Jiragiok;

Jiragiok is forbidden Noiognok and Palarop;

Palarop is forbidden Jiragiok.

Therefore, the classes Mondorop, Tondorop, Noiognok, and Palarop are each prohibited one class in addition to their own, while Tirarop and Jiragiok are prohibited two; and the exclusion is always mutual. This pattern can be explained as follows; the original classes were: I, Mondorop with Tirarop as a subclass; and II, Noiognok with Jiragiok as a subclass. Tondorop branched off from Tirarip, while Palarop separated from Jiragiok. These third subclasses separated so much from the first (Mondorop and Noiognok) that marriage became permissible, while on the contrary the middle subclass was prohibited from marriage either to the first or to the third. Marriage, then, is governed by the following schema:

Class I: sub-classes a, b, and c;

Class II: sub-classes d, e, and f;

a is forbidden b;

c is forbidden b;

d is forbidden e;

f is forbidden e;

b, however, is forbidden a and c;

e is forbidden d and f.

It is certainly peculiar that the class principle is not put into effect here in that all subclasses of each class may marry all subclasses of the other. One would

usually expect that the first section of Class I would only
marry into the first section of Class II and so on.

   Among the central tribes there are four classes:
Pultarra (A^1), Perula (A^2), Commarra (B^1), and Aponunga (B^2).
Marriage must be into another class. Furthermore, the child
of a Pultarra woman is a Perula and that of a Commarra woman
is an Aponunga (Willshire 1895, 183). The pattern is obviously as follows:

   A Pultarra man marries a Commarra woman,

      and their child is Aponunga;

   An Aponunga man marries a Perula woman,

      their child is Pultarra;

   A Commarra man marries a Pultarra woman,

      their child is Perula;

   A Perula man marries an Aponunga woman,

      their child is a Commarra;

whereby each time a circle is closed.

   As reported by Fison (1880, 34), the tribes of Mount
Gambier have two classes, Kumite and Kroki, which marry each
other reciprocally (Curr, 3:461). The Torrowotto of Central
Australia are also divided into two exogamous classes (Curr,
2:178). Classes are mentioned for some tribes without any
closer description. The Limba Karadjee have three classes,
Manderojelli, Manburlgeat, and Mandrowilli (Curr, 1:269).

   It has been mentioned that the clan system derives
from totemism, and just as the tribes reviewed above include the universe in their division of totems, so the
tribes around Port Mackay include it in their class division.

They have two tribal spheres, Yongaroo and Wootaroo; and the whole of the animated world belongs to one or the other of them (Curr, 3:45).

VI

Now that the development to tribal totemism has been traced, the question of mother right and father right can be taken up.

From the above it naturally results that the totem group must be based either on mother right or father right. It may be that mixture of animals occurs as an exception in legends, but it is monstrous and contrary to life and could never be a normal biological phenomenon. Names must therefore be chosen after the father or the mother; and it was naturally more obvious to choose names after the mother.

The grounds for mother right are thus much simpler than has so far been thought. Other circumstances may have contributed to maintaining and consolidating the system and to eliminating for a time the consideration of father right; but the principal reason was the impossibility of combining both systems.

The mother gave birth to the child and, as is common in tribes, did so away from the house, sundered it from herself, nursed it for years, and then for more years let it play around her while the husband was up to all sorts of tomfoolery. That the relation to her is regarded as decisive is so natural that the contrary must seem highly remarkable to anyone who has ever taken the trouble to imagine what savage life is like.

This being the case, however, totemic recognition of
father right was automatically excluded; and since kinship
law was identical with totemism, it too disregarded father
right. And naturally the system survived intact for a long
time due to the _vis inertiae_ of things, while on the one
hand the clan system, and on the other the family, developed
from totemism.

I have already expressed myself in various places on
the development from mother right to father right. Certainly _one_ form of development, and indeed the most original,
has until recently remained obscure to me and to other scholars, and yet the matter is exceptionally simple. The be-
liefs of the tribes of British Columbia gave me the key to
it. They have the idea that the clan descends from an original animal mother, but they also believe that the subclans
developed when the men received the new family arms at sea
or on the mountain tops from nature spirits.

The increased expansion of the clan necessitated, as
remarked above, splitting into subclans. For this, however,
no more convenient principle of division suggested itself
than naming the subclan after the father, just as, conversely, today in Switzerland the various branches of the family
are distinguished by adding the mother's name to the father's.
Therefore, if one Mrs. Bear married Mr. Raven while another
Mrs. Bear married Mr. Deer, it follows naturally that the
whole Bear clan would divide by splitting into the Raven and
Deer subclans. However, if it came to the point that the
Deer subclan was named after father Deer, the members of

the subclan might from then on feel like deer and sense in
their limbs the speed of the fleet deer and no longer the
gait of the grumbling bear. Then if one of the Deer men
married, it would be quite understandable that like his
father he might want to impress the deer nature on his child.
This process may have met with resistance for a time, but
the example undoubtedly had effect. Consequently, the subclan ultimately took up father right, and when the original
clan completely split up, mother right disappeared. Naturally, mother right would have lasted somewhat longer, depending upon how strongly the older totem system maintained itself within the different subclans. For this reason, the
shift to father right must have been especially easy among
just those tribes who dissolved into loose village communi-
ties and allowed the totem system to decay.

An additional element disintegrative of mother right
lies in the fact that a connection with the maternal relatives may no longer be maintained among tribes which are
prevented by their food sources from living in groups and
where individual families consisting of father, mother, and
child disperse in the most widely separated directions,
camping here today, there tomorrow. If it is possible for
the whole clan to live together, it will seem natural for
the child who amuses himself daily with his maternal uncle
to find a patron in him as well. However, if dearth of
nourishment forces members of the clan to split up, husband,
wife, and child must stay together, for they depend upon
one another if they are to lead a full human life.

If the dispersal of the clan becomes complete, then
the maternal uncle will no longer be known and the legal
bond to him will seem unnatural. It follows from this that
mother right will be stronger and more lasting among just
those tribes which by nature have a hordelike community,
rather than among those which are soon split up by the scarcity of food and other resources (cf. Kohler 1893, 321).
These considerations explain the relatively rapid disappear-
ance of mother right among the Australian tribes and the
long retention of the principle among the American Indians.

I have already examined mother right and father right
among the Australian tribes in another treatise (1887b, 345
ff.). To this the following may be added. Mother right is
found among tribes in New Norcia in the west (Curr, 1:322),
tribes on the Darling River (for this reason the uncle de-
cides here whether the newborn child will be allowed to live
or not [Curr, 2:197; Bonney 1884, 129]), around Port Mackay
(Curr, 3:45), on the Mary River (Curr, 3:163), at Mount
Gambier (Fison, p. 34, following Stewart, who was also
Curr's source), and the central tribes (Willshire 1895, 183).
Father right occurs among the Larrakia, near Port Darwin
(Curr, 1:252, Willshire, p. 193), the Ngurla on the De Gray
River (Curr, 1:291), the tribes at Nickols Bay (Curr, 1:298),
in Eucla (Curr, 1:402), in Gippsland (Curr, 3:546), the Dieri
and related tribes (Gason 1895, 168), the tribes in Powells
Creek (Stationmaster 1895, 177), and on the Victoria River
(Crauford 1895, 180).

As for the American Indians, mother right is found

especially among the Iroquois and all their branches, the
child being a member of its mother's clan, to which the
father does not belong (Lafitau 1724, 1:471, 558 ff., 563;
Schoolcraft 1847, 128; Morgan 1851, 84 ff.; 1870, 139, 165;
1877, 153; 1881, 5, 66; Colden 1747, 13; Hale 1883, 65),
among the Delaware and Mohegan (Loskiel 1789, 79; Dwight
1821, 4:198; Morgan 1877, 174),[14] the Wyandot (Powell 1881,
61, 63; Parkman, p. li), in general the Huron,[15] also the
Oto, Minitari, Raven, and Crow (Morgan 1877, 156, 158 ff.),
the Dakota, the Creek, Choctaw, Cickasaw, Cherokee (Parkman,
p. lii; Morgan 1877, 161 ff.),[16] in addition the Virginia
tribes,[17] the tribes in Carolina (Lawson 1711, 185),[18] the
Natchez (Waitz 1859-72, 3:108), the Navajo (Matthews 1890,
105), and the Zuni (Tylor 1896, 88).

The tribes of British Columbia have mother right;
the child has its mother's totem (R. C. Mayne, p. 258). This
is true at least so far as the northern tribes are concerned;
but, as in California, the tribes of southern British
Columbia have father right (Boas 1887a, 422). It is reported of the tribes in the interior of British Columbia
that the husband moves into his wife's home because the woman can work better in these familiar surroundings, and
that the household goods all belong to the woman (Bancroft
1883, 277).

The Cegiha Indians (the Omaha), have father right;
only the children of halfbreeds belong to their mother's
group. And the same is true of the Ponca, Iowa, Kaw, and
Winnebago (Dorsey 1884a, 225; Morgan 1877, 155 ff.). The

Mandan also have father right; the son belongs to his fa-
ther's totem (Catlin, 1:136); and the same is true for the
Caddo (Pawnee), the Miami, Shawnee, Sauk, and Blackfoot
(Kate 1885a, 375; Morgan 1877, 168 ff.). Furthermore, the
Oregon tribes have father right (Gibbs 1877, 187),[19] and as
a rule the California tribes do too (see below, p. 137).

On the other hand, mother right prevails among the
Indians of the far north--the Kutchin (Dall 1870, 197; cf.
Bancroft 1:132), the Kenai, where the closest heir is the
sister's son (Wrangell, 1:105), and also apparently the
Aleuts, where husband and wife do not live together (Badlam
1890, 71), and certainly the Tlingit and Haida (Holmberg,
p. 325; Krause, pp. 220, 312; Dall 1870, 414 ff.).[20] The
Koniag are in an intermediary state, for among them the
inheritance, although it goes to the brother, passes from
him to the son chosen by the deceased (Holmberg, p. 399).

We find a remarkable mixed system among the Innuit
(Eskimo). In theory they have father right; the oldest son
is heir, even if he is only an adopted child (Rink 1875, 25;
Boas 1888, 580-81). On the other hand, in case of divorce
the mother keeps the children (Rink, p. 25), and the newly
married couple move first into the house of the wife's parents is order to perform bride service. It is only after
the parents' death that they set up their own household
(Boas 1888, 579; Dall 1870, 402).

The various tribes draw the logical consequences
from the principles of mother right and father right as
follows. Among the matrilineal Iroquois the children have

no right of inheritance, for a man's own clan inherits from
him, but no one interferes if he gives his own children
something (Morgan 1851, 327).[21] It is expressly reported
of the Wyandot that in case of divorce the children stay
with the mother, and that a man's heir is his brother or
his sister's son, while a woman's heir is her eldest daughter (Powell 1881, 64-65). Among the Tlingit, not only is
the sister's son the first heir, but a woman loses all control over her children's freedom (Dall 1870, 414, 417, 420).
We find among the Wyandot that the husband often goes to
live in his wife's clan, even though he retains membership
in his own (Powell 1881, 63).[22] The same thing is true of
the Sauk, who otherwise have father right, for which reason
the husband must return to his own clan in the event of a
war (Long 1824, 219).

Among some tribes a man will move into his father-in-
law's house.[23] This is the case among the Gulf tribes (Jones
1873, 65),[24] the Tlingit, as long as the couple does not
become independent (Dall 1870, 415; Krause, p. 220), the
Cree (Franklin 1824, 109), and the Mandan (Wied-Neuwied
1839-41, 2:129). It also occurs among Californian tribes.
Among them, as among the Malays, there are two types of
marriage. In the regular form, governed by father right,
the woman is completely paid for. Sometimes, however, the
husband pays only half the price, in which case the man
moves into his wife's home and becomes a servant in her
household. This is the case among the Yurok (Powers 1877,
56), the Patawa (p. 98), and the Patwin (p. 221). In this

latter case it is called half-marriage. The custom of
changing households is also reported for the Yokut, although
here a man has power of life and death over her person
(Powers 1877, 382).

Naturally, among tribes with mother right, it is the
relatives of the woman who have the decision, at least the
principal decision, over approving the marriage. Among the
Iroquois, the mother arranges the marriage (Morgan 1851,
321 ff.; Heckewelder, p. 257); and among the Creek the
bride's female relatives, in particular the mother, are applied to. The brother and mother's brother are also asked,
but the father usually is not (C. Swan 1855, 5:268; Jones
1873, 65).

Among peoples with mother right, when names are
chosen after ancestors, then characteristically it is the
name of a maternal relative which is chosen. Among the
Haida (Krause, p. 310), the mother' brother's name is selected; and this is true too among the Tlingit, but with the
modification mentioned immediately below (Dall 1870, 414;
Krause, p. 217).

Some forms showing transition to father right have
already been mentioned above. The following transitional
forms occur among the Tlingit. First, a child will be
given the name of a maternal ancestor, but later the name
of one of his paternal ancestors will be added to it (Dall
1870, 414; Krause, p. 217). Secondly, it is usually a son
or grandson who inherits a shaman's talent, and with it his
office and the requisite implements (Dall 1870, 425; Krause,

p. 284).

The couvade, evidence of a developing father right,
also occurs among, for example, the California tribes. Here
the father may not leave the house for four days after the
birth of his child (Wrangell, 1:87), sometimes even for as
long as fourteen to twenty days, and he must abstain from
eating many foods (Boscana 1846, 283; cf. Bancroft, 1:412).

A complete childbed for men is reported for the
tribes of southern California. A report from 1739 says:

> Among the Californians was found the same bar-
> barous monstrosity that we read of with laughter
> in the history of Brasil. The women who had just
> given birth went to the water to bathe themselves
> and their children; then without sheltering them-
> selves in any regard, they went about their usual
> business, going to the woods for firewood and to
> search for food, and worked at whatever else the
> husband required. In the meantime, this barbarian,
> pretending to be fatigued and suffering, retired
> to his cave or stretched out under a tree and re-
> mained very sheltered for three or four days
> [Venegas 1: 94].

There are also traces of the couvade among the Innuit,
where a man and his wife may not take part in the Sedna festival in the year of the birth of their child (Boas 1888,
605, 611).

VII

We find, therefore, both mother right and father right among
the Indians and among the Australian Aborigines. However,
since we cannot well doubt the unity of origin of all the
Australian tribes on the one hand and of all the Indian
tribes on the other, and since a similar diversity of basic
principles could surely not have existed within the organ-

ization of the original tribe, it is certain that only one
of them can have been the original social principle. This
conclusion is so much the more certain, as this diversity of
principles occurs right within some tribal groups like the
Algonkian, and since some tribes which are closely related
to each other, like the Ponca and the Oto, have systems
based on opposite principles.

That the original principle was mother right is proven
by the following considerations:

1. Those given above (sec. VI, this chapter) regarding the formation of the totemic community.

2. Historical proof that some cultures have changed
from mother right to father right; whereas, so far as I
know, no case of a change in the opposite direction has yet
been found. The historical proof in question is provided
by the Malay tribes, where it can be shown step by step how
mother right changed with the adat kamanakan[25] into father
right. The same can be shown for African (Kohler 1893, 321
ff,; 1895c, 3 ff.) and American Indian tribes, particularly
the Algonkian and the Shawnee of whom it can be proved that
they once had mother right (Morgan 1877, 166, 170).

3. That it is factually more probable that mother
right changes into father right than vice versa. The splin-
tering community cannot for very long tolerate a situation
in which its productive members are organizationally separated from those persons (wife and children) to whom they
are bound by the inevitable circumstances of life, particularly when there is any scarcity in the means of subsistence.

And this situation is especially insupportable when the search for gain is no longer merely a momentary search for consumables, but has become a continuous striving for wealth. What was remarked in the preceding section obtains here. Therefore, any colonization entails that the man takes his wife and children with him, that he thus effectively removes them from her family.

4. The fact that institutions like the abduction of women and bride purchase, which historical ethnology has proven to exist, inevitably bring about father right. The extensive formative influence of these factors is often seen in the two marriage types which depend upon whether or not brideprice is paid (concerning American tribes in this regard see the preceding section).

5. That among tribes like the Tlingit, where the ancient institution of totemism has maintained itself with particular vitality, mother right is in full flower.

6. And by institutions reminiscent of a different arrangement in earlier periods, such as are particularly prominent among American Indians. As has been remarked, the Omaha have father right, but:

(a) It is not the father but the brother and mother's brother who exercise authority over the daughters. These are consulted if the daughter is to marry (Dorsey 1884a, 268), and they chastise her if she goes astray (p. 365).

(b) Inheritance indeed goes to the sons, but if these are lacking it then goes to the brother, sister, mother's brother, and sister's son (Dorsey 1884a, 367).

(c) The former existence of mother right is also
proved by the circumstance that the prohibition of marriage
is not limited to the agnatic line. For marriage is not only
forbidden within one's own clan (which is at the same time
the clan of the father, father's father, and so on), it is
also excluded in the mother's clan and in the subclans of
the paternal and maternal grandmother and great-grandmother,
and it is excluded with the sister's daughter (Dorsey 1884a,
256 ff.).

The Omaha have, then, the following survivals of
mother right: (a) the avunculate, (b) subsidiary inheritance
right, and (c) various marriage prohibitions. Among them,
the avunculate in particular can also be found in the related
Iowa tribe (Morgan 1870, 158).

Observation of the Australians and the Indian tribes
thus gives us certain proof that at least these great tribal
spheres have wrested themselves from mother right to father
right and that mother right was original. That this allows
us to draw a similar conclusion for other peoples too is
obvious. And should anyone refer us, on the contrary, to
various peoples of a lower cultural level who have father
right, we must remark that this evidence has no significance;
for the reference to it shows that completely incorrect
method, censured above, which lacks all scientific basis.

VIII
Totemism leads directly to group marriage. If one animal
marries another, one totem another, it automatically results
that the men of one marry the women of the other and vice

versa. Any man bearing the insignia of totem A marries women bearing the insignia of totem B, and vice versa.

      This arrangement, however, leads to men marrying their
daughters, whereas mother and son on the one hand and brother and sister on the other share the same totem and marriage between them is excluded. But a great innovation is
brought about by further restriction on marriage. At all
events, marriage of father and daughter ceases when father
right appears, since father and daughter now belong to the
same totem--whereby the previous prohibition deriving from
mother right on relations between mother and son is retained.
But limits are set to relations between father and daughter
even before the development of father right. And various
systems are then formed, in the simplest of which each totem group splits into three generation levels. One generation level always marries into the corresponding level of
the other totem group, or it is allowed to skip a generation
level, but only in a way that insures that the union of father and daughter is always excluded. How this occurs is
explained below (chap. 3, sec. VIII).

      The accuracy of this picture of the development of
totemism is also attested by the fact that the same process
is repeated in the decline of totemism and the rise of the
tribal system. The tribe is divided into several generation
levels, whereby the older generation level marries into the
older, the younger into the younger; and this is why the
example of the Australians is so exceptionally instructive
(see above, sec. V).

Another type of marriage which begins to be rejected is marriage of father-in-law with daughter-in-law or of mother-in-law with son-in-law, because in these cases the father would be uniting with the same woman as does his son, and the mother with the same man as does her daughter. This is held to be unnatural, by analogy with the previous prohibitions. How one proceeds here is shown by the example of the Omaha. Among them a man may not marry a woman who belongs to the subclan of his son's wife, and a woman may not marry a man who is her son-in-law (Dorsey 1884a, 257).

These are distinctions which have developed within the totem groups. The whole history of group marriage is a history of the restriction of marriage between clans, by placing specific rules on marriage with certain of their subclans (concerning cross-cousin marriage, see chap. 3, sec. IX).

However, the fact that group marriage is connected with totemism is important. Wherever we find features reminiscent of totemism, we are also reminded of a former group marriage, and the probability appears that group marriage was present here as well; and this probability can be strengthened on further grounds.

3
Group Marriage among the American Indians, Australians, and Dravidians

AMERICAN INDIANS AND DRAVIDIANS

I

Dorsey's researches among the Omaha (1884a) belong, if not
to the most important, at least to the most useful contributions in this area. In particular, his relationship tables, which he prepared from the most exact inquiries, are
absolutely basic for any investigator. The admirable consistency that they show in the development of a specific
initial idea demonstrates with certainty that we are not
being confronted here with the product of arbitrariness,
chance or insufficiency, but with a natural phenomenon per-
taining to the human race and faithfully expressed in relationship terminology.[1]

In the following, I will make use of Dorsey's and
Morgan's tables. I have taken the designations of the kinship types from the Omaha language, but I have omitted
Dorsey's detailed diacritical spellings, which are unimpor-
tant for our purpose.

Group marriage is found among American Indians in
three forms: (1) in the version in which members of the

same generation marry one another (brothers on the one side
with sisters on the other), or (2) as in the Omaha version,
in which a man also marries his wife's aunt and niece, or
(3) as in the Choctaw version, in which a woman marries both
her husband's uncle and his nephew.

From the first (pure) form, which is also that of
the Australian Aborigines and the Dravidians, arises the
general type of classificatory kinship terminology. From
the second and third versions spring different and singular-
ly complicated arrangements, which are closely examined below (secs. III and IV; cf. Bernhöft 1888).

II

I will present first the following general data on classificatory kinship, taken from the Omaha language.

    I. father = father's brother,

             = the agnatic grandfather's brother's son,

             = the agnatic great-grandfather's brother's
                grandson.

Which is shown by the following figure:

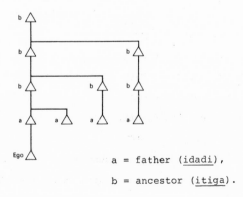

a = father (<u>idadi</u>),

b = ancestor (<u>itiga</u>).

(The same is true for the languages adduced by Morgan 1870, table II, nos. 61, 166, 207.)

It is remarkable that the degree of kinship is not further distinguished among the ancestral generations, just as there are no terms for descendants below grandchildren; only three ascending or descending generation levels are recognized.

II. mother = mother's sister,

= mother's mother's sister's daughter,

= mother's mother's mother's sister's grandmother.

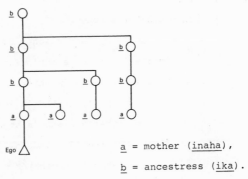

a = mother (inaha),

b = ancestress (ika).

The same is shown in the evidence given by Morgan (1870, table II, nos. 139, 196, 225).

III. Further, every wife of a man addressed as in I (idadi) is called mother (inaha), every husband of a wo-man addressed inaha is called father (idadi)(cf. Morgan 1870, table II, nos. 62, 140; see also below sec. V).

IV. grandfather = grandfather's brother,

= father's father's father's bro-ther's son.

grandmother = grandmother's sister,

            = mother's mother's mother's sister's

            daughter.

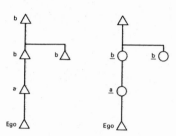

b = ancestor,
    (<u>itiga</u>),

<u>b</u> = ancestress
    (<u>ika</u>)

The same is also shown by Morgan (1870, table II, nos. 165,
206, 195, 224).

      V. son = brother's son,

            = father's brother's son's son,

            = mother's sister's son's son.

     VI. daughter = brother's daughter,

               = father's brother's son's daughter,

               = mother's sister's son's daughter.

    VII. grandson = brother's grandson,

               = father's brother's great-grandson.

   VIII. brother = son of the father's brother or his

               equivalent,

               = son of the mother's sister or her

               equivalent.

     IX. sister = daughter of the father's brother or his

             equivalent,

             = daughter of the mother's sister or her

             equivalent.

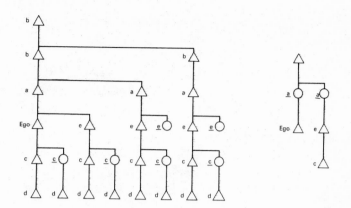

b = ancester (<u>itiga</u>), a = father (<u>idadi</u>), c = son (<u>ijinge</u>),
d = grandson (<u>ituepa</u>), <u>a</u> = mother (<u>itiga</u>), <u>c</u> = daughter (<u>ijange</u>)
e = brother (<u>ijice</u>), <u>e</u> = sister (<u>itange</u>).

Compare Morgan's table II (1870), for V (nos. 29, 75, 169,
209, 153), for VI (nos. 31, 77, 171, 155), for VII (nos. 33,
83, 173, 210), for VIII (nos. 63-66, 167, 168, 208, 141-144),
for IX (nos. 69-72, 197, 198, 226, 147-150).

The tribal law of the American Indians, like that of
the Australians, distinguishes sister's sons from brother's
sons. The former are not regarded as sons, but have their
own name: they are nephews and the daughters are nieces.
This is true however only when Ego is male. For a female
Ego, the reverse is true; brother's son is called nephew
and sister's son is called son. In both cases the terms
brother and sister are to be understood in the classificatory sense mentioned above. That a female Ego regards

sister's son as son is shown by Morgan's table II (nos. 53, 55, 80, 82, 158, 160).

For a male Ego:

X. nephew = sister's son,
= father's brother's daughter's son,
= mother's sister's daughter's son.

niece = sister's daughter,
= father's brother's daughter's daughter,
= mother's sister's daughter's daughter.

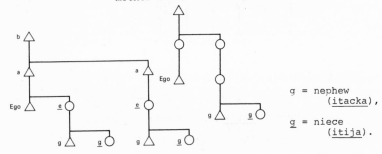

q = nephew (itacka),

q̲ = niece (itija).

The same is shown by Morgan's table II (nos. 37, 39, 79, 81, 157, 159).

For a female Ego:

nephew = son of brother (and equivalent),

niece = daughter of brother (and equivalent).

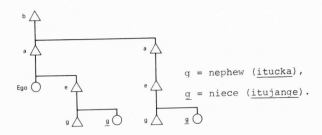

q = nephew (itucka),

q̲ = niece (itujange).

The same is found in Morgan's table II (nos. 45, 47, 76, 78, 154, 156).[2]

Among the Indians (like the Australians), while the father's brother is equivalent to father and the mother's sister is equivalent to mother, there is a special term for mother's brother and father's sister.

XI. uncle = brother of mother (and her equivalent).

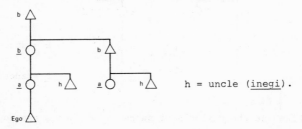

h = uncle (inegi).

Compare Morgan, table II, nos. 113, 186, 219.[3]

XII. aunt = sister of father (and his equivalent).

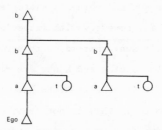

Compare Morgan, table II, nos. 87, 176, 213.

XIII. Among many tribes, however, uncle is also equivalent to the father's sister's husband (see below sec. V).

XIV. aunt = mother's brother's wife.

The above distinctions are not continued in the older generations; on the contrary equations are made among
them. Therefore grandmother's brother = grandfather, grandfather's sister = grandmother (cf. Morgan, table II, nos.
175, 185).

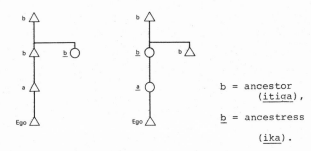

b = ancestor
(itiga),

b = ancestress

(ika).

Likewise the children of nephews and nieces are equivalent
to grandchildren (Morgan, table II, nos. 41-44, 49-52).

XV. A designation for male and female cousin cannot
be dispensed with in this classificatory kinship. To be
sure, father's brother's son and mother's sister's son are
called brother. How is it, however, with father's sister's
son and mother's brother's son, that is, with uncle's son
and aunt's son? Since the uncles and aunts are distinguished
and have special names, it is consistent to have special
terms for their children too. This is not true, of course,
for the Omaha and Choctaw, from whom we must abstract mo-
mentarily; but it is true for a great number of American
tribes, as is shown by Morgan's table II (nos. 89-92, 115-
118). And the same is true concerning female cousins (nos.
95-98, 121-124).

XVI. However, the children of cousins are treated

like siblings' children.

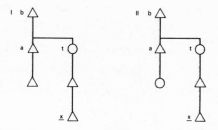

In case I, Ego calls "x" son, as if he were a brother's son; in case II, the female Ego calls "x" her nephew, as if he were her brother's son. Conversely, in case
III, Ego calls "x" nephew, while in case IV, the female Ego
calls him son.

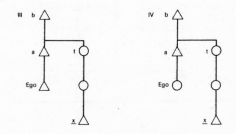

And it is similar in the following cases:

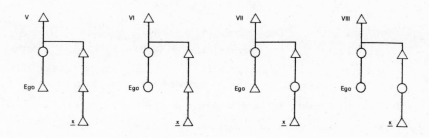

In case V, "x̲" is called son; in VI, he is called nephew.
In case VII, he is called nephew; in case VIII, he is called
son.

The above is confirmed by Morgan's tables, although
there are some variations in his material. The tribes
which have the Omaha system (numbered 18-24, 46-55) and
those which have the Choctaw system (numbered 26-36), both
of which do not have a concept for the cousin, must be left
out of consideration.

For case I, see Morgan, table II, nos. 101, 103; for
II, nos. 102,104; for III, nos. 105, 107; for IV, nos. 106,
108; for V, nos. 127, 129; for VI, nos. 128, 130; for VII,
nos. 131, 133; and for VIII, nos. 132, 134.

In this way, the distinction is continued as the generations progress, as is shown in the following figures.

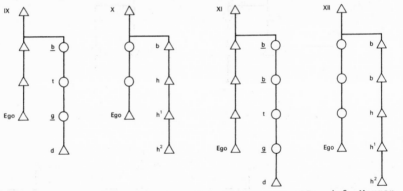

(cf. Morgan, II,   (cf. Morgan, II,   (cf. Morgan, II,   (cf. Morgan, I
nos. 175-82)   nos. 185-92)   nos. 211-15)   nos. 217-21)

An observation must be included here, in which it
will be necessary to take a glance at the Dravidian kinship system. There is a certain consistency, in the case

mentioned above, in treating male cousin's son like the
brother's son, and female cousin's son like sister's son.
However, there is another possible way of looking at this
situation. In case I above (p. 151), we might regard "x"
as the son of a male cousin, but since the tie to Ego is
through the aunt "t" we might call him nephew rather than
son. Likewise, in case IV, it might be argued that "x"
could be regarded as the female Ego's nephew because the tie
to her is mediated by her father "a". Similar arguments
could be made in cases V and VIII. In fact, this is the way
in which the Dravidians have reasoned. They call "x" in
case I (the father's sister's son's son) nephew (Morgan
1870, table III, no. 101); and "x" is called nephew in cases
IV (Morgan, table III, no. 106), V (no. 1027), and VIII (no.
132). Cases II, III, VI, and VII are excluded here since,
as a consequence of the rule of cross-cousin marriage (see
below sec. IX), "x" in these cases is necessarily equivalent
to Ego's son (table III, nos. 102, 105, 128, 131). In any
case, it is interesting how, as a consequence of these circumstances, the Dravidians have ended up with exactly the
contrary results to those of the American Indians.

     The Indians call "x" son in cases I, IV, V, and VIII,
while they call him nephew in cases II, III, VI, and VII.
The Dravidians, on the other hand, call "x" nephew in the
first series of cases, and son in the second.

     For the Dravidians there occur some deviations in
cases like IX and X. In case IX, if Ego is male, the figure
labeled "d" will in some instances be called son, in others

nephew (table III, no. 179). For, if the cousins have
married, then Ego and "g" are siblings and the latter's son
will be Ego's nephew. But if there has been no cousin marriage, Ego may marry "g" (his second cousin), and the child
will be the son of both.

If Ego is female, then there are the same deviations,
but the situation works itself out conversely. If there has
been cousin marriage, then Ego and "g" are sisters, and sister's son is called son. If cousin marriage has not taken
place, then Ego and "g" are second cousins, and the child is
treated like that of a cousin, as in the situation in case
IV, hence as Ego's nephew (table III, no. 180).

In case X, if there is a male Ego, the figure labeled
"h^2" is always regarded as nephew (in Tamil and Telugu), although if there has been cousin marriage, one would actually
expect Ego and his counterpart "h^1" to be brothers; the child
"h^2" would, as brother's son, be called son (no. 189). If
there is a female Ego, the child is designated in Tamil and
Telugu as son (no. 190).

In case XI, the figure labeled "d" is called nephew
by a male Ego (no. 215). In case XII, the child "h^2" is
also supposed to be called nephew, though no further information is given (no. 221).

So much for the simple classificatory form of relationship system. It is based on group marriage, in which
the generations are strictly kept distinct. The brothers
AAA marry the sisters bbb, while the brothers BBB marry the
sisters aaa. The children from the first marriage have all

AAA men as their fathers (group fathers) and all bbb women
as mothers (group mothers); and these children are all siblings (group siblings). Each man regards his brother's son
as son, each woman her sister's son as son. A similar situation obtains for the second marriage between BBB men and
aaa women.

On the other hand a male Ego uses a distinct term for
his sister's son and female Ego a distinct term for her brother's son, because in both cases the child is the product
of the opposite group. There are also distinct terms for
uncle and aunt. A son of AAA men and bbb women will regard
BBB men as uncles and aaa women as aunts (members of the opposite group). The uncle and aunt terms imply just this,
that these are relations belonging to the opposite section.
Cousin terms result in the same way.

III

Australian group marriage generally developed according to
the above principle of classificatory kinship--as I have
already shown in my work on Australian law (1887a). The
same is true for Dravidian group marriage, as demonstrated
by Morgan's tables, but as will be shown among the Dravidians, cousin marriage causes some peculiarities.

We find the following equations among the Dravidians--
Tamil, Telugu, and Canarese--(all numbers referring to Morgan's table III):[4]

F = FB = FFBS = FFFBSS (Morgan's table III, nos.

61, 166, 207).

M = MZ = MMZD = MMMZDD (nos. 139, 196, 225);

= FBW = FFBSW = FFFBSSW (nos. 62, 140).

PF = FFB = FFFBS (nos. 165, 206).

PM = MMZ = MMMZD (nos. 195, 224).

S = BS (m.s.) = FBSS (m.s.) = FFBSSS (m.s.) =
    FFFBSSSS (m.s.) = MZSS (m.s.)(nos. 29, 75, 169,
    209, 153).

D = BD (m.s.) = FBSD (m.s.) = FFBSSD (m.s.) = MZSD
    (m.s.)(nos. 31, 77, 171, 155).

CG = BCS = FBCCS = FFBCCCS = FFFBSSSSS (nos. 33, 83,
     173, 210).

B = FBS = FFBSS = FFFBSSS (m.s.) = MZS (nos. 63-66,
    167-168, 208, 141-144).

Z = FBD = MMZDD = MMMZDDD (f.s.) = MZD (nos. 69-72,
    197-198, 226, 147-150).

Nephew = ZS (m.s.) = FBDS (m.s.) = MZDS (m.s.) = BS
         (f.s.) = FBSS (f.s.) = MZSS (f.s.) (nos. 37,
         79,157,45,76,154).

Niece = ZD (m.s.) = FBDD (m.s.) = MZDD (m.s.) = BD
        (f.s.) = FBSD (f.s.) = MZSD (f.s.) (nos. 39,
        81, 159, 47, 78, 156).

S = ZS (f.s.) = FBDS (f.s.) = MZDS (f.s.) (nos. 53,
    80, 158).

D = ZD (f.s.) = FBDD (f.s.) = MZDD (f.s.) (nos. 55,
    82, 160).

uncle = MB = MMBS = MMMBSS (nos. 113, 186, 219).

aunt = FZ = FFZD = FFFZDD (nos. 87, 176, 213).

cousin = FZS = FZD = MBS = MBD (nos. 89-92, 95-98,
         115-118, 121-124).[5]

However, the American Indians have introduced two
important modifications, producing greater complexity, which
I call the Omaha and Choctaw forms.

Concerning the Omaha, Dorsey gives us the precise report that group marriage occurs in the version in which a
man marries or is permitted to marry not only his wife and
her sister, but also his wife's nieces and aunts. These
women are all regarded as real or potential wives (Dorsey
1884a, 261). This fact provides the key to a series of terminological peculiarities found among the Omaha and a group
of closely related tribes, including the Ponca, Iowa, Oto,
Kau and Osage (concerning the linguistic relations of the
tribes, see Powell 1885-86, 115 ff.; for the following, cf.
Bernhöft 1888, 39 ff.), and also among the Winnibago and a
group of Algonkian tribes. These are tribes nos. 18-24 and
46-55 in Morgan's tables, those he classed together as the
Missouri and the Mississippi groups, respectively.

As far as this type of kinship system is concerned,
we are best informed about the particulars of the Omaha system by Dorsey. Regarding the others, we have only Morgan's
tables to rely upon, which are not quite so extensive, but
despite some individual differences, provide us with enough
facts to establish a regular structure.

If a man marries a woman, her aunts and nieces (the
various "a"s in the following diagram), then his child
(Ego) will call all four women labeled "a" his mother, producing the following terminological equations:

I. M = MFZ = MBD = MBSD

II. F = MFZH = MBDH = MBSDH

III. B = MBZS = MBDS = MBSDS

IV. Z = MFZD = MBDD = MBSDD

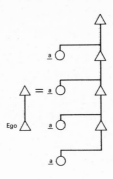

a = mother
    (<u>inaha</u>).

V.   MB = MBS = MBSS[6]

VI. ZS = MFZDS = MBDDS = MBSDDS (also = FZS [m.s.])

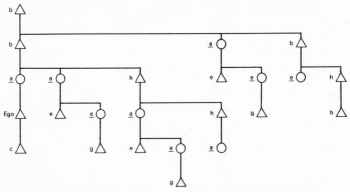

a = mother (<u>inaha</u>),   h = uncle (<u>inegi</u>),

b = ancestor (<u>itiga</u>),   e = brother (<u>ijice</u>),

e = sister (<u>itange</u>),   g = nephew (<u>itacka</u>).

The above is demonstrated as follows. Since Ego's

father has the women designated "a" as wives, they are also
Ego's mothers, giving these equations:
M = MFZ = MBD = MBSD (proving the above equations).
Consequently "a"s sons are also Ego's brothers, producing
the following:
MFZS = MBDS = MBSDS (proving the third set of equations
above, and therefore the fourth set is also proved).

Furthermore, since all "a" women are regarded as
mother by Ego, their brothers are also his uncles (unless
they are regarded as ancestors). Consequently the fifth
set of equations is proved.

Finally, since MBDD is my sister, her son "g" is my
nephew; and since MFZD is also equivalent to my sister, her
son (MFZDS) is also my nephew, thereby justifying the sixth
set of equations.

Furthermore, since MBS = MB, then FZS is equivalent
to nephew, as can be seen in the following figure.

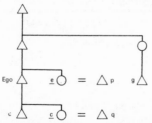

Here "g" regards Ego ("g"'s MBS) as his uncle (MB),
and as a consequence Ego regards "g" as his nephew (ZS).
However, in our idiom "g" is Ego's FZS; hence FZS = nephew
(ZS).

MBZ is always equivalent to mother, and since "g"

regards Ego as uncle (MB), then he also regards "e̲" (Ego's
Z) as mother. Similarly, following the above principle
(that MBS = MB), "g" regards "c" as uncle and "c̲" as his
mother.

And since mother's husband is always equivalent to
father, "p" and "q" are regarded by "g" as father and therefore they regard "g" as son.

But this does not yet exhaust the question. In the
figure page 158 (second figure), if we were to take "c" as
Ego, then the above considerations concerning mother could
be applied to grandmother (since my mother is my son's
grandmother). Thus, the women marked "a̲" in that figure
would be regarded as grandmother by "c." Since according
to the above (p. 150), grandmother's brother = grandfather,
every man marked "h" would be regarded by "c" as grandfather,
from which we derive a new equation:

since MBS = MB, then sons of grandfathers (i̲t̲i̲g̲a̲)are
also grandfathers (excluding men called fathers);
furthermore, since MBD = M, then daughters of grandfathers are also grandmothers.

The same does not hold of the son of daughters of
the grandmother. These are again equivalent to father and
aunt (FZ) as in the following figure:

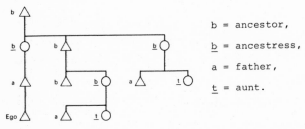

b = ancestor,

b̲ = ancestress,

a = father,

t̲ = aunt.

However, if they are related to ego through mother
rather than through father, they will be equivalent to
mother and uncle (MB) as in the following figure:

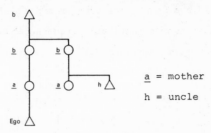

a = mother

h = uncle

For the equations of series I, see Morgan's table II,
nos. 121-24, according to which, in tribes nos. 18-24, 46-
52, 54, and 55, MBD = M, and nos. 129-30, according to which
the MBSD = M. For series II, see nos. 125-26, which give
the equations MBDH = F. For series III, see table II, nos.
131-132, showing for tribes 18-24, 46-52, 54, and 55 that
MBDS = B. For series IV, see nos. 133-34, according to
which MBDD = Z. For series V, see nos. 115-18, which for
the same tribes give the equations MBS = MB, and nos. 135,
137, where MBSS = MBSSS = MB (in one of the tribes, with the
delightful additional specification, "the small uncle").
Also refer to nos. 189, 190, 193, where MMBSSS = MMBSSSS =
MB.[7] For series VI, nos. 89, 91, 95 and 97 indicate that
FZS = ZS and FZD = ZD. Morgan's table II, nos. 121, 122,
129, and 130, show that MBSD (hence MBD) = M; and nos. 90,
92, 96, and 98 show that FZS (f.s.) = S. Morgan, nos. 125-26
show that MBDH = F.

These tribes have no terms for male and female cousin;

what we mean by these concepts is for them a conglomeration
of kinship relations. They regard male and female cousin,
depending upon position, as brother and sister, nephew and
niece, uncle and mother, or even as son and daughter. This
circumstance results inevitably from the above equations.
Compare the following figures.

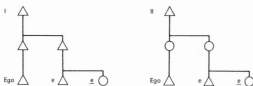

That "e" is equivalent to brother and "e̲" to sister
results from the general principles of classificatory kinship (see above sec. II, equations VIII and IX).

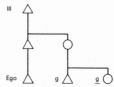

That "g" is equivalent to my nephew (ZS) and "g̲" to
my niece (ZD) (according to equation VI above), derives from
the fact that Ego is their uncle (MB), in consequence of the
principle that MBS = MB.

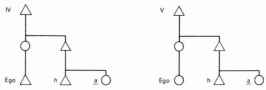

According to equation V (MB = MBS), "h" is my uncle,
and according to equation I (M = MBD), "a̲" is my mother
(Morgan, table II, nos. 115-18, 112-24).

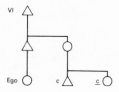

Ego regards "c" as son, since Ego is regarded by "c" as mother (MBD = M); thus Ego also regards "c̲" as daughter (nos. 90, 92, 96, 98).

The situation is continued in the same way in the following generations. Since in figure III, "g" is equivalent to nephew, then his son is equivalent to nephew's son, and thus in turn to grandson (sec. II, no. XV, Morgan, nos. 101, 103). Since in figures IV and V, "h" is equivalent to uncle, then his son (following the Omaha principle in which MBS = MB) is also equivalent to uncle (nos. 127, 128). Furthermore, since "h" is equivalent to uncle, his daughter, as the sister of an uncle, is equivalent to mother (nos. 129, 130). Since "a̲" is equivalent to mother, her son is equivalent to brother (as follows from Dorsey). In figure VI, since "c" equals son, his son is equal to grandson (nos. 102, 104).

The situation is also carried out consistently in the older generations.

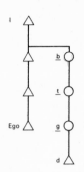

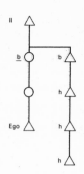

(See Morgan, table II,   (See Morgan, table II,
nos. 175, 176, 178, 181, 182).   nos. 185, 186, 187, 189, 190, 193).

However, Morgan's inventories contain a mistake. According to principles set out above in which MBS = MB, MMBS =
grandfather, we would assume in figure I that "t̲" would regard Ego (her MBSS) as uncle (MB). Ego then should regard
her as niece (ZD). And in figure II, Ego should regard the
three men marked "h" as his grandfathers. The case is similar with Dorsey, whose material gives us Morgan's results
only if in figure II the person marked "b" were a woman (because the equation of male ancestor's son with ancestor is
not continued through a female link), or if the person marked
"b̲" were a man, in which case "b" would no longer be a MMB
but a normal MFB (grandfather). In figure I, Dorsey's
material gives Morgan's results only when we replace Ego's
FF with his FM.[8]

Finally:

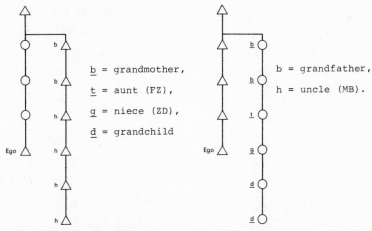

b = grandmother,

t = aunt (FZ),

g = niece (ZD),

d = grandchild

b = grandfather,

h = uncle (MB).

(Compare Morgan's table II, nos. 211-16).

(Compare Morgan's table II, nos. 217-22).

IV

The Choctaw group of tribes stand in opposition to the Omaha group. Among them, group marriage also takes place in the upper and lower generations, but in an inverse way. It is not the man who marries his wife, her aunt, and her niece, but the woman, who marries her husband, his uncle, and his nephew (ZS, cf. Bernhöft 1888, 22 ff.). We do not have direct confirmation for this, as we do for the Omaha, but it is clearly shown by Morgan's tables that it occurs among his tribes nos. 26-36, the Minitari, the Crow, Choctaw, Chickasaw, Creek, Cherokee, Pawnee, and Arichara.

The Choctaw version of group marriage produces the following equations:

I.   FMB = F.   IX.   MB = B;

II.   FZS = F.   MBW = BW = W.

III.   FZ = grandmother (or aunt).   X.   BS (f.s.) = grandson;

IV.   FZH = grandfather.   ZS (m.s.) = B;

V.   FZD = grandmother (or aunt).   ZSW = BW = W;

VI.   FZDS = F (or B);   ZD = Z;

       FZDH = grandfather.   ZDH = ZH = brother-in-law.

VII.   FZSS = B;   XI.   FFZD = grandmother;

       FZSW = M.   FFZDS = F (grandfather);

VIII. MBS = S;   FFZDD = M (or grandmother).

       MBD = D;   XII. MMBSS = S;

       MBSW = daughter-in-law;   MMBSSS = grandson.

       MBDH = son-in-law;

       MBSS = grandson;

       MBDS = grandson.

     These equations are demonstrated by the following
figure.

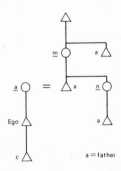

a = father

     Ego's mother "a" married the three persons marked
"a," consequently all three are Ego's fathers. We would

regard the upper "a" as FMB, the lower "a" as FZS, which
automatically produces the equation: F = FMB = FZS (those
in series I and II above).[9] In addition, the sister of the
upper "a," as we represent her, is Ego's grandmother, demonstrating equation III (FZ = grandmother and also aunt) and
consequently also equation IV (FZH = grandfather). Upper
"a"'s sister's daughter is lower "a"'s mother, and since
Ego regards both of these men as father, equation V is
demonstrated (FZD = grandmother). However, this woman, "n,"
is also Ego's aunt (FZ), demonstrating equation VI (FZDS =
F; FZDH = grandfather). Likewise, the ZS of the upper "a"
is equivalent to the middle "a," my father therefore his
son is equivalent to my brother and his wife is equivalent
to my mother, proving equation VII (FZSS = B; FZSW = M).
Furthermore, Ego is the MBS of the lower "a," but at the same
time his son, therefore equation VIII is shown (MBS = S;
MBD = D).

     This situation results in equation IX (MB = B; MBW =
BW); for any "a" is always MB to the next lower "a," but
all "a" men have the same wife and will be both uncle and
brother to another "a" man, showing that MB = B. This equation produces further the equation MBW = BW. However there
is another possible equation. Since most "a" men have the
same wife, any "a" will have his own wife and that of his
MB, thus MBW = W.

     Further, since the mother of the lower "a" is equal
to the sister of the middle "a" and since Ego regards both
"a" as his fathers, this same woman is also Ego's grand-

mother and aunt (as in equation III). Conversely, Ego is
equivalent to her nephew (BS) and grandson, showing equation
X (BS [f.s.] = grandson).

On the other hand, ZS (m.s.) is equivalent to brother,
since Ego always regards the sister's son of an "a" as another
"a," and, according to the above, several "a" count as brothers to each other. This result also follows from equation
IX; since uncle is equivalent to brother, nephew must also
be equivalent to brother, as brotherhood is reciprocal.
Correspondingly, sister's daughter equals sister, sister's
son's wife equals brother's wife or own wife, since middle
"a" (ZS of upper "a") has the same wife as upper "a."

If we draw a line down from Ego and call his son "c,"
then we may conclude from the above that the upper "a" is
equivalent to the father's father of "c"; "n̲" is equivalent
to the sister's daughter of upper "a," and is thus also
equivalent to the father's father's sister's daughter of
"c." However, "n̲" is also mother of lower "a" and thus
Ego's grandmother and the great-grandmother of "c." But
great-grandmother is equivalent to grandmother; therefore
series XI is demonstrated (FFZD = grandmother, FFZDS = F,
FFZDD = M [or grandmother or aunt]).

The mother's mother of lower "a" regards upper "a"
as brother; and since both lower and upper "a" are fathers
to Ego, he is son to both of them, and consequently series
XII is demonstrated (MMBS = S). This equation is not
actually found in the terminologies, but we do encounter it
at another level (MMBSS = S).

Now if we look at the terminologies in Morgan's table II, we discover that, disregarding a few understandable deviations (for example mother instead of grandmother), they are admirably consistent.

I   cannot be shown in the terminologies.

II   is found in nos. 89-92. For one tribe the FZS is distinguished as "small father." Nos. 93-94, show FZSW = M, sometimes also "small mother" or stepmother.

III   is found in no. 87. FZ is called grandmother, mother, and aunt.

IV   is found in no. 88. FZH is called grandfather, father, "small grandfather," stepfather, or second father.

V   is found in nos. 95-98. FZD is called grandmother, mother, and aunt.

VI   is found in nos. 105-6. FZDS is called father, "small father," and brother. Nos. 99-100 show that FZDH is called grandfather, father, "small grandfather," and stepfather.

VII   is found in nos. 101-2. FZSS is called brother. Nos. 93-94 show that FZSW is called mother, and also "small mother."

VIII   is shown by nos. 115-18, 121-24. MBS is called son and grandson. MBD is called daughter and granddaughter. Nos. 119-120 show that MBSW = daughter-in-law. Nos. 125-26 show that MBDH = son-in-law. Nos. 127-28 show that MBSS = grand-

son (see also nos. 129-30). Nos. 131-32 show
that MBDS = grandson.

IX   is shown by no. 113. To be sure the equation of
      uncle with brother occurs only among two of the
      Choctaw type tribes, the Minitari and the Crow;
      but that this equation was formerly more strong-
      ly felt is proven by no. 114, MBW = BW (even
      daughter-in-law). The equation MBW = W occurs
      among the Pawnee.

X   is shown by no. 45. BS (f.s.) is called grand-
      son or child. No. 37 shows that ZS (m.s.) is
      called brother; no. 39 shows ZD is called sister.
      These latter two apply, of course, only for the
      Minitari and Crow and by analogy to series IX.
      No. 38 shows that ZSW = BW among the Crow and
      that ZSW = W among the Arickara, and that ZSW =
      granddaughter among other groups. No. 40 shows
      that ZDH equals brother-in-law among the Mandan
      and the Minitari (cf. no. 255).

XI   is shown by no. 176. FFZD is called grandmother
      or aunt. No. 177 shows that FFZDS = F (also
      "small father"). No. 178 shows that FFZDD
      is called grandmother, mother and aunt. Nos.
      179-80 show that FFZDDS = B or F ("small father,"
      or even grandfather). Nos. 181-82 show that
      FFZDDD is called sister or aunt. No. 214 shows
      that FFFZDDD is called grandmother, aunt, or
      sister.

XII is shown by nos. 187-88. MMBSS is called son.

This can also be derived from nos. 189-94. No.

220 shows that MMMBSSS = S, which can similarly

be derived from nos. 221-22.

The Choctaw tribes have no distinct terms for cousin.
The male cousin is called either brother, father, or son.
The female cousin is called sister, grandmother, aunt, or
daughter. This is demonstrated by the following figures.

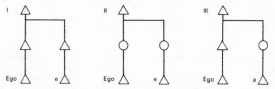

In accordance with the basic rules of classificatory
kinship, "e" is equivalent to brother. In figure III, "a"
(FZS) is equal to father, in keeping with equation II above.

For the same reason, "c" in figure IV (MBS) is equivalent to son, in accord with equation III above.

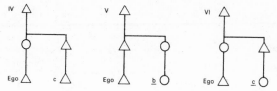

In figure V, "b" is equivalent to grandmother, mother,
or aunt, in accordance with equation V. In figure VI, "c"
is equivalent to daughter, as results from equation VIII.

Similarly in the following generations, since (according to figure III) "a" equals father, the son of "a"
is equal to brother. Since (from figure IV) "c" is equal
to son, the son of "c" is equal to grandson. Both of these

conclusions can be seen to derive from the equations in the
series VII and VIII above. Furthermore, since (in figure
V) "b" is the same as grandmother or mother, her son will be
equal to father or brother, as can be seen in equation VI.
And finally, since (in figure VI), "c" is equivalent to
daughter, her son is the same as grandson, as in equation
VIII.

The following figures extend into even further
generations.

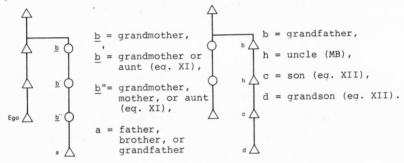

(Compare Morgan, table II,   (Compare Morgan, table II,
nos. 175-82).   nos. 185-92).

(Compare Morgan, table II,   (Compare Morgan, table II,
nos. 211-15).   nos. 217-21).

V

The same rules which govern kinship also govern affinity.

The general principle of classificatory kinship produces

these equations:

    I.   FBW = M.   V.   FBSW = BW.

    II. MZH = F.   VI.   MZSW = BW.

    III. BSW = daughter-in-law. VII. MBW = FZ.

    IV. BDH = son-in-law.   VIII. FZH = MB.

For:

    I.   Since FB = F, then his wife equals mother ([Mor-
gan, table II, no. 62], sometimes also stepmother or aunt [FZ]).

    II.   Since MZ = M, then MZH = F ([no. 140], sometimes
also stepfather, "small father," uncle [see
sec. II above]).

    III.   Since BS = S, then his wife equals daughter-in-
law ([no. 30], rarely also granddaughter, sister-in-law).

    IV.   Since BD = D, then her husband equals son-in-
law (no. 32).

    V.   Since FBS = B, then his wife equals BW ([no.
67], rarely wife, once also sister [cf. no. 68]).

    VI.   Since MZS = B, then his wife equals BW ([no.
145], once wife).

    VII.   Since the group marriage of AAA men with bbb
women and BBB men with aaa women is reciprocal,
"B"'s wife is also "A"'s sister. Thus MBW = FZ
([no. 114], also stepmother).

VIII. For the same reason FZH = MB ([no. 88], also

father, stepfather; for the Omaha group the

situation is different [see p. 179 below]).

Niece's husband and nephew's wife have no distinct
term of their own; they are also called son-in-law and
daughter-in-law (nos. 38, 40, 46, 48). Similarly, son-in-
law's father and mother are designated son-in-law and daughter-in-law.

The group marriage of AAA brothers with bbb sisters
results in the following equations (cf. Bernhöft 1888, 22):
(a) W = WZ; (b) W = BW (m.s.); (c) H = HB; (d) H = ZH (f.s.).
Equation (a) is found among the Pawnee and the related Arickara (both belong to the Caddo tribe; cf. Powell 1885-86, 61),
the Cheyenne, the Crow, and the Minitari (no. 260). Equation
(b) is true of one of the Pawnee tribes, of the Arickara,
and of the Mandan (no. 262). Therefore, one of the Pawnee
tribes and the Arickara also have the equation W = FBSW (no.
67), and for the same Pawnee tribe W = MZSW (no. 145).
Equation (c) occurs among two Pawnee tribes (no. 254), (d)
among one of them (no. 256).

It should be noted that the Creek call the woman in
(a) and (b) and the man in (c) and (d) "the present occu-
pant" (nos. 254, 256, 260, 262, 31).[10]

Most tribes however have distinct terms so that the
wife's sister is no longer called wife but "potential wife,"
and the husband's brother is no longer called husband but
"potential husband," with the same terms being applied to
brother's wife and sister's husband.

The Omaha are a typical case. Among them wife is
called "igaqca," potential wife "ihanga;" hence ihanga = WZ
and BW (m.s.). Husband is called "iegcange," potential husband "icie," hence icie = HB and ZH (f.s.). All of the above
is shown by Dorsey's tables.

That the real meaning of ihanga is "potential wife"
and the meaning of icie is "potential husband" may be clearly deduced from the Omaha type of group marriage. For since,
among them, a man marries not only wife's sister but her
niece and aunt as well, these latter, as will be shown, will
also be designated as ihanga, and a similar argument can be
made regarding icie. Likewise the brother of ihanga is
called brother-in-law, the sister of icie sister-in-law,
from which it can be clearly concluded that these terms in
fact express the potential relationship of marriage.

This conclusion also results from the following equation. Since wife's sister is a potential wife, and husband's
brother is a potential husband, son-in-law is not only the
husband of daughter or niece but also the brother of this
husband; and daughter-in-law is not only the wife of son or
nephew but also the sister of this wife. These conclusions
are strictly substantiated by Dorsey's tables.

On the other hand, among the Omaha the husband's sister is called "icika" (sister-in-law), as is the brother's
wife (woman speaking). Wife's brother is called "itaha"
(brother-in-law), as is the sister's husband (man speaking).
Both equations result from the reciprocity of group marriage;
therefore the terms for brother- and sister-in-law are

reciprocal, as are those for siblings.

We encounter this point of view, if not everywhere,
at least among most tribes.

I.   WZ = BW (m.s.) = potential wife (Morgan, table
        II, nos. 260, 262).

II. HB = ZH (f.s.) = potential husband (nos. 254, 256).

III. HZ = BW (f.s.) = sister-in-law (nos. 261, 263).

IV. WB = ZH (m.s.) = brother-in-law (nos. 257, 255).

Another explanation for the equations given at the
beginning of this section derives from those given here.
Since Ego calls not only his WB but also his ZH brother-in-
law, then his child calls both uncle, and the same child calls
both FZ and MBW aunt. Therefore uncle (MB) also equals FZH,
aunt (FZ) also equals MBW (Morgan, table II, nos. 88, 114).
Furthermore, nephew is also equivalent to WBS and HZS (this
is also deducible from Dorsey's tables, if one allows for
the idiosyncrasies of the Omaha system).

Cousin's wife is called by the same term as brother's
wife, cousin's husband by the same term as sister's husband,
because no further distinction is made--this is true naturally only for those tribes which have developed the concept of
male and female cousin (nos. 93-94 [compared with 262-63],
99-100 [compared with 255-56], 119-20, 125-26).

VI

So much for the expression of affinity under the general
rules of classificatory kinship. In this area both the
Omaha and the Choctaw types have their own singularities,
and we will now deal with these. First it is useful to look

at the Omaha type in close detail.

A

I. <u>Wife's sister is potential wife</u> in the above classificatory sense. However, according to the rules of Omaha kinship, the sister concept extends even further. Since MBD =
M (according to equation I, sec. III above), then MBDD = Z,
as does MBSDD (equation IV, sec. III). Ego may marry all of
these sisters of his wife--should that not be too many for
him. These conclusions result inevitably from Dorsey's
tables.

However, according to Omaha kinship, not only is Ego's
wife's sister a potential wife, but so are his wife's aunt
and niece. The term "potential wife" is also to be understood in the classificatory sense developed above (secs. III,
IV). Therefore, Ego may also marry his initial wife's FFFSD,
if he wishes. The same thing is true for the niece (sec. IV);
Ego may also marry his WFFSSD, if he wishes and if she is not
too young. This latter may be deduced directly from Dorsey's
table, and the first could certainly be deduced if the tables
were extensive enough.

II. Furthermore, <u>brother's wife is potential wife.</u>
In fact, the Omaha say that the dead brother's wife is still
regularly taken as an additional wife (Dorsey 1884<u>a</u>, 258; cf.
below sec. XIII). Here too brother is meant in the broader
sense given it in Omaha kinship. Therefore, among the Omaha
MBDSW is also potential wife as could be seen in Dorsey's
tables if they were sufficiently extensive.

III. A man calls the <u>sons</u> of all actual and potential

wives within the range of Omaha kinship, his sons; this
term is applied therefore also to WZDS and WFZS (Dorsey
1884a, table II).

IV. <u>The brothers</u> of all these women are brothers-in-
law (<u>itaha</u>) for a male Ego,[11] their <u>fathers</u> are fathers-in-
law, their <u>mothers</u> are mothers-in-law. All of these concepts are to be understood in the broader sense employed by
the Omaha.

These usages may overlap. If Ego marries his WFZ,
then his first wife's father is the brother of this second
woman and thus simultaneously brother-in-law and father-in-
law. The latter term would be given precedence.

However, concerning the designations father-in-law
and mother-in-law, Morgan's table shows that most tribes
have special terms for them, while wife's grandfather is
called grandfather or old man or even father-in-law. Among
the Omaha in particular father-in-law and mother-in-law seem
to be given special terms (father-in-law is called old man),
while wife's grandfather is called grandfather (Morgan, nos.
235-38). On the other hand, according to Dorsey's tables
even father-in-law and mother-in-law are called grandfather
and grandmother, as are ascending relations from them and as
are wife's uncles. The term for grandfather is <u>itiga</u>, that
for grandmother is <u>ika</u>. The inconsistency disappears when
one considers that Morgan's terms, in particular the name
"old man," are undoubtedly popular variants or terms of
familiarity.

V. <u>Brothers-in-law's</u> (itaha) <u>sons</u> are also brothers-in-law. The reason for this is obvious.

Ego △ = ○   p △

p △   p ○

Since "p" is my potential wife, then her brother,
the lower "p," is as much my brother-in-law as the upper "p."

VI. The husbands of my potential wives are my brothers; for originally the brothers as a group married the
sisters, nieces and aunts as a group.

VII. Brother-in-law (itaha), however, according to
the above is also equivalent to sister's husband (male speaking). Here again sister is to be understood in the widest
sense given it in Omaha kinship.

However, the Omaha equations of wife with wife's niece
and with wife's aunt also become relevant here. Therefore
Ego's ZH equals Ego's sister's aunt's husband (ZFZH or simply
FZH) and Ego's sister's niece's husband (ZBDH or simply DH).
Now since Ego's ZFZ is Ego's own FZ, then Ego's FZH = ZH =
brother-in-law (itaha).[12] Furthermore, since Ego's sister's
niece (ZBD) is the equivalent of Ego's own daughter (whether
in fact his own or his brother's), then Ego's DH = ZH = brother-in-law; however DH is also equivalent to son-in-law, and
this latter terms takes precedence.

B

I. Conversely, a woman calls her husband's brother, potential
husband (icie). And the use of this latter term corresponds
with the enlarged meaning of the term brother in Omaha kin-

ship (which is broader than the general classificatory meaning). According to equation III, sec. III, MBDS = B among
the Omaha; therefore HMBDS is also _icie_, which unavoidably
results from Dorsey's tables.

    II. However, a woman also calls her sister's husband,
potential husband (_icie_). Here too sister is to be understood in the wider sense given it in Omaha kinship. But she
also calls, and this is again characteristic of Omaha kinship, her niece's husband and her aunt's husband potential
husbands, which is the converse and the result of the fact
that a man calls his wife's aunts and nieces wife, and, if
he wishes, he may marry them. This fact is also to be deduced from Dorsey's first table.

    III. The sons of all potential husbands are called
son, according to the above; and a woman calls her potential
husbands' sisters, sisters-in-law (_icika_). Since according
to equation III at the end of sec. V above HZ = BW, then the
sons of sisters-in-law are equivalent to brother's sons (in
keeping with the general rules of classificatory kinship).

    As for the parents-in-law, what has already been said
about them above is true here too. The terms _itiga_ and _ika_,
grandfather and grandmother, are already found in Morgan's
tables. However, the terms for parents-in-law, which vary
according to whether a married or unmarried woman is speaking, are not at all the same among all the tribes; rather,
as is shown by Morgan's table II (nos. 231-32 compared with
235-36), there are several idiosyncratic variations here.

    A woman calls the wives of potential husbands her

sisters, nieces, or aunts, because originally all the brothers as a group married the sisters, aunts, and nieces as
a group.

IV. A woman, furthermore, calls her **brother's wife**
her **sister-in-law** (*icika*), whereby again brother is to be
understood in the wider Omaha sense, because as just mentioned BW = HZ.

V. These additional equations will be explained in
subsection D below:

> (a) ZHZ = granddaughter;
>
> (b) BWB = grandfather;
>
> (c) HZH = grandfather;
>
> (d) WBW = daughter-in-law.

C

Since there are no distinct terms for cousins in Omaha kinship, the equation of cousin's wife with brother's wife
(above, last paragraph, sec. V) cannot be generally true
here. Of course, wherever cousin is equivalent to the brother, as in the case of the FBS or the MZS the equation obviously holds (cf. Morgan, nos. 67, 68, 145, 146, 262, 263).
However, when the cousin is equivalent to nephew, thus the
FZS, then, as is shown by Dorsey's table I and Morgan's table
II (no. 93), cousin's wife is equivalent to daughter-in-law.

Where cousin equals uncle, thus when he is MBS, then
cousin's wife equals aunt (Morgan, nos. 119-20). If cousin
equals son, thus when Ego is a woman and the cousin is the
FZS, then his wife is equivalent to daughter-in-law (Morgan,
no. 94).

The same principles obtain for the cousin's husband.
When the cousin equals the sister, her husband is equivalent
to ZH (Morgan, nos. 73-74, 151-152, 255-256). When the cousin equals the niece (FZD [m.s.]), her husband is equal to
son-in-law (Morgan, no. 99 and Dorsey's table I). When the
cousin is equal to mother (MBD), her husband is equal to
father (nos. 125-26). When the cousin is equal to daughter
(FZD [f.s.]), her husband is equivalent to son-in-law (no.
100).

D

Within the Omaha family, not only are the wives of the son,
nephew, and grandson and of the aunt's son (since FZS = ZS,
equation VI, sec. III) regarded as <u>daughters-in-law</u>, but so
are the sisters, aunts, and nieces of all of these women; for
these women are the potential wives of sons and nephews.

However, Ego's WBW is also daughter-in-law, as can
be seen in the following figure.

Ego is the husband of "<u>w</u>" and potential husband of
"<u>v</u>;" however, "<u>v</u>" is the aunt of "p," and "p" is therefore
her nephew, and "s," as nephew's wife, is her daughter-in-
law. But since Ego is the potential husband of "<u>v</u>," then

"s" is also Ego's daughter-in-law (cf. sec. VII below). Of
course, "s" is also Ego's mother-in-law because "p" is also
Ego's wife, and she is the daughter of "p" and "s."

Dorsey and Morgan show that both equations actually
exist. In Dorsey's information "s" is termed daughter-in-
law (itini); in Morgan's information (table II, no. 265) she
is ika, grandmother or mother-in-law. We have here then one
of the world's most astonishing curiosities. The same person may be at the same time daughter-in-law and mother-in-
law.

II. The daughter's husband in the wider sense appropriate to Omaha ideas is son-in-law. However, Ego's
niece's husband and his granddaughter's husband (cf. Morgan,
nos. 99-100) as well as his aunt's daughter's husband (since
FZD = ZD), are also son-in-law.

The additional equation of son-in-law with sister's
husband would also be possible, since ZH is also DH (as in
the equation above, sec. VI, subsec. A, where DH = brother-
in-law). However, since the Omaha type tribes have a specific name for the brother-in-law, this term takes precedence.
The equation occurs though among three other tribes, which
will be discussed below.

III. Father-in-law is equal to father's father-in-
law. This is because no further distinction is made here.
This fact leads to the following situation.

The man labeled "z" is the father-in-law of "c" and

also Ego's father-in-law. Ego is the father-in-law of lower "ǫ", and also that of upper "ǫ"; hence "z" is Ego's father-in-law and upper "σ" is Ego's son-in-law (cf. Dorsey
1884a, table II and p. 255; it must be kept in mind though
that the father-in-law there is *itiga*, grandfather).

　　　IV. Daughter-in-law's brother is equivalent to grandson. Son-in-law's sister is equivalent to granddaughter.
This is because in descending degrees of kinship and affinity
everyone who does not bear a special term is called grandson
or granddaughter.

　　　From this fact derive the following four equations
already promised:

　　　(a) ZHZ = granddaughter (Dorsey 1884a, 255); for ZH
is also DH (husband of the first woman's niece), thus he is
my son-in-law and son-in-law's sister is granddaughter, according to the above.

d = granddaughter

　　　(b) From this fact it results that Ego is the grandfather of "d." This results in the equation that BWB =
grandfather (woman speaking). BWB is however equivalent to
HZH; for WB = ZH (above equation IV, end of sec. V). BW =
HZ therefore BWB = HZH.

　　　(c) If we place the latter into the equation given
above then it results that HZH = grandfather.

$$\text{Ego}\ \bigcirc\ =\ \triangle_{\text{w}}\quad \underline{\text{o}}\bigcirc\ =\ \triangle_{\text{b}}$$

Therefore "b" is Ego's grandfather, which is shown
with admirable consistency by Dorsey's table II.

(d) However, grandfather is equivalent to father-in-
law. Consequently the inverse is true; WBW = <u>daughter-in-
law</u>, as was already demonstrated in a different way in this
subsection.

We have thus dealt with the riddles of Omaha kinship.

VII

Unfortunately, we lack a Dorsey for the Choctaw group of
tribes. We must depend upon Morgan's tables, and these are
incomplete for the affinal terms. Among the Choctaw type
tribes, a woman marries the brother, uncle, and sister's
son of her first husband (sec. IV above), thereby producing
the following equations:

I.   MBW = W.

II. ZSW = W.

The first equation, however, is still to be found
among only one of the tribes, the Pawnee (Morgan, table II,
no. 114). Among all the other tribes (tribes nos. 26-29)
MBW = BW (cf. table II, no. 262), which is explained by the
fact that among all these tribes MBW is actually equivalent to
BW, but the equation BW = W has been given up, as was already remarked in section V above. BW is now only equivalent
to potential wife. But among the Pawnee the equation BW =
W has been retained, and therefore also the equation W = MBW.

The second equation (ZSW = W) may be encountered a-
mong the Arickara (no. 38), but it has been given up elsewhere in favor of the equations ZSW = BW and ZSW = daughter-
in-law. The first equation results from the above equation
BW = potential wife, but the second is a borrowing from
other tribes which do not have a Choctaw system (see sec.
V).

Among the Choctaw too the equation cousin's wife =
BW does not obtain, since they have no distinct terms for
cousins. The two exceptions to this generalization are the
normal features of classificatory kinship in which FBS and
MZS = B, and their wives therefore equal BW. Otherwise,
among the Choctaw (see sec. IV above), the cousin is either
equivalent to father (as FZS), and therefore his wife
equals mother (Morgan, nos. 93-94; also "small mother" or
stepmother), or he is equivalent to son (as MBS) and therefore his wife equals daughter-in-law (nos. 119-20).

The same thing is true for the female cousin and her
husband. Thus FZD = grandmother (or mother) and her husband
equals grandfather (also called "small grandfather," stepfather or father; cf. Morgan nos. 99-100). MBD = D and her
husband equals son-in-law (nos. 125-26).

So much then for the Choctaw. The Pawnee and Arickara
show an idiosyncracy (Morgan, nos. 34-36); while they otherwise are like the Choctaw group, they show influence from
the Omaha group in one point. It was remarked in the preceding section that in the Omaha system, the equation ZH =
son-in-law is possible (since Ego's daughter is also his wife).

This equation no longer occurs among the Omaha tribes, but
it is found among the Pawnee and the Arickara (Morgan, no.
255). This feature is explained by the fact that the Pawnee and the Arickara not only allowed a woman to marry her
husband's uncle and nephew, but also permitted a man to marry his wife's aunt and niece. The equation is then a consequence of this marriage practice, and will be dealt with
in the next section.

Among the same tribes then the following equation
obtains, MZDH = son-in-law (Morgan, nos. 151-52). This is
self-evident since MZD = Z, hence MZDH = ZH = son-in-law.
Likewise FBDH = son-in-law (Morgan, nos. 73, 74) because
FBD = Z.

VIII

If we consider again the nature of the Choctaw and Omaha
systems as a whole, then we may see the following points.
Neither system is fortuitous or arbitrary; both rest on two
firm principles. It seems indeed that given these two far-
reaching principles, a combination of both, or even a greater or lesser degree of implementation of them, but certainly no other system was possible.

These principles are the following:

(a) marriage partners may be taken from only one
other clan;

(b) no marriage into this clan may take place which
would result in a parent-to-child relation between the
spouses.

Otherwise, the two systems are distinguished in that

the Choctaw system derives from mother right and the Omaha
system from father right. In the first system the totem is
received from the mother, in the latter from the father.
(see pp. 133-34, also Bernhöft 1888, 32 ff., 39 ff.).
Given these premises, we can be certain that only these two
systems are possible.

If we assume that mother right obtains, then it is
only possible for a man to marry a woman and her sister in
another clan, taking sister in the classificatory meaning,
of course. Marriage with wife's mother and daughter would
be automatically prohibited, the latter because it would
constitute marriage between father and daughter, the former
because if a third marriage took place with the initial
wife's sister this would mean marrying the second wife's
daughter and thereby one's own daughter.[13] The terms mother and daughter are naturally to be understood in the
classificatory sense, whereby M = MZ, D = ZD.

In our idiom therefore marriage may take place with
the wife's sister, mother's sister's daughter, and grandmother's sister's daughter's daughter, but not with her
mother or mother's sister and also not with her daughter or
sister's daughter. However, there would be an obstacle in
the way of marriage with the initial wife's brother's daughter or father's sister, since they belong to different clans,
if we assume mother right. Hence only marriage with wife
and her sisters is possible.

On the other hand, a woman may marry her husband's
sister's son and his mother's brother. Marriage with the

husband's father and son would be excluded because this
would bring about marriage between mother and son and in addition because there would be a difference of clan. Here
too the terms are to be understood in the classificatory
sense. Both problems would be avoided in the case of marriage with the sister's son and with the mother's brother.
In these cases the clan unity would be maintained because
mother's brother's clan is always the same as that of the
sister's son. This then is the situation in the Choctaw
system.

The Omaha system develops in a similar way from the
presupposition of father right. A woman in this system may
marry only her husband's brother but not his brother's son
or his father's brother; for such arrangements would lead to
marriage between mother and son. She also may not marry his
mother's brother or sister's son because (given father right)
these belong to another clan.

On the other hand, a man may marry not only his wife's
sister, but also her brother's daughter and her father's
sister, since on the one hand these belong to the same clan
and on the other there is no danger here of a union between
father and daughter.

A combination, as is found among the Pawnee and the
Arickara, is possible provided that one family is ordered
by father right and the other by mother right. Here a woman
whose family is governed by father right may marry a man and
his sister's son and mother's brother, provided that his
family is governed by mother right (for in this case these

persons would all belong to the same clan). And conversely the man could marry the woman, her brother's daughter,
and her father's sister (since, given father right, they
would all belong to her clan). Who gets the children depends on whether father right or mother right is considered
the predominant principle. This explains why we find among
those two tribes a combination of the Choctaw and the Omaha
systems.

In general, the admirable way in which these systems
are implemented should bring various truths to light. The
idea that classificatory kinship terminolosy has any other
basis than consanguinity is definitely refuted. Just try
to explain the features of Choctaw and Omaha kinship by
means of any other system!

Furthermore, the clearly pronounced details of these
systems show on the one hand that nature works with astonishing consistency, even in the ethnological question of choice
of spouse. On the other hand, these details show that the
tribes have a sufficiently intuitive understanding of these
principles to designate kinship relations in terms of them,
and hence that primitives have, in this regard, reached a
sufficient degree of intellectual development to allow the
conclusion that they have gone through a long and fundamental
process of evolution. This is otherwise demonstrated, as
remarked above, by their languages, which are often formed
with admirable delicacy and logic.

Opinions to the effect that classificatory kinship
merely reflects residential patterns or is based on the

poverty of language or the confusion of ideas, need consequently be given no further consideration. History has
left, in the exceedingly complicated and yet admirably consistent Omaha and Choctaw systems, the clearest proof that
group marriage is basic to classificatory systems. Therefore, anyone who fails to begin with the admittedly difficult study of these systems is not in a position to give an
authoritative judgment on the question. For this reason
alone we may bypass Mucke and Westermarck.

IX

Group marriage leads directly to cousin marriage, provided
that the principle of marriage within the same generation
is maintained.

Let us suppose that in the two groups A and B, the
AAAA men marry the bbbb women and the BBBB men marry the
aaa women. If we now assume that (given mother right) the
children of the first group are BBBB, while those of the
second are aaaa, and if we assume that normally AAAA all
belong to the same generation and are thus regarded as
siblings and that the same is true for the bbbb of the other
group, then BBBB and aaaa are related to each other as
cousins; for BBBB are the children of A and B, while aaaa
are the children of B and a. They are related then according to the formula: as the son of A, B marries a, the
daughter of a; and as the son of b, B marries a, the daughter
of B. Hence brother's son marries sister's daughter, and
likewise brother's daughter marries sister's son.

As is well known this form of cousin marriage is
widespread. It is especially important among the Dravidians,
whose kinship terminology is based on it. When sister's
child and brother's child regularly marry each other, the
following equations are the result, which according to Morgan's table III occur among the Dravidian tribes (Tamil,
Telugu, Canarese, of course with variations):

    I.   WF = MB (table III, no. 235);

          HF = MB (no. 231).

   II.   both mothers-in-law = FZ (nos. 236, 232).

  III.   son-in-law = nephew (nos. 239-40);

          daughter-in-law = niece (nos. 241-42).

   IV.   nephew's wife (ZSW [m.s.], BSW [f.s.]) = D

          (nos. 38, 46);

          niece's husband (ZDH [m.s.], BDH [f.s.] = S

          (nos. 40, 48).

    V.   FBSW = cousin (nos. 67-68);

          FBDH = cousin (nos. 73-74);

          MZSW = cousin (nos. 145-46);

          MZDH = cousin (nos. 151-52).

   VI.   FZSW = Z (nos. 93-94);

          FZDH = B (nos. 99-100);

          MBSW = Z (nos. 119-20);

          MBDH = B (nos. 125-26).

VII.   FZSS (m.s.) = nephew (no. 101);

       FZSS (f.s.) = S (no. 102);

       FZDS (m.s.) = S (no. 105);

       FZDS (f.s.) = nephew (no. 106).

VIII. MBSS (m.s.) = nephew (no. 127);

       MBSS (f.s.) = S (no. 128).

IX.   MBDS (m.s.) = S (no. 131);

       MBDS (f.s.) = nephew (no. 132).

X.   HB = cousin (no. 254);

       WB = cousin (no. 257);

       WZ and HZ = cousin (nos. 260-61).

XI.   WZH = cousin (no. 258);

       WBW = Z (no. 265);

       HZH = cousin (no. 259);

       HBW = sister (no. 264).

XII.   ZH = cousin (nos. 255-56);

       BW = cousin (nos. 262-63).[14]

The accuracy of these equations is shown by the following figures:

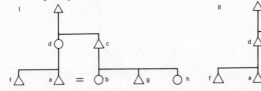 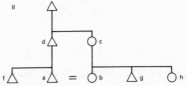

Since "a" marries "b", then "c" (in figure I) is both uncle
and father-in-law of "a"; and "c" (in figure II) is both
aunt and mother-in-law of "a." And conversely the same is
true of "d" in both figures in relations to "b." Similarly "a" (in both figures) is both nephew and son-in-law of

"c," and "c"'s daughter "b" is the wife of "a." In this way
the equations I-IV are produced.

The equations V and VI are shown in the following.

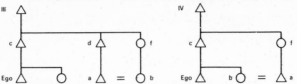

In figure III, "a" marries "b;" since "b" is Ego's cousin,
the wife of "a" (FBSW) is equivalent to cousin. Ego's sister could not marry "a" for reasons explained immediately
below. On the other hand, in figure IV, Ego's sister marries "a," hence FZSW = Z, etc.

Regarding equation VII, the following must be taken
into consideration.

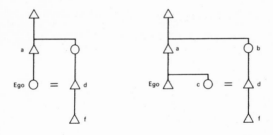

When Ego is male, his sister marries "d" and her child "f"
is his nephew. When Ego is female, she marries "d" herself
and "f" is her son. The same reasoning obtains for equations VIII and IX. Equation X derives from the preceding
figures I and II in this way. The person labeled "f" is at
the same time the cousin of "b" and her husband's brother;
and similarly "g" is both the brother of "b" and the cousin

of "a."

Equation XI (WZH = cousin) is striking. One would
actually have expected him to be equivalent to brother,
since "h" (in figure I and II) must marry a brother of "a"
(a brother either in our sense or in the classificatory
sense, e.g., MZS). The same inconsistency occurs concerning the husband's sister's husband. On the other hand the
following equations are consistent, WBW = Z because "g" (in
figure I and II) must marry a sister of "a," and HBW = Z
because "f" must marry a sister of "b."

Equation XII results automatically. Sister marries
her (and also Ego's) cousin; brother marries his (and Ego's)
cousin.

Naturally cousin marriage may only occur when the
connecting parents are of the opposite sex. When they are
of the same sex, the cousins (FBD, MZD) are siblings and
marriage is therefore, prohibited—or, in the language of
totemic law, they belong to the same totem. In fact, the
following equations are also found among the Dravidians:

father-in-law = MB (but father-in-law ≠ FB);

mother-in-law = FZ (but mother-in-law ≠ MZ);

son-in-law = ZS (m.s.); BS (f.s.)(but not vice versa;

cf. Morgan, table III, nos. 239-40, 37,

45, 29, 53).

These distinctions are also a consequence of the arrangement
explained at the beginning of this section.

X

A number of tribes with group marriage have at an early

stage already given up cousin marriage. It is easy to
understand how this came about. While formerly the whole
generation level "A" married the whole generation level "b,"
now both groups split into two and each subgroup marries
only the corresponding subgroup; consequently:

$A^1A^1A^1$ marry $b^1b^1b^1$, and the children are $\underline{B}^1$;

$A^2A^2A^2$ marry $b^2b^2b^2$, and the children are $\underline{B}^2$;

$B^1B^1B^1$ marry $a^1a^1a^1$, and the children are $\underline{a}^1$,

$B^2B^2B^2$ marry $a^2a^2a^2$, and the children are $\underline{a}^2$.

The children of "$\underline{B}^1$" no longer marry the children of "$\underline{a}^1$,"
but "$\underline{B}^1$" marry "$\underline{a}^2$" and "$\underline{B}^2$" marry "$\underline{a}^1$."

By this procedure, cousin marriage is avoided. In
fact, it is not common among American Indians and is, indeed, completely forbidden among a whole series of tribes.
This is said to be the case for the Huron (Sagard-Théodat
1865:113), the southern tribes, for example the Cherokee
(Adair 1775, 190; C. C. Jones 1873, 68), the tribes in
Carolina (Lawson 1711, 186), Californian tribes, for example
the Gualala (Powers 1877, 192), and tribes of British
Columbia (J. G. Swan 1874, 13).

Consequently, among these groups we do not find the
equations, father-in-law = MB, son-in-law = ZS, ZSW = D,
brother-in-law = cousin, WBW = Z.

Some features reminiscent of them as survivals still
appear among a few tribes. Among the Cree tribes (in Morgan's table II, tribes nos. 37-39) father-in-law = MB (nos.
231, 235) and mother-in-law = FZ (nos. 232, 236; this is
also true for some other tribes), without these equations

being carried any further.

The apparent equations among the Dakota, which others have already cited, of FZSS (f.s.) = S (table II, no. 102) and MBSS = S (no. 128), rest on a translation error made by Morgan; for in both cases, the expression metoushkä (and so on) does not mean son but nephew, as can be seen by referring to other parts of the table (nos. 37, 9).[15]

However, that such an equation does occur among the Iroquois tribes, is the result of a special set of circumstances which will be reviewed in section XI below.

We may also sporadically encounter the equations, WBW = Z and HBW = Z (nos. 264-65) among the Winnebago, Menomini, and one Algonkian tribe (nos. 24, 52, 64), also in this case without being carried further.

Naturally, it would be impossible for cousin marriage to develop among those tribes who, as a consequence of marriage into the upper and lower generation levels, did not develop the concept of cousin. Since among tribes with an Omaha system, our term "cousin" is equivalent to brother, nephew, uncle, or son, and since among tribes with a Choctaw system it corresponds to brother, father, or son, cousin-marriage would have resulted in marriage with niece, mother, and daughter, which is obviously out of the question (chap. 2, sec. VIII).

Consequently, cousin marriage may still be recognized among the Indians only in rare survivals. Of course we do encounter second-cousin marriage among the Pawnee and the Arickara (cf. Bernhöft 1888, 29), which from the above discussion may be seen as a natural, historical development.

If we continue the series started at the beginning
of this section, we come to the point where finally "a^2"
and "$\underline{B}^1$" marry, and likewise "$\underline{B}^2$" and "$\underline{a}^1$." Now if we place
the husband on the left and the wife on the right, the fol-
lowing equations result:

$\underline{a}^1$ marries $\underline{B}^2$, and the child will be $\underline{BB}^2$;

$\underline{a}^2$ marries $\underline{B}^1$, and the child will be $\underline{BB}^1$;

$\underline{B}^1$ marries $\underline{a}^2$, and the child will be $\underline{aa}^2$;

$\underline{B}^2$ marries $\underline{a}^1$, and the child will be $\underline{aa}^1$.

When in this generation "$\underline{aa}^1$" and "$\underline{BB}^1$" again marry
and "$\underline{aa}^2$" and "$\underline{BB}^2$," then the marriage of the grandchildren
of siblings is given.

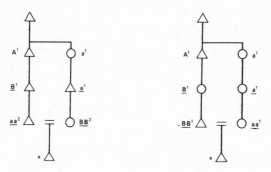

From this marriage, the following equations in Pawnee and Arickara law result, FFF = MB, since "A^1" is the
uncle of "$\underline{a}^1$" and therefore also uncle (great-uncle) of his
descendants, and since for the same reason "A^1" calls "x"
nephew, then great-grandfather = MB, great-grandson = ZS
(Morgan, table II, nos. 3, 13-14, 35, 51). For the same
reason MMBSSSS is called nephew (nos. 193-94), which, since

Ego is regarded by the latter as grandfather, we should of
course have first expected in the following generation
(great-grandfather = uncle, not grandfather = uncle).

XI

The Hawaiian type of group relationship, which is produced
by sibling marriage, results in the following equations:

   ZS (m.s.) = S (Morgan, table III, no. 37);

   BS (f.s.) = S (no. 45);

   FZ = M (no. 87);

   MB = F (no. 113);

   FZH = F (no. 88);

   MBW = M (no. 114);

   male cousin = B (nos. 89-92, 115-18);

   female cousin = Z (nos. 95-98, 121-24);

   cousin's wife = Z (nos. 93-94, 119-20);

   cousin's husband = B (nos. 99-100, 125-26);

   son-in-law = S (nos. 239-40);

   father-in-law = F (no. 231);

   brother-in-law = B (no. 257).

These equations are more or less thoroughly implemented in the Hawaiian system. They indicate group marriage
prior to totemic distinction, to which we will not here
give closer attention.

Traces of such former sibling marriage, which would
not have been governed by any totemic division, are to be
found among a few North American tribes (cf. Bernhöft, pp.
46 ff.). They appear first of all among some Athapaskan
tribes (the Tinne; i.e., northern tribes; cf. Powell 1885-

86, 51). Two Athapaskan tribes are consistent in having the equation, ZS (m.s.) = S (Morgan, table II, nos. 37, 39, 79, 81, 157, tribes no. 65-66). Among several tribes we find the equation, BS (f.s.) = Z, namely among four Athapaskan, three Algonkian, and some Iroquois tribes (Morgan, nos. 45, 47, 76, 78, 154; tribes no. 2-7, 61-67).[16]

Similar equations may also be found:

(a) FZ = M;

(b) MB = F;

(c) FZH = F;

(d) MBW = M.

Of these equations, (a) is found among two Algonkian tribes (Morgan, table II, no. 87, tribes 61 and 62; the terms used are stepmother and "small mother"), and among five Iroquois tribes (nos. 2-5 and 7).[17] Equation (b) is found nowhere, while (c) occurs among three Algonkian and one Athapaskan tribes (table II, no. 88, tribes 61-63, 67; the term is stepfather) and among the Iroquois and among a Dakota tribe (tribes 1-7, 9; their terms are father or stepfather).[18] Equation (d) is found among an Algonkian tribe (no. 114, tribe 63) and two Iroquois tribes (tribes 4 and 5).

Furthermore, the equation of cousin with brother occurs among several Athapaskan tribes, which as we have already seen show traces of sibling marriage (table II, nos. 89-92, 115-18, tribes 64, 66-68). The equation of cousin with sister is also found among them (nos. 95-98, 121-24, tribes 66-68). It could be that these equations have other grounds, but if other traces of sibling marriage can be

found, then this should be considered the reason for them.
They also occur among some other tribes, one Iroquois tribe
(tribe 7), and among a Rocky Mountain tribe (56) as well as
among several Algonkian tribes (59, 61-63).

On the other hand the equation of cousin's wife
with sister and cousin's husband with brother is almost
completely lacking. Among some Iroquois tribes it happens
that a woman calls the son of a cousin (of FZS or MBS) son
instead of nephew (table II, nos. 102, 170 for tribes 2-7
and no. 128 for tribes 2-5, 7).[19]

The further equations of son-in-law with son,
father-in-law with father, and brother-in-law with brother
do not occur or occur only in isolated cases (cf. Bernhöft,
p. 47). Nevertheless, I should like to dismiss here the
equation of father-in-law with father, which occurs among
one Choctaw tribe, since it appears to be only a variation
of the common father-in-law = grandfather.

Thus, if we look at the whole, we may perceive a
certain systematic consistency among some Athapaskan, Algonkian, and Iroquois tribes. Sibling marriage is most
likely to have occurred among the Athapaskan; in fact it is
said of some northern tribes, particularly the Koniag, that
brother and sister have sexual relations.[20] On the whole,
we can only take notice here of traces which do not yet
lead us to certain results.

XII

The classificatory system also occurs in its essential out-
lines among the northern Indians, insofar as our information

is adequate: thus among the natives of Slave Lake (Morgan 1870, 234), on the Mackenzie River (1870, 236), among the Kutschin (p. 239), the Tukuthe (p. 239) and among the British Columbian tribes (p. 247).

On the other hand there is hardly any trace of classificatory kinship nomenclature left among the Innuit (Eskimo); at most, grandfather's brother is also called grandfather and niece's husband is called son-in-law, nephew's wife is called daughter-in-law and cousins' husband and wife are called siblings' husband and wife (pp. 276-77; Dall [1877, 117] confirms this lack of classificatory kinship, so far as his information is sufficient).

The Eskimo have long since given up totemic clan organization, and their language and family idea have taken another path without, however, allowing all traces of a former institution of group marriage to disappear.[21]

XIII
Group marriage has left clear traces not only in the language but also in the life of the Indians, and I think that it is possible to find enough proof to support the conclusion which I drew from the relationship terminologies that they once had such an institution. The following kinds of proof are present: (I) group marriage relations which are still in effect; (II) potential, occasionally occurring group-marriage relations, (a) at death, (b) during festivals, and (c) in ceremonial situations; (III) relations which are similar to those of group marriage.

I. Group marriage is reported to be present among

the Omaha, and this by an observer like Dorsey, whose re-
liability is above all doubt.   Dorsey says (1884a, 261) in
his concise, naively convincing way:

> The maximum number of wives that one man can
> have is three, e.g., the first wife, her aunt,
> and her sister or niece, if all be consanguini-
> ties ... When a man wishes to take a second
> wife, he always consults his first wife,
> reasoning thus with her: "I wish you to have
> less work to do, so I think of taking your
> sister, your aunt, or your brother's daughter
> for my wife ..." Sometimes the wife will make
> the proposition to her husband: "I wish you
> to marry my brother's daughter, as she and I
> are one flesh." Instead of "brother's daughter,"
> she may say her sister or her aunt.[22]

The woman's relation to her husband's brother becomes apparent at the death of her husband. Dorsey (1884a,
258) says: "A man takes the widow of his real or potential
brother in order to become the stepfather ... of his brother's children."

The man's relation to his wife's sister is also
especially prominent in case of death. "When the wife is
dying, she may say to her brother, 'Pity your brother-in-
law. Let him marry my sister.'"

The nature of group marriage shows itself very
clearly here. The whole group of women who may be married
is predetermined for every man, should he not be satisfied
with only one or two. Similarly, the husband's brother is
designated for the woman when her husband dies. The levirate is a survival of group marriage; the husband's brother
takes his place, at least when he dies. Correspondingly,
it also happens among some tribes that they have another
term for the father's brother to be used for the time being,

but that they immediately call him father or stepfather as
soon as their actual father dies. This is so for the tribes
of British Columbia, as Morgan mentions (1870, 248): "My
father's brother I call Is-se-malt. After the death of my
own father I call him my step-parent, Es-tlu-es-tin." The
same thing holds of mother's sister, who after the death of
one's own mother immediately becomes es-tlu-es-tin.

Thus we have certain proof of the actual existence
of group marriage relationships among the Omaha. Now if we
observe how their whole kinship system rests on this form of
group marriage, that is, marriage with wife, her sister, her
aunt, and her niece, and how the kinship terminology derives
unavoidably from this equation of the several women, then we
have completely valid proof for the fact that the kinship
terminology rests on group marriage and may be explained only
in this way, not only among the Omaha but anywhere there is
a similar system. Since there are quite a number of tribes
which have the Omaha system, and since on the other hand the
Choctaw system is only a reflection of the same thing in the
opposite direction, then group marriage is as certainly
proved for all the peoples with this type of kinship system
as it is possible for anything to be proved in historical
terms.

We have a specific, indubitable report about the
Osage (relatives of the Omaha) from Nuttal (1821, 185):

> That curious species of polygamy . . . is like-
> wise practised by the Osages, by which the man,
> who first marries into a family, from that period
> possesses the control of all the sisters of his
> wife, whom he is at liberty either to espouse
> himself or to bestow upon others.

We also find group marriage in practice among other
tribes. Among the Crow, the husband has a right to all the
sisters of his wife (Morgan 1877, 160). De facto polyandry
is reported of one Iroquois tribe (Lafitau 1724, 1:555).
Among the Ojibwa, the men marry by preference several sisters if they want several wives (P. Jones 1861, 81). In
fact, by their kinship terminology the Ojibwa belong to
those nations in which a man only marries sisters but not
their nieces or aunts, hence to the group marriage type,
who keep their marriages within the same generation level,
and hence to those nations who, as a result of this, have
cousin terms. The same is true of the Algonkin (Lafitau 1,
599).

Marriage with several sisters is also reported of
the Mandan and the Minitari (for the Mandan, whoever marries
the oldest daughter has a right to all her sisters; Lewis
and Clark 1893, 557; Wied-Neuwied 1839-41, 2:130), of which
the latter at least belong to the Choctaw group. Marriage
of several sisters is also reported of tribes in Louisiana
(also peoples of the Choctaw group; Hennepin 1688, 38).
The same is true for those in Carolina, where one marries
several sisters and brother's widows too (Lawson 1711, 186),
and the same for the Californian tribes (Bancroft 1883,
1:388 ff.). Among the Nez Percé in the interior of British
Columbian territory, it is said that "marrying the eldest
daughter entitles a man to the rest of the family, as they
grow up;" and if a woman dies, "her sister or some of the
connexion, if younger than the deceased, is regarded as

destined to marry him" (Alford, pp. 654 ff.). Similarly,
among the Apache, the husband has the right to the wife's
younger sisters, and possibly to other clan women (Bourke
1890, 118).

Among the Tlingit and the Koniag, there is a custom
of auxiliary husbands. These are the brothers or near
relatives of the husband (Holmberg 1855-63, 316, 399). As
long as the husband is present, they stay away; on the other
hand, they have the right to take the place of the real
husband in his absence, but lose the right as soon as he
returns (Holmberg, p. 399). They share in the costs of upkeep, and therefore if a relative of the husband commits
adultery with his wife, he is also declared an auxiliary
husband and must then contribute to her upkeep (Holmberg,
p. 316). This constitutes a clear proof that the woman
originally belonged to the husband's relatives as a group,
on account of which even later adultery by one of them still
has a very special significance.

Langsdorff (1812, 2:43) refers to a similar arrangement among the Aleut, to whom in a wider sense the Koniag
also belong. It is reported of the Innuit that sometimes
several men have a wife in common (Ross 1835, 356, 373). A
further symptom not to be left out of consideration is that
the cousins are in practice equivalent to siblings. This is
true of the Ojibwa (Long 1824, 171); and an observer of the
previous century tells of the Cherokee, "the whole tribe
reckon a friend in the same rank with a brother, both with
regard to marriage and any other affair in social life"

(Adair 1775, 190).

So much for marriage with members of the same group. An interesting reaction against this occurs in Wyandot law; here the man may indeed practice polygamy, but the women must belong to different clans (Powell 1881, 63; it is also reported of the Eskimo that a man may not marry two sisters [Lyon 1824, 256]). This is a reaction against marriage with several sisters, which also occurs elsewhere and which is explained by the fact that the relative position of the several women tends to be unequal and this inequality in rights is felt to be particularly difficult by a sister.

II. (a) It is very common that a brother or sister take the place of a deceased spouse.

Among the Ojibwa a man may take his brother's widow as wife, and she then shortens her period of mourning. Otherwise she must carry the clothing bundle representing her husband around with her throughout the whole period of mourning; only then may she, should her husband's brother reject her, marry another (Yarrow 1879-80, 184-85; Long 1824, 171).[23] The brother of the deceased husband has a right to the widow among the Apache too, but he must avail himself of this right within a year (Bourke 1890, 118).

We learn of the Huron, Delaware, and Iroquois that a widower usually marries the sister of a dead wife, and a widow is maintained or married again by a relative of the husband (Lahontan 1703, 2:141; Lafitau 1724, 1:560; Loskiel 1789, 83). Among the Californians too, the widow falls to the lot of the husband's brother (Venegas 1739, 1:94). Even among the Eskimo, the brother marries the widow of the deceased brother (Klutschak 1881, 234).

How much this levirate right is connected with the presence of polyandry is shown in the life of the Tlingit. Here the wife has sexual relations with her husband's brother as auxiliary husband even during the first husband's lifetime, as has just been mentioned, and she goes to him, if she becomes a widow (Dall 1870, 416; Krause 1885, 221).

(b) An orgiastic lack of constraint in sexual intercourse is very common at certain festivals and initiation rites, which certainly indicates former unions between male and female groups.

Among the Mandan, when there is a dearth of game, festivals are celebrated where they give the women to the old men (Lewis and Clark 1893, 221; Wied-Neuwied 1839-41, 2:181). At initiation into the secret society the woman is surrendered to the initiator (Wied-Neuwied, 2:140, 143, 277; the same thing occurs among the Huron [Lafitau 1724, 1:581]). Wanton relations during festivals are reported for the Californian tribes (Venegas, 1:93). Such communal orgies are particularly common in the North, among the Aleut (Dall 1870, 399) and especially among the Innuit (Eskimo). At certain festivals, the latter have sexual relations without any discrimination, due to a religious custom (Egede 1763, 160; Boas 1888, 605; Nordenskiöld 1886, 463); and in East Greenland there is the lamp-extinguishing game, where such things take place (Nansen 1891, 146).

(c) The surrendering of women on the basis of sacral

principles is similarly widespread. The woman is given to
the priest, who deflowers or copulates with her in substi-
tution for her whole clan. In the tribes of upper California,
the woman had to give herself to every sorcerer she met
(Boscana 1846, 276). Among the Eskimo, the woman must give
herself to the Angekok, particularly when she is sterile
(Egede 1763, 161; cf. Nansen 1891, 145), and the Kinipetu
Eskimo have a clear _jus primae noctis_ (Klutschak 1881, 234;
cf. Kohler 1883, 287).

III. Group marriage leads to sexual relations between groups, from which the woman is extracted by individual
marriage. It is therefore understandable that before marriage a free sexual traffic obtains, which is frequently
limited so that sexual relations may only occur with a particular clan, and close relatives and one's own totem group
must be avoided. This group marriage was the rule in primordial times. Now it is limited through individual marriage because the woman who formerly was available to the
whole group is from now on in the possession of only one
man. However, prior to marriage, unrestrained intercourse
continues to be possible.

Unrestricted sexual relations before marriage is
absolutely confirmed for almost all Indian tribes, including
the Huron and Wyandot (Parkman 1867, xxxv; cf. Lafitau 1724,
1:584). We do learn of the latter, that the mother and her
relatives exercise a control over the daughter and punish
her in case of excess (Powell 1881, 66). There is unrestrained
sexual relations before marriage reported for the Iroquois

(Lahontan 1703, 2:130; Parkman, p. xlv), the Attiguatan
(Champlain 1830, 1:383; Sagard-Theodat 1865, 111 ff.), the
Mandan (Wied-Neuwied 2:131), and the Carolina tribes (Law-
son 1711, 187).

It also occurred among the southern tribes, where
a maiden's reputation increased when she had many lovers,
though she was not supposed to have a child (C. C. Jones
1873, 69; concerning the Creek, cf. C. Swan 1855, 5:272).
The maidens might also be loaned out for a time (Hennepin
1688, 35), which was the immediate result of the fact that
group relation was finally regarded as something which is
allowed only with special permission. Similarly among the
Natchez, intercourse before marriage counted among a maiden's
titles to fame, while a wife was required to be virtuous
(Domenech 1862, 509).

It is expressly reported of the Comanche that premarital relations are permitted, but they must be kept
within the clan (Kate, 1885a, 390). Premarital commerce is
also common among the California tribes, such as the Karok
(Powers 1877, 22). Among the Pomo, the young maidens are
even considered to be common property (Powers, p. 157),
while fidelity is demanded from wives. The same holds true
for other tribes there. It is reported by one observer that
intercourse must remain within the same clan (Wrangell,
1:88). Free sexual contact also occurs among the Oregon
tribes (Gibbs 1877, 199), as well as among the Chinook
(Bancroft 1883, 1:242), but in particular among the tribes
of the North.

It is reported of the Aleut women that they are regarded more as mates than as wives (Ritter 1862, 255).
Among the Koniag the greatest licentiousness holds sway
(Bancroft, 1:81 ff.), and the same things are related of
the Haida (Poole 1872, 312). This is also said about the
Innuit (Murdoch 1892, 419), and is especially true among
the Kaviak, where the unmarried may have intercourse without
reproach (Dall 1870, 138).

A famous traveler relates of the Greenlanders that
a maiden who has a child out of wedlock assumes a special
headdress, but that this contributes not to her shame but
to increasing her reputation (Nansen 1891, 143), while
Egede (1763, 161) gives more favorable reports from some
tribes.

However, even regarding the period after marriage,
the wife's restraint is maintained only insofar as the hus-
demands it. Therefore, the trading and loaning of wives is
common. This is not necessarily to be regarded as a survival of communal possession of women; it can also be the
result of the political law and will therefore be discussed
elsewhere (Kohler 1897a). On the other hand, a former
communal marriage system is very likely to encourage the
idea of such trading and loaning. And if cutting off the
nose or biting off the ear of an unfaithful wife is a punishment frequently practiced, in many cases laxer relations
seem to reign.

One of the first travelers to visit the Indians,
Champlain, at the beginning of the seventeenth century

(1830, 383), relates of the Attiguatan: "After nightfall,
the young maidens run from one hut to the other, as do the
young men on their side, who take them wherever it pleases
them, sometimes without any violence"--a report which is
also repeated by Sagard-Théodat (1865, 111, 115).

Among the Californians, scaring techniques are
used--disguises, magic, and similar things--to terrorize
the women in order to preserve their subjection and fidelity.
For example, a sorcerer may shout curses from time to time,
swing a rattlesnake around, and so on (Powers, p. 160).
These belong to the many means of deceit by which the men
of primitive tribes are accustomed to secure their control
of women.

XIV

Concerning group marriage and cousin marriage among the
Dravidians, I can first draw on Bernhöft's exposition (1891)
and on the existing Indian reports on the matter. Group
marriage is the kule kanyâpradânam of the Brihaspati, which
is described there as a custom still existing among the
southern peoples (Jolly 1896, 47).

Toda polyandry in particular is well known and has
been put above all doubt by Marshall's observations (1873).
The manner of contracting such a polyandrous marriage is
most interesting and shows us that even group marriage does
not exclude bride price. One brother acquires a wife for a
keikuli, a bride price; the others obtain their share by re-
imbursing the first brother for the corresponding share of
the bride price (Marshall, p. 213).

Bernhöft has already justly remarked that where polyandry is mentioned, it is usually based on group marriage which has, however, been transformed into polyandry, several brothers marrying one woman, as a result of the frequent murder of female children.

However, it is shown by the report of the investigator who has studied the Toda most intensively, namely Marshall (p. 206), that among them both group marriage (that is, several brothers marrying several sisters) and polyandry occur. Marshall says that when several wives are present, each husband treats every child of one of these woman as his own. The presence of group marriage is thereby demonstrated by a completely indisputable observer.

Its presence may also be deduced from the report that the brother takes the dead brother's widow to himself (p. 207). Now if this brother enters into communal possession of women with an already married brother, then the situation again occurs in which several women are married to several men.

We encounter polyandry then as a survival among the Bhil in Panch Mahal, insofar as intercourse between the older brother and the wife of the younger brother is not prohibited (Kohler 1892, 68). Further evidence of the communal possession of women in South India is given by J. D. Mayne (1878, 58).

Among the Nayar, group marriage has become alternating marriage, in which the woman does not have several husbands at the same time, but is accustomed to changing

them after shorter or longer periods--a situation which is
so well known that a further description may be omitted
(Kohler 1892, 67, and the works cited there).

Polyandry is further established for the Sinhalese,
also in the form in which a man often takes a supplementary
partner (Kohler 1889a, 233; Jolly 1896, 44); and here too
it occurs along with normal cousin marriage (Kohler 1889a,
233). Among the Tottyar in Madura, it is reported of the
polyandrous relationship that brother, uncle, and nephew
take a wife in common (Dubois 1825, 5). This would lead to
similar relationships as in the Choctaw form of group marriage. However, this version seems only to be local, for
we do not find the kinship terminology structured in the
Choctaw fashion among the Dravidians.

For example, we do not find the equation FZ = grandmother; she is called aunt (Morgan 1870, table III, no. 87).
Similarly BS (f.s.) is not called grandson but nephew (Morgan, table III, no. 45); ZS (m.s.) is not called brother but
likewise nephew (no. 37). But they do have the cousin concept unknown to the Choctaw type (nos. 89-92, 115-18), and
so on.

Dravidian group marriage therefore implies an equivalence of the generation levels, to which in fact the
practice of cousin marriage also leads. We have already
spoken of this type of cousin marriage, it is also found
among the Gond (Kohler 1889b, 144) and among the Komti in
Dharwar (Kohler 1892, 72).[24]

Finally, the polyandry of the Himalayan peoples

will just be mentioned here because these tribes fall outside our area of consideration (cf. Kohler 1887c, 229; for
the Jats, Kirkpatrick 1878, 86,[25] and for a general discussion see Stulpnagel 1878, 134). Here too bridewealth may
be paid by several brothers acting together.

XV

American and Dravidian communal possession of women corresponds to the communal possession of goods.

Among the American Indians in general, see Powell
(1885-86, 34). Among the Iroquois, not only did the land
belong to the clan as a whole, which then apportioned it to
the individual families for cultivation (fields were re-
distributed every twenty years [Hale 1883, 50]), but there
was also a tradition of unlimited hospitality (Morgan 1851,
327 ff.; 1881, 45; cf. Margry 1879, 1:345 ff.; Loskiel 1789,
19 ff.). Even in this century they still built houses from
fifty to one hundred feet in length, in which several
families lived together in different sections with separate
hearths. The inhabitants practiced communism in subsistence;
a matron divided the food among the hearths (Lafitau 1724,
2:10 ff.; Morgan 1870, 119, 121; 1881, 32; 1851, 315 ff.; cf.
Loskiel 1789, 69).

Thus Champlain relates of the Attiguatan (early in
the seventeenth century) that they lived in very large huts
with twelve hearths and twenty-four households, at the back
of which the (doubtless communal) provisions were stored
(Champlain 1830, 1:373). Sagard-Théodat reports of the
Huron (1865, 81 ff.) that the huts had up to twelve hearths

and twenty-four families (always one family to the right
and one to the left of the fire). The same may be ascer-
tained of the Mandan (Catlin 1841, 82-83; Wied-Neuwied,
2:127), the Creek, the Shoshoni (Morgan 1881, 68, 73; 1870,
489), the Pueblo (Peet 1888, 351 ff.) and the British
Columbian tribes (Dawson 1888, 926).

We find the same system among the Chinook, where
three to four families lived together communally (Lewis and
Clark, pp. 783, 767). And the same is found among the
northern tribes, for example, the Koniag (Holmberg, p. 376).
Communistic hospitality is thus widespread everywhere and
is to be found, for example, among the Mandan (Catlin 1841,
1:122), the Creek (Bartram 1793, 466) and the northern
tribes such as the Aleut (Wrangell, 1:205).

A peculiar remnant of communism if found among the
British Columbian tribes. If one totem comrade meets
another, he may show him the picture of the totem and on
the basis of it request a gift from him (R. C. Mayne, p.
258)--totem communism.

Clan-owned territory, as already mentioned for the
Iroquois, occurs also among other peoples with agriculture;
whereby in some cases the field tools belong to the individual and in other cases are communally owned. Among the
Wyandot, tilled land belonged to the tribe, which in turn
every two years apportioned it among the clans, who then
divided it again among the families (Powell 1881, 65).
House, hunting, and fishing utensils belonged to the individual, but larger canoes were totem property (Powell, p.

65); and unlimited hospitality was also the custom (Sagard-
Théodat 1865, 66 ff., 70).

Grain-based agriculture involving the periodic shift-
ing of residence is already reported by Champlain (1830,
1:374, 391) for the beginning of the seventeenth century
and for the eighteenth century by Lafitau (1724, 2:107).
The Creek worked their fields communally. Each person was
given the product of a piece of land specifically apportioned to him, but he then customarily put a part of this
into the king's granary to help form a reserve of provisions
for people whose own ran out (Bartram, p. 485 ff.).

However, communism also occurs frequently among hunters. Among the Dakota, anyone who killed game had to
share it with whoever he met (Prescott, in Schoolcraft
1851-57, 4:60). This communistic sharing of the products
of one's labor is still more widespread among the northern
tribes. Among the Aleut, in times of dearth someone who
killed an animal or anyone else who possessed food was
obligated to share it with those in need; these would sit
on the shore and would wait for the hunter's return. They
would not expressly ask for anything; they waited silently
and spoke only the word akh, "thank you" (Wrangell, 1:183).

Innuit law is especially characteristic of all of
these communistic arrangements. For them, hunting implements, the axe, the knife, sewing equipment, and the tent
belong to the individual and the family; other implements
and the house belong to the household, which consists of
several families. As for the most important thing, the

hunt, a large kill (whale) is shared by all. Everyone cuts
out what he can; so that occasionally someone may wound
someone else. A middle-sized catch, particularly seal, belongs to the village, that is the settlement, at least in
so far as each household may take possession of a part of
it (there are differing customs governing this division).
A small catch belongs to the members of the house (Rink 1875,
30; Boas 1888, 582; Bessels 1884, 873; Nansen 1891, 100-103;
Nordenskiöld 1886, 468 ff.; Klutschak 1881, 233, cf. Kohler
1889c, 86). In other words, game is shared as far as its
size and the requirements of consumption allow.

For the Eskimo there is also (1) communal possession
of food for the several families living in one house, (2)
the obligation to give up a surplus to needy members of the
village, (3) unlimited hospitality, and (4) absence of re-
sponsibility by the borrower for anything lost or damaged
(Rink, p. 30; Egede, p. 148; Nansen, pp. 99, 100, 107).

Among the Eskimo tribes, for example those of Point
Barrow, this communistic sharing seems to have been curbed,
perhaps under the influence of European trade. The catch
belongs here only to those taking part in the hunt, and it
sometimes occurs therefore that individuals--for example,
the umialik (Boat owner)--may acquire greater wealth than
other tribe members (Murdoch 1892, 429). We establish here
a development toward the right of individual ownership, as
we have seen elsewhere in marriage.

So far we have dealt with the American tribes. Among
the Dravidians we find the same appearance of communistic

ownership. Among the Toda the land belongs to the whole village. Cattle are private possessions, but milk is used in the first place communally, and only what is left over is returned to the individual men according to the number of their animals (Marshall 1873, 206; cf. Watson and Kaye 1868-75, 8:433-34).

Among the Nayar, family possessions (the tarwad) are under the discretionary control of the head of the family (J. D. Mayne, pp. 200, 271). We also encounter communal arrangements among the Sinhalese, where brothers having a wife in common share in an especially close federation of property, so that if a brother dies, another brother united to him in this way takes precedence in inheritance over others not so united (Kohler 1889a, 233, 236). The same situation is found in the Himalayas (Stulpnagel 1878, 135).

We may conclude that community in marriage, as in property, is a distinct sign of an earlier phase of humanity.

AUSTRALIAN ABORIGINES

XVI

I have already devoted an extensive exposition to the group marriage system in Australia (1887a, 321 ff., 325 ff.). Later reports and research have led to complete confirmation of what was set out there.

Of course, opposition has been raised to my formulation (which is the same as that given by Fison and Howitt) by Curr in his book The Australian Race. Curr's work does contain something of value in its collection of material, though the data he brings together there are quite incomplete,

and the vocabularies in particular give us so little of the
relationship terms that they are almost useless for juristic
purposes.

The conclusions Curr draws from his material are unmethodical, his presentations suffer from an improper generalization, and his notion that the Australians derive from
Africa--which he especially infers from similar words in
Australian and African languages--gives evidence of anything
but right method and critical handling of the material.

Fison, admittedly, has not always expressed himself
clearly enough; so we may point out that group marriage is
no longer the normal condition of the Australians and that
on the whole we see it as a phenomenon of the past, still to
be encountered only in residual forms which are its survivals.
But even if it is true that one or the other of Fison's reports is to be taken with caution, Curr has disproved nothing
with his completely unmethodical procedures, and everything
which has been said about the existence of group marriage
still stands. If some authors nevertheless believe that
the group marriage theory may be disputed simply on the basis
of Curr's latest conclusions, without bothering to subject
his comments to any critical test, then they show just that
lack of critical ability which is customary among those
people who hold themselves capable of making a sound judgment
without any technical study of comparative jurisprudence.

Curr (in his manner which grasps only the surface of
contemporary circumstances) appeals to the fact that, according to Australian law, the husband is considered the absolute

owner of his wife and is entitled to exchange her or offer
her sexual services to another man (Curr, 1:109; cf. Kohler
1887a, 327; Gason 1895, 170; Stationmaster 1895, 178; Willshire 1895, 183; Matthews 1895, 187; Foelsche 1895, 194).
No one would deny this, but the crucial point is that it is
dominance by the husband which has forced the development
away from communistic ownership of women, just as the distinct
and jealously guarded landownership of our farmers on their
small farms also derives from former communal ownership of
land.

Above all, the custom of lending one's wife still
bears the traces of the earlier communal marriage relationships; for among some tribes there is still a custom that
the wife is given by preference to the husband's brother, as
Curr himself reports (1:109, 110)--which is very strong
evidence of former group marriage. This custom has a completely different character than that of offering the wife
to a guest. Among the natives of Gippsland (3:546), it is
said:

> There is reason to believe that custom sanctioned
> a single man cohabiting occasionally with his
> brother's wife; and also a married man with his
> wife's sister. A man spoke of his sister-in-law
> as puppar-worcat, which means another wife; and
> when a wife died, her sister not unfrequently
> took her place.

This is also confirmed by the evidence I have presented elsewhere (Kohler 1887a, 326). Schürmann (1879, 223)
says of the Port Lincoln tribe in South Australia that here
the women are reciprocally lent to others and continues:

> As for near relatives, such as brothers, it may
> almost be said that they have their wives in

common. While the sending out of the woman for
a night seems to be regarded as an impropriety
by the natives themselves, the latter practice
is a recognized custom, about which not the least
shame is felt. A peculiar nomenclature has arisen
from these singular connections; a woman honours
the brothers of the man to whom she is married
with the indiscriminate name of husbands; but the
men make a distinction, calling their own individual spouses yungaras, and those to whom they
have a secondary claim, by right of brotherhood,
kartetis.

Elsewhere too relations of communal intercourse with
several men still exist. This was recently confirmed again
by Gason (1895, 169), one of the finest observers, regarding
the Dieri. A woman often has eight to twelve secondary
husbands (pirraura), and jealousy is forbidden on penalty
of strangulation. Crauford (1895, 181) remarks of the
tribes on the Victoria River: "If a strange woman is cap-
tured from another tribe or from the whites, all the men
have connection with her, one after the other until, as a
rule, the woman dies."

It is also reported elsewhere that women are so often
exchanged that they circulate through a great number of
men of a tribe (Matthews 1895, 187).

Many reports also say that the widow goes to the
brother of the deceased. This may have a different basis
in that it may rest on inheritance law; however, since the
widow usually goes to the brother (not, for example, to the
stepson) and since inheritance law otherwise is hardly
developed, this custom may be taken as an important indication that remnants of a former communalism still exist here.
There are a series of reports about this in Curr and the
Journal of the Anthropological Institute (vol. 24) which

demonstrate further what I have already set out (Kohler
1887a, 349, 363). Among the tribes of Nicols Bay the widow
goes to the husband's brother (Curr, 1:298), and the same
is true for the tribes in Port Darwin (Foelsche 1895, 194),
the York District (Curr, 1:338), on Halifax Bay (Curr, 2:425),
on the Belyando River (3:21), in Peak Downs District (3:65)
and among the Dieri (to the older brother; Gason, p. 170).
This even occurs among tribes where the widow must carry
the bones of the dead man around with her for a period, as
in Peak Downs District (Curr, 3:65).

The argument for the existence of group marriage from
the periodic communal orgies at festive occasions is in no
way disproved; this fact was recently confirmed regarding
the Dieri by the exceptional observer Gason (p. 173). I do
not see how Curr (1:109) can apodictically assert to the
contrary, "Amongst the Australians there is no community of
women!" And how can this simply be repeated by German
authors?

Concerning the most important evidence to be drawn
from the relationship terms, Curr has unfortunately given
us only a small list of usable terms. When he attempts to
draw conclusions from the fact that there are terms for
uncle, aunt, nephew, niece, son-in-law, and brother-in-law
in the lists (1:140), and when he thereby attempts to cast
doubt on the scientific impartiality of a scholar like
Fison (1:142), then we must merely take note of it. Where
could a classificatory family like those of the Indians and
Australians exist, which had no names for the mother's

brother, father's sister, sister's child (man speaking),
brother's child (woman speaking), husband's sister and wife's
brother? In any case, the consistent development of this
law of group relationship leads to such terms; and if some
of the American Indian tribes deviate from them, these are
to be considered understandable variations. The Australians
had to develop cousin terms, since in marriage they always
stayed within the same generation; and hence such monstrous
kinship distinctions as were developed by the Omaha and the
Choctaw remained unknown to them.

Curr (1:137) even supposes that the equation of
father with father's brother, etc., rests on the fact that
after the mother's death the children go to her father's
brother and that the latter belongs to the same clan as her
father, while the mother's brother does not. This argument
is obviously quite inadequate. Why is the mother's sister
called the same as mother, the sister's son the same as son
(woman speaking)? Why is the wife's sister the same as wife
and the wife's sister's husband equivalent to brother? Curr
is here arguing from individual, unrelated data; whereas in
fact a harmonious system of nomenclature is present.

Although he speaks of a poverty of language, which he
says does not yet differentiate (1:135), he himself gives
enough examples of the richness of the terminology. Why is
this principle carried through so consistently? What does
it matter here that some languages use the same word for
wood and fire, for milk and water, for night and dark? One
could draw similar conclusions from the fact that we use

the word "church" for templum and ecclesia and the word
"See" (sea and lake) for mare and lacus, "wine" for both
natural and artificial wines. The Australians consider wood
as a provider of fire, and milk and water are nourishing
fluids for them.

In order to given an indication of the richness Australian languages show regarding kinship terms, I will note
that the author's vocabularies demonstrate there are commonly special terms for older and younger brother and for older
and younger sister. The Dieri even make the following distinction: a child is addressed as athamura, but it is consistently referred to as athamura-wauka ("small athamura").
Father is addressed as apiri, but referred to as ginni
(1:135-36). Sometimes a son is called by a different term
depending upon whether it is a man or a woman who is speaking,
for example, athamura and athani, yimmu and kumma (1:141).

Another objection asks how someone could come to call
the mother's sister "mother," since there could be no doubt
about who actually gave birth. The argument rests on that
complete misunderstanding of the idea of group marriage which
I illustrated in section IV of chapter 1.

It is not the uncertainty of paternity which leads to
equating father and father's brother, but the idea that the
child is the whole group's child; hence that the men of the
group are its fathers and the women its mothers, as I have
explained above (end of sec. II, this chapter). The historian must put himself into the modes of thought of the periods
he is concerned with and may not modernize their institutions.

What should we make of this comment by Curr (1:134)? "A
woman calls her sister's male child son as a mode of
speech." Is this comment itself anything other than "a mode
of speech"?

The only things of value in Curr are the special examples which the author quotes in order to refute. The
evidence produced by Fison and Howitt and my own (taken from
them and from A. S. P. Cameron) are not to be shaken. Some
doubt could exist in regards to the Dieri, where we have inferred the following schema (1887a, 342):

> apiri = F, FB;   athamura(ni) (ni is a suffix meaning
>   "my") = S, BS (m.s.);
>
> andri = M, MZ;   athani = S, ZS (f.s.).

According to new reports by Gason, the following is
supposed to be true: a man calls not only his brother's son,
but also his sister's son athamura (meaning son); and a
woman calls not only her sister's son, but also her brother's
son athani. In addition there is the term for brother.
According to the reports used by Fison (p. 61), nihini means
brother, father's brother's son, and mother's sister's son;
while Curr's information (also based on Gason) says the FBS,
FZS, MZS, and MBS are called kankau or athata, depending on
whether he is older or younger than Ego.

This situation is explained by Gason's word list in
Woods (1879, 294) which shows that nihi is the older brother
(ni here is a prefix meaning "my"), kaku means the older
sister, athata the younger brother or sister.

According to this it now seems that Gason's report to

Curr is inexact, at least in so far as here <u>kaku</u> is given
for older brother and sister (in the classificatory sense),
while in fact the older brother is called <u>nihi</u>, the older
sister <u>kaku</u>. More weight must certainly be given Gason's
report in his paper in Woods, and the expression <u>nihi</u> is
confirmed by the Reverend Homan (Fison and Howitt, p. 61).[26]
However, if this is the case, then a certain doubt must still
be permitted whether the equation of brother with father's
sister's son and mother's brother's son, as is given in this
report by Gason, is completely correct. Only the equation
of B = FBS, MZS corresponds to the classificatory system.
If the reports are accurate, then we would have here precisely one of those cases, easily explained by the fluidity of
these languages, where an idiomatic irregularity was produced by the disintegration of the original form of the
family.

I will illustrate this point with the following example, which Curr presents in his own work. As is well
known, among primitive peoples it is almost universally considered dangerous to utter the name of a deceased person
(e.g., among the Mary River tribes; Curr, 3:166) because they
feel there is a mysterious relation between a person and his
name and they therefore fear that the spirit of the deceased
will come and do mischief. Among some tribes this leads to
the remarkable practice that when someone dies who happens
to bear the name of some object, the term for this object is
changed so that its original name no longer needs to be used
(3:580 ff.). Curr remarks (3:581) here:

About twenty-five years ago the equivalent of
kangaroo was Poonminmir, which name a girl also
bore. The girl died, and <u>wardakow</u> became the
term for kangaroo, as the name of the dead could
not be uttered for many years, in accordance with
a custom which seems to be universal in Australia.[27]

Curr otherwise presents some further and more exact

vocabularies. According to one of them (1:139 ff.), one

tribe uses <u>wimbara</u> for children and brother's children (male

speaking) and for children and sister's children (woman

speaking). A man calls his sister's children <u>gainguja</u>, a

woman her brother's children <u>wahraja</u>. The terms are employed

of course in conformity with the classificatory system. In

contradiction to it is only the fact that the mother's sis-

ter is called differently (<u>mahluja</u>) than the mother

(<u>nummahka</u>).

Among the Larrikia tribe (1:138 ff.), <u>lemurk</u> means son

and brother's son (man speaking), <u>ni</u> son and sister's son

(woman speaking), all in conformity with the classificatory

principle; for it is natural and occurs among many tribes

that the woman calls the children by a different name than

the man.

It is likewise in conformity with the classificatory

principle that a man calls his sister's son and daughter

<u>nagunye</u> and <u>alagunye</u>, the woman her brother's son <u>lemurk</u>

(whereby the coincidence with the above designation <u>lemurk</u>

is certainly striking).

It is also appropriate that a child calls its mother

<u>wuding</u>, its mother's sister <u>wudy</u> or <u>wuding</u> (which is doubt-

less the same word), while the designations for father

(<u>peppi</u>) and father's brother do not completely conform--the

latter is called nuggetty and peppai (perhaps it should also
be peppi, so that it is only a question of variant record-
ing).

        In general, this case shows us how language differen-
tiates itself. First a term distinguishing two relations
develops in addition to the one they hold in common; peppai
was doubtless originally peppi. This distinguishing term
then gradually gains precedence as more need for differen-
tiation arises; and this explains the distinction in the
previous case.

        What Fison (p. 61) established following Bridgman
about the tribes at Port Mackay is confirmed by Curr (3:45),
who draws upon Bridgman and Bucas. Here father and father's
brother are called tabu(nera) (or yabu?), mother and mother's
sister yunga(nera), son and brother's son (man speaking)
wulbura, brother and father's brother's son cuta(nera).

        Correspondingly, Curr (2:47) says that one calls
every member of one's own subclass brother, excepting those
who belong to a higher generation level, who are then called
father, and every woman from the subclass of wife is called
wife (3:47, 50). How could group marriage be better confirmed? The idiom of another tribe, the Mulula (1:139),
is out of order. Both men and woman call the sister's
daughter luckinthunmin, and the father's sister as well as
the mother's sister are called yeruen.

        When special terms for cousins in opposition to
brothers exist in some tribes (1:141), this is in accord
with classificatory principles. In this regard the following

must be remarked. As is well known, Australian languages
distinguish between FBS and MZS on the one hand (called
brothers) and FZS and MBS on the other (called cousins).
The Australian group marriage gives no support for using
the terms brother or sister for these latter relations.

Now, because of the incompleteness of his report, it
is not possible to determine in every case whether the tribes
for whom Curr reports cousin terms all still maintain this
distinction. We can do so in one case, and this shows at the
same time what sort of methods Curr used and what is to be
granted to his polemic against Fison. We have more exact
information from Taplin (in Woods, p. 52; a work which
appeared in 1879, long before Curr) for the Narrinyeri on
the lower Murray River, to whom Curr (1:141) also refers.
Curr lists the following: brother is gelane, tarte; sister
is maranwe, tarti; male cousin runde, female cousin nguyanowi.
In fact, however, the situation is this: B, FBS, MZS =
gelane[28] or tarte, depending on whether he is older or
younger than Ego; Z, FBD, MZD = maran(ow)i or tarte, with
the same distinction.

On the other hand nguayane (nguyanowe) means indeed
cousin, but only as MBC or FZC. The same is the case with
uncle; here Curr lists, FB = wanowe, MB = ngoppano. Taplin
says on the contrary that FB = F (nanghai) and the MB and
FZH = wanowe, thus completely in accord with the principles
of classificatory kinship. Likewise, MZ = M (nainkowa),
while FZ = barno.

The expression ngoppano for uncle, which does not occur

in Taplin (p. 52), seems to be another more differentiated
term for the MB, so that wanowe and ngoppano both refer to
the MB, thus not at all to FB.

That the language certainly has a tendency toward new
distinctions is proved by the circumstance that the BS = S
(porlean), but in order to distinguish him from son, he is
also called wayatte and ngoppari (according to whether he
descends from the older or the younger brother; Taplin, p.
52, says, "A title to distinguish them from my own
children").

Regarding the Encounter Bay tribes, Woods's vocabulary
(pp. 169 ff.) is unfortunately not scientifically enough
prepared to allow such checking. However, the same as for
the Narrinyeri can be assumed from the close relationship
of the tribes and from the similarity of several of the
terms.

Cousin marriage is not implemented among the Australians. So far as we know, we do not find the equation MB =
father-in-law; ZS = son-in-law; for example, it does not
occur among the Dieri, where the MB is called kaka, the
father-in-law thuru (Woods, p. 294). Neither is it found
among the Narrinyeri, where MB = wanowe; father-in-law =
yullundi; ZS = ngarra; son-in-law = yullundi; ZD = nanghari
and daughter-in-law = mayareli. So much then for classificatory kinship.

4
Conclusion

That the American Indians, the Dravidians, and the Australians originally had group marriage may now be considered certain. That all the peoples of the earth originally had group marriage appears irrefutable if we consider the following points: (1) the connection between group marriage and totemism, and how the one derives from the other; (2) how these not at all closely connected peoples developed matching group-marriage systems with only individual variations and characteristic features; (3) that these are peoples whose totemism indicates a special originality for their culture, above all the American Indians; and (4) that totemism presents itself to us in nearly all human activities, institutions, legends, idioms, as an ancient and later abandoned system.

Whether totemistic group marriage is the oldest institution remains the question. We have left undecided until now the question of whether there may formerly have been a condition where promiscuous intercourse was customary within the totem group or before any such groups formed. Humanity's true life and history could only have begun when the division into totem groups and the strict regulation of marriage among

them had been instituted and therefore had provided the pre-
conditions for any further development, that is to say the
joining together of the masses leading to unity in diversity
and diversity in unity.

We have demonstrated traces of an original practice of
sibling marriage, but these traces are not strong enough to
make the inference of its existence a scientific probability
rather than a mere possibility. It has been scientifically
proved, though, that totemistic group marriage lies at the
starting point of our civilization. Anyone who would like
to dispute it will have to follow us on to the field of
Morgan's tables. General skepticism has no scientific
importance.

Thus, as we have seen, the worship and awe of the
totem animal by the members of the clan, that is, the
uniting of the social community in the animal cult, was one
of the most important phenomena in the history of our
species.

Notes

Editor's Introduction

1. Claude Lévi-Strauss, "Preface de la deuxième édition," in Les Structures élémentaires de la parenté (Paris, 1967), see p. xxiv; "Preface to the Second Edition," in The Elementary Structures of Kinship, trans. Bell, Sturmer, and Needham (London, 1969), see p. xxxvi.

2. Rodney Needham, "The Mota Problem and its Lessons," Journal of the Polynesian Society 73 (1964): 302-14, see p. 313; idem, "Remarks on the Analysis of Kinship and Marriage," in Rethinking Kinship and Marriage, ed. Rodney Needham (London, 1971), pp. 1-34, see p. 14.

3. Below pp. 89, 187-88; Emile Durkheim, "Zur Urgeschichte der Ehe, Prof. J. Kohler," L'Année Sociologique 1 (1897): 306-19; cf. idem, 9 (1904): 378-80.

4. The coruscation, however, is not Kohler's alone. It was anticipated in several quarters, as is explained in section

X of this Introduction and was set out quite explicitly by Bernhöft in the work cited by Kohler in the relevant passage. The common misconception that it was Durkheim who made the discovery in correcting Kohler should now be laid to rest; see A. R. Radcliffe-Brown, "The Study of Kinship Systems," Journal of the Royal Anthropological Institute 71 (1940): 1-18, see p. 14. It is the historical conjunction of Kohler's detailed examination and Durkheim's seminal critique which make Kohler's work of especial interest. Durkheim advanced upon Bernhöft and Kohler in dismissing the group marriage hypothesis, which in the views of the latter two men intervened between the rule of descent and the terminology and was the immediate explanation of the form of the nomenclature.

This translation may be offered as well as an admonition and as a reminder that not everything that is best in social anthropology is owed alone to the French sociological school.

5. E. Rabel, "Josef Kohler," Rheinische Zeitschrift für Zivil- und Prozessrecht 10 (1919): 123-33, see p. 123; Arthur Kohler, "Vorwort," in Josef Kohler-Bibliographie, ed. Arthur Kohler and Victoria Eschke (Berlin-Grünewald, 1931), p. viii; Roscoe Pound, "The Scope and Purpose of Sociological Jurisprudence," Harvard Law Review 25 (1911/12): 140-68, see p. 155.

6. Lehrbuch der Rechtsphilosophie (Berlin, 1909). Philosophy of Law, trans. Adalbert Albrecht (New York, 1921).

7. William Seagle, "Kohler, Joseph [sic.] (1849-1919)," in
Encyclopaedia of the Social Sciences (New York, 1932),
8:587-88, see p. 587; Arthur Kohler, Josef Kohler, p. viii.

8. Leonhard Adam, "In memoriam Josef Kohler," Zeitschrift
für vergleichende Rechtswissenschaft 38 (1920): 1-30, see p. 8.

9. Arthur Kohler, Josef Kohler, p. v, n 2. Albert Osterrieth, Josef Kohler, ein Lebensbild (Berlin, 1920), p. 32n.

10. Osterrieth, Josef Kohler, pp. 17, 21; Josef Kohler, Aus
Vier Weltteilen: Reisebilder (Berlin, 1908), pp. 123-46.

11. Wilhelm Sauer, "Josef Kohlers Lebenswerk: zur Veröffent-
lichung der Bibliographie von Arthur Kohler," Archiv für
Rechts- und Wirtschaftsphilosophie 25 (1931): 107-11, see
p. 108.

12. Arthur Kohler, Josef Kohler, p. viii. The American was
Professor John H. Wigmore of the University of Chicago.

13. Adam, "Josef Kohler," p. 24.

14. Ibid., p. 25; Arthur Kohler, Josef Kohler, p. ix, n 8.;
Osterrieth, Josef Kohler, p. 13.

15. Arthur Kohler, Josef Kohler, p. 159; Albert Kocourek,
"Editorial Preface," in Josef Kohler, Philosophy of Law, pp.

pp. xv-xxiv, see p. xxiii.

16. Kocourek, "Editorial Preface," p. xxiv.

17. Festgabe zum 70. Geburtstag Josef Kohlers am 9 März 1919
(Berlin, 1919). Archiv für Strafrecht und Strafprozess 67
(1919). Festgabe für Josef Kohler zum 70. Geburtstag, dar-
gebracht von Freunden, Schülern und der Verlagshandlung
(Stuttgart, 1919). Zeitschrift für vergleichende Rechtswissenschaft 37 (1919).

18. Kurfürstendam 216, Berlin W 15.

19. Rabel, "Josef Kohler," p. 123; Osterrieth, Josef Kohler,
p. 5.

20. Kohler's whole scholarly career and especially his in-
quisitive researches into the legal systems of so many other
nations, contemporaneous and ancient, fully attest to his
cosmopolitan humanism. A further indication of his freedom
from the narrowness of some of his colleagues is his friendly
predisposition toward Jews (Osterrieth, Josef Kohler, p. 32n.).

21. Carl Zuckmayer gives an evocative description of the
euphoria and willingness to engage in a national purpose
which seized Germany in the first weeks of the mobilization
after Sarajevo and then slowly turned sour, as it doubtless
did in other nations as well. Als wär's ein Stuck von mir

(Wien, 1966), pp. 185-213. Only a few men of the character
of a Karl Liebknecht or the German-American George Grosz re-
sisted every pressure to join in the war effort. H. L.
Mencken cynically commented, "The amazing slanging which
went on between the English professors and the German professors in the early days of the late War showed how little
even cold and academic men are really moved by the bald
truth, and how much by hot and unintelligible likes and dis-
likes. The patriotic hysteria of the War simply allowed
these eminent pedagogues to say of one another openly and to
loud applause what they would have been ashamed to say in
times of greater amenity, and what most of them would have
denied stoutly that they believed." "The Genealogy of Eti-
quette," in Selected Prejudices (London, 1926), p. 137.

22. Osterrieth, Josef Kohler, p. 26; Arthur Kohler, Josef
Kohler, p. vi.

23. Josef Kohler, Vom Lebenspfad: Gesammelte Essays (Mannheim, 1902), p. 4; Osterrieth, Josef Kohler, pp. 6-7.

24. Josef Kohler, Vom Lebenspfad, p. 6; Osterrieth, Josef
Kohler, p. 7.

25. Josef Kohler, Vom Lebenspfad, pp. 14 f.; Osterrieth,
Josef Kohler, pp. 7-8.

26. Josef Kohler, Vom Lebenspfad, p. 27; Osterrieth, Josef

Kohler, p. 8.

27. Josef Kohler, Vom Lebenspfad, p. 29; Osterrieth, Josef
Kohler, p. 9.

28. Osterrieth, Josef Kohler, pp. 10-11. Josef Kohler,
Deutsches Patentrecht (Mannheim, 1877-78). Kohler already
had a family at this time. He married Ida Pflüger in 1873;
the couple eventually had two sons, Arthur and Rudolf.

29. Published in Würzburg. This book was translated into
Russian in 1895. A second, revised German edition was published in Berlin in 1919.

30. Kohler was an enthusiastic admirer of the Italian Re-
naissance, which seems to have restricted his response to
the Baroque. Tolstoi and the later Ibsen never appealed to
Kohler, though he admired Peer Gynt and the works of Strind-
berg. He lost his taste for Zola. In art he admired Italian
painting, in music Wagner, Chopin, and Beethoven. He disliked
Mozart and Schiller, both idols for his father. Osterrieth,
Josef Kohler, pp. 7, 13, 29n.

31. Josef Kohler, "Das wichtigste Ereignis in meinem Leben,"
Berliner Morgenpost, 24 December 1911; Osterrieth, Josef
Kohler, p. 13.

32. The frontispiece photograph was made in Tarasp-Vulpera,

Switzerland, after the move to Berlin, in 1900 or 1901, when
Kohler was 52 or 53 years old. Arthur Kohler, Josef Kohler,
p. vii.

33. Osterrieth, Josef Kohler, p. 13.

34. Aus Vier Weltteilen (1908).

35. Rabel, "Josef Kohler," p. 125; Osterrieth, Josef Kohler,
p. 21.

36. Osterrieth, Josef Kohler, pp. 20-21.

37. Sauer, "Josef Kohlers Lebenswerk," p. 108; Rabel, "Josef
Kohler," p. 125.

38. Rabel, "Josef Kohler," p. 125.

39. Adam, "Josef Kohler," pp. 15-16; Osterrieth, Josef Kohler,
p. 25; Sauer, "Josef Kohlers Lebenswerk," p. 110.

40. Philosophy of Law (New York, 1921), p. xliv.

41. Ibid, pp. 14, 22. "Vom Positivismus zum Neu-Hegelianis-
mus," Archiv fur Rechts- und Wirtschaftsphilosophie 3 (1909/
10): 167-72, see pp. 169-70. For the following compare also
"Wesen und Ziele der Rechtsphilosophie," and "Rechtsphilosophie und Rechtsvergleichung," Archiv für Rechts- und Wirt-

schaftsphilosophie 1 (1908): 3-15, 192-99; "Rechtsphilosophie
und Universalrechtsgeschichte," in Franz von Holtzendorff
and J. Kohler, eds., Encyklopädie der Rechtswissenschaft
(Berlin, 1903), 1:1-69.

42. Philosophy of Law, p. 19.

43. "Vom Positivismus," p. 170, Philosophy of Law, p. 20.

44. Philosophy of Law, p. 49; "Vom Positivismus," p. 171.

45. "Vom Positivismus," p. 171.

46. Philosophy of Law, pp. 20-21.

47. Ibid, pp. 21, 26.

48. Prehistory, chap. 1, sec. II; "Zur Rechtsphilosophie und
vergleichenden Rechtswissenschaft," Juristisches Litteraturblatt 7 (1895): 193-201.

49. "Die Geschichte im System des Neuhegelianismus," Archiv
für Rechts- und Wirtschaftsphilosophie 3 (1909/10): 321-25,
see p. 322.

50. Philosophy of Law, p. 21.

51. "Geschichte," pp. 322-23.

52. Ibid, p. 324.

53. "Aufgaben und Ziele der Rechtsphilosophie," Archiv für Rechts- und Wirtschaftsphilosophie 3 (1909/10): 500-508, see pp. 505-6, 508; Philosophy of Law, p. 26.

54. "Vom Positivismus," p. 168; Prehistory, chap. 1, sec. III. This may be compared with Freud's attempt to identify the categorical imperative with personal taboos. Totem und Tabu (Vienna, 1913); Totem and Taboo, trans. James Strachey (London, 1950), p. x. Kohler's version best accommodates another form of categorical imperative--prescriptive marriage systems--to which topic this book makes a contribution. Rodney Needham, "Prescription," Oceania 43 (1973): 166-81.

55. "Soziologie und Rechtsphilosophie," Archiv für Rechts- und Wirtschaftsphilosophie 4 (1910/11): 558-63.

56. "Aufgaben und Ziele," p. 505.

57. Ibid, pp. 504-5.

58. Philosophy of Law, pp. 4, 5.

59. "Aufgaben und Ziele," pp. 505-6; Philosophy of Law, p. 50.

60. Einleitung in eine Naturwissenschaft des Rechts (1872).

61. Leonhard Adam, "Josef Kohler und die vergleichende Rechtswissenschaft," Zeitschrift für vergleichende Rechts-wissenschaft 37 (1919/20): 1-31, see p. 25-7.

62. Adam, "Josef Kohler," p. 26.

63. Prehistory, chap. 1, sec. III.

64. Seagle, "Kohler, Joseph," p. 588.

65. Adolf Lasson, "Kohlers Rechtsphilosophie," Archiv für Rechts- und Wirtschaftsphilosophie 2 (1909): 318-26; trans-lated by Albert Kocourek and published in the appendix to Kohler's Philosophy of Law, pp. 319-332 (see p. 329).

66. Adam, "Josef Kohler," p. 12; Josef Kohler, Philosophy of Law, p. xliv.

67. Adam, "Josef Kohler," pp. 10, 22.

68. The reader may conveniently refer to Claude Lévi-Strauss, Le Totémisme aujourd'hui (Paris, 1962); Totemism, trans. Rodney Needham (Boston, 1963); Arnold van Gennep, L'État actuel du problème totémique (Paris, 1920); Alexander A. Goldenweiser, "Totemism, an Analytical Study," Journal of American Folk-lore 23 (1910): 179-293; idem, "Form and Con-tent in Totemism," American Anthropologist 20 (1918): 280-95; James J. Frazer, Totemism (Edinburgh, 1887).

69. John Long, Voyages and Travels of an Indian Interpreter and Trader ... (London, 1791).

70. Albert Gallatin, "A Synopsis of the Indian Tribes of North America," Archaeologia Americana, Transactions and Collections of the American Antiquarian Society 2 (1836): 1-422.

71. Scott Nind, "Description of the Natives of King George's Sound (Swan River Colony) and Adjoining Country," Journal of the Royal Geographical Society of London 1 (1831): 21-51; Sir George Grey, Journals of Two Expeditions of Discovery in North-West and Western Australia, during the years 1837, 38, and 39, 2 vols. (London, 1841).

72. John F. McLennan, "The Worship of Animals and Plants," Fortnightly Review, 6 (12 of old series) (1869): 407-27, 562-82; 7 (13 of old series) (1870): 194-216.

73. Goldenweiser, "Totemism," p. 266.

74. Ibid., p. 267.

75. Claude Lévi-Strauss, Le Totémisme aujourd'hui.

76. Lewis H. Morgan, Systems of Consanguinity and Affinity of the Human Family (Washington, 1870), pp. 480-94.

77. Ibid., pp. 484-85; Lewis H. Morgan, Ancient Society
(New York, 1877), pp. 425, 517.

78. Morgan, Systems, pp. 10-11.

79. J. F. McLennan, Studies in Ancient History Comprising
a Reprint of Primitive Marriage, ed. D. McLennan (London,
1876), pp. 366.

80. C. N. Starcke, The Primitive Family (London, 1889), pp.
186-87, 207. For a general survey of this question, see
Rodney Needham, "Editor's Introduction," in C. Staniland
Wake, The Development of Marriage and Kinship (Chicago,
1967): pp. xxxiii-xxxvii.

81. Edward Westermarck, The History of Human Marriage, 2d.
ed. (London and New York, 1894), pp. 85, 539. Compare Sir
John Lubbock, The Origin of Civilization and the Primitive
Condition of Man (London, 1971), p. 113.

82. Nind, "Description of the Natives," pp. 37-38.

83. Lorimer Fison and A. W. Howitt, Kamilaroi and Kurnai:
Group-Marriage and Relationship, and Marriage by Elopement;
the Kurnai Tribe (Melbourne, 1880), pp. 50-51.

84. Ibid., pp. 127-28.

85. Ibid., p. 51.

86. Ibid., p. 160.

87. Edward M. Curr, The Australian Race, 4 vols. (Melbourne, 1886-87), 1: 109.

88. Fison and Howitt, Kamilaroi, pp. 58-59.

89. Curr, The Australian Race, 1: 125.

90. Ibid., p. 142.

91. Ibid., p. 126.

92. John Mathew, "The Australian Aborigines," Journal and Proceedings of the Royal Society of New South Wales 23 (1889): 335-449, see p. 404.

93. Westermarck, Human Marriage, p. 57.

94. Ibid., p. 96.

95. Ibid., p. 113.

96. C. Staniland Wake, The Development of Marriage and Kinship (London, 1889); new ed. by Rodney Needham, Classics in Anthropology (Chicago, 1967), see pp. 13, 52 of new ed.

97. Prehistory, chap. 1, sec. III; Paul and Fritz Sarasin, Die Weddas von Ceylon (Wiesbaden, 1893).

98. J. F. McLennan, Primitive Marriage: An Inquiry into the Origins of the Form of Capture in Marriage Ceremonies (Edinburgh, 1865); new ed. by Peter Rivière, Classics in Anthropology (Chicago, 1970).

99. Ancient Society, pp. 511-15.

100. Kamilaroi, p. 79; Needham, "Editor's Introduction," p. xxvii.

101. Wake, Marriage and Kinship, p. 25.

102. Sir Henry Maine, Ancient Law (London, 1861).

103. Wake, Marriage and Kinship, p. 25.

104. Starcke, The Primitive Family, p. 28.

105. Ibid., p. 50.

106. Ibid., p. 118.

107. Ibid., p. 120.

108. Wake, Marriage and Kinship, p. 16.

109. Ibid., p. 17.

110. Northcote W. Thomas, Kinship Organisations and Group Marriage in Australia (Cambridge, 1906), pp. 16, 23; see Kohler's reply, "Nochmals uber Gruppenehe und Totemismus," Zeitschrift für vergleichende Rechtswissenschaft 21 (1908): 252-66, see pp. 253-54.

111. Compare Needham, "Editor's Introduction," p. xxxvii.

112. Ernst Grosse, Die Form der Familie und die Formen der Wirtschaft (Freiburg, 1896); Émile Durkheim, "Die Formen der Familie . . ., Ernst Grosse," L'Année Sociologique 1 (1897): 319-32, see p. 319.

113. E. E. Evans-Pritchard, Theories of Primitive Religion (Oxford, 1965), p. 111.

114. Darwin in a letter to Alfred Russel Wallace, 22 December 1857. Francis Darwin, ed., The Life and Letters of Charles Darwin, 3 vols. (London, 1887), 2: 108. Compare Needham, "Editor's Introduction," pp. xvi-xvii; "Nor is there any good reason, for that matter, why we should abstain from even the wildest or most tenuous conjectures, so long as we know what we are doing and do not commit ourselves to any of them without proper grounds."

115. Prehistory, chap. 1, secs. II and III.

116. Chap. 1, sec. III. Kohler here states the importance
of marriage institutions as a form of communication between
groups; the same idea which Lévi-Strauss made famous in the
closing pages of his monograph The Elementary Structures of
Kinship.

117. Prehistory, chap. I, sec. II. See E. B. Tylor, "On a
Method of Investigating the Development of Institutions:
Applied to the Laws of Marriage and Descent," Journal of the
Anthropological Institute of Great Britain and Ireland 18
(1889): 245-72. See also Westermarck's comments on these
principles and defense of himself in "Méthode pour la recherche des institutions préhistoriques, à propos d'un
ouvrage du professeur Kohler," Revue internationale de
sociologie 5 (1897): 444-57.

118. Prehistory, chap. 2, sec. III.

119. See Needham, "Editor's Introduction," p. xx.

120. Sally Falk Moore, "Oblique and Asymmetrical Cross-
Cousin Marriage and Crow-Omaha Terminology," American Anthropologist 65 (1963): 296-311, see p. 298.

121. Prehistory, chap. 2, secs. VI and VII.

122. Chap. 2, sec. VI; chap. 3, sec. VIII.

123. Chap. 2, sec. VII.

124. Starcke, The Primitive Family, pp. 59-60; Daryll Forde, "Double Descent Among the Yakö," A. R. Radcliffe-Brown and Daryll Forde, eds., African Systems of Kinship and Marriage (London, 1950), pp. 285-332; F. A. E. van Wouden, "Locale groepen en dubbele afstamming in Kodi, West Sumba," Bij- dragen tot de Taal-, Land- en Volkenkunde 112 (1956): 204-46.

125. McLennan, Studies in Ancient History, p. 124.

126. Starcke, Primitive Family, p. 127.

127. Cf. Needham, "Editor's Introduction," p. xxv; Arnold van Gennep, Mythes et légendes d'Australie (Paris, 1906), pp. xxvi-vii.

128. George P. Murdock, Social Structure (New York, 1949), p. 44.

129. Edmund Leach, "More about 'Mama' and 'Papa,'" in Rod- ney Needham, ed., Rethinking Kinship and Marriage (London, 1971), pp. 74-98, see p. 76-77.

130. Rodney Needham, "Terminology and Alliance I," Sociolo- gus 16 (1966): 141-57, see p. 141; "Terminology and Alliance II," Sociologus 17 (1967): 39-53, see p. 48.

131. Chap. 3, sec. VIII.

132. Chap. 3, sec. XI.

133. Morgan, Systems, p. 391.

134. Fison, Kamilaroi, p. 76. Dumont, "Dravidian Kinship
Terminology as an Expression of Marriage," Man 53 (1953),
no. 54. Needham, "Editor's Introduction," pp. xxvii, xxviii;
idem., "Introduction," in Rethinking Kinship and Marriage,
pp. lix-lxvi. In another place Fison says the terms "uncle,"
"aunt," and "cousin" should never be used; "The Classificatory System of Relation," Journal of the Anthropological Institute of Great Britain and Ireland 24 (1895): 360-371, see
pp. 366-67.

135. Refer to Rodney Needham, "Remarks on the Analysis of
Kinship and Marriage," in Needham, ed., Rethinking Kinship
and Marriage, pp. 1-34, see pp. 18-22. For the definitive
statement on the distinction between prescriptive and nonprescriptive systems and something of the history of the
notion of obligation, see Needham, "Prescription," Oceania
43 (1973): 166-81. A neglected but striking essay which
would have been of use to Kohler, had he taken advantage of
it, is Basil H. Thompson's "Concubitancy in the Classificatory System of Relationship," Journal of the Anthropological
Institute of Great Britain and Ireland 24 (1895): 371-87.
In this he reports the discovery on Fiji of "a system of

obligatory marriage." He describes the aim of his paper as
being to approach the Fijian system "from the point of view
of compulsory or obligatory marriage." He then proposes a
term to express "this central idea of obligation." Having
rejected the first term which presented itself to him,
"orthogamy," as indicating "rather propriety than obligation,"
he resorts to a literal translation of the Fijian name for
the category for obligatory marriage, veindavolani (from vei,
affix of reciprocity, davo, "to lie down"). "Until, therefore, a better term is found to indicate the practice I shall
speak of the relationship in which the marriage is obligatory as 'concubitancy'" (pp. 371-72). The Fijian kinship
nomenclature, he remarks (p. 372), indicates two types of
relatives: consanguines and relatives through marriage. Of
concubitants, he says, they "are born husband and wife, and
the system assumes no individual preference could hereafter
destroy the relation." He then goes on with a perceptive
observation which effectively forestalls certain modern
sophistry, "but the obligation does no more than limit the
choice of the mate to one or other of the females who are
concubitants with the man who desires to marry. It is thus
true that in theory the field of choice is very large, for
the concubitous relation might include third or even fifth
cousins" (p. 375). He also speaks of the oppressive in-
tolerance of the system, for even where there is a deviation
from the concubitant mate, "the system goes on, refusing to
admit the injury done to it." "If a man dares to choose a
woman other than the wife provided him his disobediance

avails him nothing"; for the woman becomes a recognized concubitant and "all her relatives fall into their places as if
she had actually been born his concubitant" (p. 374). When
discussing possible origins of the system, he considers the
interesting possibility that once both classes of cousins-
germane were prohibited, but "the desire for alliances among
chief families," etc., "may have chafed against the prohibitions until these were so far relaxed as to allow the marriage of cousins in the degree most effective for promoting
an interchange of property" (p. 381). In an accompanying
analysis of the nomenclature, Fison remarks that <u>veindavo-
lani</u> "expresses a <u>right</u>, and an <u>obligation</u>, as well as a
<u>qualification</u>"; Fison, "The Classificatory System," p. 367.

136. Louis Dumont has in fact recently questioned the commonly assumed structural identity of the Dravidian and
Kariera systems; "Sur le vocabulaire de parenté Kariera,"
in Jean Pouillon et Pierre Maranda, eds., Échanges et com-
munications: Mélanges offerts à Claude Lévi-Strauss (Paris,
1970), vol. 1, pp. 272-86. Kohler might have started from
the Malay (Hawaiian) system. This, however, is cognatic and
strategically the least satisfactory form for comparative
analysis.

137. Following established convention, only the initial
letter of each word is given; so that FZS reads "father's
sister's son." Sister is indicated by <u>Z</u> in distinction from
<u>S</u>, son.

138. Taken from chap. 3, sec. II. They are repeated with some additions in the Dravidian system analyzed on pp. 155-56.

139. Émile Durkheim, "Zur Urgeschichte der Ehe. Prof. J. Kohler," L'Année Sociologiaue 1 (1897): 306-19, see p. 316.

140. Ibid., p. 312.

141. Ibid., p. 316.

142. Durkheim, "Zur Urgeschichte," p. 318. Westermarck in a review used by Durkheim in preparing his own, said, "Group marriage is certainly very different than polygamy," and, "So far as I know, in all the American ethnography, there is not a single example of actually existing group marriage." Westermarck, "Méthode pour la recherche," pp. 454-55.

143. This is not quite right as prescriptive systems embody a marriage rule, but Kohler's syllogism is toppled when its premise is shown to be false.

144. Durkheim, "Zur Urgeschichte," pp. 314-15.

145. Morgan, Systems, pp. 475-76.

146. Fison, Kamilaroi, p. 26n.

147. Starcke, Primitive Marriage, p. 195.

148. Cf. Needham, "Editor's Introduction," p. xxxvii.

149. Lowie, however, prefers to see it as an expression of
a rule of exogamy. R. H. Lowie, Culture and Ethnology (New
York, 1917), "Terms of Relationship," pp. 98-180, see esp.
pp. 154-56.

150. Ibid., pp. 150, 156; cf. Needham, "Remarks on the
Analysis," p. 22.

151. Lowie, "Terms of Relationship," p. 105.

152. Spier, "The Distribution of Kinship Systems in North
America," University of Washington Publications in Anthropology 1 (1925): 69-88, see p. 73.

153. Morgan, Systems, p. 191.

154. Fred Eggan, "Historical Changes in the Choctaw Kinship
System," American Anthropologist 39 (1937): 34-52.

155. Needham, "Remarks on the Analysis," p. 14.

156. An example of how little can be said in advance from
isolated equations is provided by a terminology recorded on
Alor. It is one of three recorded from the same language,
all of which display an identical form and are associated
with identical institutions (patrilineal descent and symmetric

alliance). Unlike the other two, this terminology makes
lineal equations involving cross-cousins; MBS = MB and
FZD = FZ. The most striking feature of this example is
that the equations are commonly accepted to be the minimum
defining features respectively of Omaha and Crow terminologies; yet they occur within the same terminology. Clearly
no good purpose would be served in separating this terminology from the other two in order to assimilate it to either
the Crow or the Omaha type. The example would also tend to
call into question the conclusion that Crow-Omaha lineal
equations are inconsistent with symmetric alliances. Rodney Needham, "The Mota Problem and its Lessons," Journal of
the Polynesian Society 73 (1964): 302-14, see p. 312; R. H.
Barnes, "Two Terminologies of Symmetric Prescriptive Alliance
from Pantar and Alor in Eastern Indonesia," Sociologus 23
(1973): 71-89.

157. Radcliffe-Brown, "The Study of Kinship Systems."

158. Louis Dumont, "Marriage in India: the Present State of
the Question," Contributions to Indian Sociology 5 (1961):
75-95, see p. 93. Another charge against Radcliffe-Brown's
principle is that insofar as it derives terminological unity
from solidarity, it explains a feature of classification by
an emotion. Rodney Needham, "An Analytic Note on the Structure of Siriono Society," Southwestern Journal of Anthropology
17 (1961): 239-55, see p. 249 n. 39 and works cited there.

159. W. H. R. Rivers, Kinship and Social Organization (London, 1914); E. W. Gifford, "Miwok Moieties," University of California Publications in American Archaeology and Ethnology 12 (1916): 139-94.

160. For example, Louis Faron, "The Dakota-Omaha Continuum in Mapuche Society," Journal of the Royal Anthropological Institute of Great Britain and Ireland 91 (1961): 11-22; S. F. Moore, "Oblique and Asymmetrical Cross-Cousin Marriage," American Anthropologist 65 (1963): 296-311.

161. A. L. Kroeber, "Classificatory Systems of Relationship," Journal of the Royal Anthropological Institute of Great Britain and Ireland 39 (1909): 77-84, see p. 84.

162. Radcliffe-Brown, "The Study of Kinship Systems," p. 58; G. P. Murdock, Social Structure, pp. 123-24; Lévi-Strauss, The Elementary Structure of Kinship, pp. 360-63.

163. Robert and Barbara Lane, "On the Development of Dakota-Iroquois and Crow-Omaha Kinship Terminologies," Southwestern Journal of Anthropology 15 (1959): 254-65; David B. Eyde and Paul M. Postal, "Avunculocality and Incest: The Development of Unilateral Cross-Cousin Marriage and Crow-Omaha Kinship Systems," American Anthropologist 63 (1961): 747-71.

164. Rodney Needham, "Gurage Social Classification: Formal Notes on an Unusual System," Africa 39 (1969): 153-66; idem.,

"Remarks on the Analysis of Kinship and Marriage," pp. 14-17;
Lévi-Strauss, "The Future of Kinship Studies," p. 19.

165. Robert McKinley, "A Critique of the Reflectionist
Theory of Kinship Terminology: The Crow/Omaha Case," Man 6
(1971): 228-47, see pp. 228, 244-45; Lévi-Strauss, "The
Future of Kinship Studies," p. 19. McKinley's article contains an accomplished summary and critique of many previous
attempts to account for Crow-Omaha systems.

166. Lévi-Strauss, "Preface to the Second Edition," p.
xxxviii; idem., "Future of Kinship Studies," p. 19.

167. Lévi-Strauss, "Preface to the Second Edition," pp.
xxxvi, xli.

168. McKinley, "Why do Crow and Omaha Kinship Terminologies
Exist? A Sociology of Knowledge Interpretation," Man 6
(1971): 408-26, see p. 424.

169. Ibid., p. 444.

170. This interpretation is not perfectly true of the Omaha.
Refer for example to the use of the terms itiga: MFF, MF;
and inegi: MB, MBS, etc.

171. McKinley, "A Critique," p. 245.

172. Louis Dumont has referred to the "profound malaise" in
that form of anthropology which considers "certain institutions as fundamental and others as expressing or solving
some imaginary 'contradiction' between them"; see "Marriage
in India," p. 78.

173. McKinley, "Why," p. 414.

174. Robert Lowie, "Exogamy and the Classificatory System
of Relationship," American Anthropologist 17 (1915): 223-39,
see p. 233; idem., "The Omaha and Crow Kinship Terminologies,"
Verhandlungen des XXIV. Internationalen Amerikanisten-Kon-
gresses 1930 (Hamburg, 1934): 103-8, see p. 103.

175. McKinley, "A Critique," p. 231.

176. Floyd G. Lounsbury, "A Formal Account of the Crow- and
Omaha-type Kinship Terminologies," in Ward H. Goodenough,
ed., Explorations in Cultural Anthropology (New York, 1964),
351-93, see p. 381.

177. Alan D. Coult, "Lineage Solidarity, Transformational
Analysis, and the Meaning of Kinship Terminology," Man 2
(1967): 26-47, see pp. 26, 28; Sol Tax, "The Social Organization of the Fox Indians," in Fred Eggan, ed., Social
Anthropology of North American Tribes (Chicago, 1937), pp.
243-82.

178. Lounsbury, "A Formal Account," p. 351.

179. Tax, "Fox Indians," p. 254.

180. Edmund Leach, "More about 'Mama' and 'Papa,'" in Rodney Needham, ed., Rethinking Kinship and Marriage (London, 1971): 75-98, see p. 75.

181. Kocourek, "Editorial Preface," in Kohler, Philosophy of Law, pp. xx-xxi.

182. Starcke, The Primitive Family, pp. 124-25.

Chapter 1

1. Concerning this and cannibalism among animals, compare Steinmetz (1896, 35 ff., 48 ff.).

2. For full details, see the Sarasins, whose historical reconstruction, however, is again frequently too uncritical.

3. They mention Virchow's work on the Vedda (1881), while my presentation (1889a, 213) has remained unknown to them.

4. Sarasin (p. 458 ff.). Divorce occurs only among the village Vedda (p. 475).

5. Sarasin (p. 490). In addition, the father is supposed

to give a portion of the family's hunting ground to the son
at his marriage, which can hardly be regarded as decisive,
however.

6. Concerning the various meanings of nepos, the matter is
not so simple as the author (p. 96) assumes. Concerning the
change of meaning of nepos, compare Bachofen (1886, 91 ff.).

7. Pp. 40, 41. Mucke (p. 168) also seems to assume a connection between orda and Erde ("earth").

Chapter 2

1. Totemism in Central and South American will not be
dealt with here. For the moment it is enough to refer to
the Geajiros (Kohler 1887b, 381 ff.) and Arawak (Ernst 1887,
439 ff.).

2. Powell (1881, 59). For the Huron see especially Hale
(1883, 55); they had deer, hawk, and snake totems.

3. Morgan (1881, 7); compare Parkman (p. lv), who adds for
an earlier period a potato totem. That some changes occurred
with time is shown by Beauchamp (1886, 83 ff.).

4. Morgan (1881, 7, 55), Schoolcraft (1847, 69, 128), Hale
(1883, 53), Parkman (p. 302); see also Catlin (pp. 103 ff.)
and Colden (p. 1).

5. Morgan claims there are fourteen totems (1881, 170), and ten among the Miami (p. 10) and thirteen among the Shawnee (p. 168).

6. They had a fish, snake, buffalo and eagle feather dance (Schoolcraft 1851-57, 277).

7. [Kohler misrepresents Boas's report here. Boas actually says, "They met with some kind of spirit, who gave them his emblems."--R.H.B.]

8. [Actually, Yehl turns himself into a raven after obtaining the sun and before releasing it. Nothing is said of this in connection with acquiring water, which is merely attributed to a "stratagem."--R.H.B.]

9. [Dall says, "fowls, animals and fish."--R.H.B.]

10. Compare Kohler (1895b, 49). [In this passage, Kohler speaks of two avenues of disintegration of the earlier clan or family based totemism. The one avenue is an expansion of the totemic identification to the point where the origin of the entire nation or even of humanity in general is traced back to an animal--in some cases all men are regarded as deriving from one animal, all women from another. A second avenue, which he takes up again here, is found in the Manitu cult, where an individual is identified with a special animal. He suggests that the emergence to prominence

of the individual cult may proceed in step with the disintegration of the original totemic system.--R.H.B.]

11. The word "Manitu" is borrowed from the language of the
Algonkian; in the language of the Iroouois and the Huron
the spirit is called okin and otkon (cf. Champlain, 1:385
ff.).

12. On this subject compare Dorman (1881, 226 ff.), Heckewelder (p. 424), Marouette (p. 57), Parkman (p. lxx), Loskiel (p. 53). Loskiel says, "An Indian who has received no
protective spirit in his dreams is despondent and feels
forsaken." Concerning the Carolina tribes see Lawson (p.
195), who lists eagle, panther, and allioator spirits; for
the Michigamie see Schoolcraft (1851-57, 5:196), concerning
the Ojibwa see Tanner (p. 289) and Hoffman (1885-86, 163).
Among the latter, the protective spirit reveals itself to
the youth after a long period of fasting. The same is true
among the Californian tribes (Boscana, p. 271), where dream
life is inhanced through narcotics. For the Kwakiutl see
Boas (1896, 438 ff.). The same notion is found in the belief that one carries an animal in the body, as is found
among the Mandan and the Minnitari (Wied-Neuwied, 2: 190,
270).

13. Parkman (p. lxxi); see also Lewis and Clark (p. 208) for
the Mandan, Hunter (p. 351) for the Missouri tribes, Hoffman (p. 163) for the Ojibwa. The latter carry the picture

of the protective spirit around the neck or in a medicine
sack. Whoever has the bat as his protective spirit carries
its skin in a sack (Tanner, p. 289).

14. Related tribes, namely the Ojibwa and Potawatomi have
gone over to father right (Morgan 1877, 106 ff.; see sec.
VII, this chapter).

15. Compare Champlain's report from the beginning of the
seventeenth century (1:384). "[Their children] never succeed to their valuables; rather their heirs and successors
are their sister's children."

16. Among the Creek, the office of chief is inherited
through the uterine side (C. Swan 1855, 273).

17. According to Strachey (writing at the beginning of the
seventeenth century), the office of chief is inherited by
the brother and by the sister's sons, but never by the son
(p. 70).

18. The succession to the offices of chief is also governed
by mother right (p. 195).

19. Especially the Nez Percé (cf. Alford 1855, 652), among
whom the son inherits magic and the office of chief.

20. Even the slave, when set free, belongs to his mother's

totem (Holmberg, p. 331).

21. Concerning this deviation from mother right, see my
article (Kohler 1893, 322).

22. It is also interesting that, according to Morgan 1870,
table II (nos. 240, 241), among the Delaware the father-in-
law calls his son-in-law his hunter and his daughter-in-law
(?) his cook, which indicates the obligation of service
within the house of the affines.

23. Among the Kwakiutl a man inherits his father-in-law's
family emblem (Boas 1896, 437).

24. Among the Creek, son-in-law and daughter-in-law (?) are
called unhutisse, which Morgan (table II, nos. 239-42),
translates as "my hanger-on."

25. [The adat kamanakan is the rule of customary law whereby
the sister's child or kamanakan inherits--R.H.B.]

Chapter 3

1. Dorsey's excellent and very detailed information on
kinship also confirms in a superb way Morgan's Omaha terms,
though one naturally has to allow for Morgan's still somewhat primitive, Anglicized spellings and also for the fact
that he places the particle wi ("my") before the words.

2. There is an error in the translation given in table II, no. 78. For tribes 10-24, the terms are mistakenly translated "daughter" instead of "niece," which is made clear by comparison to table II, nos. 47, 39, 81, 201. In addition, Morgan gives the same term for nephew, male speaking ("a" = ZS) and female speaking ("a" = BS), while Dorsey gives different terms in each case for both nephew and niece.

3. The table is after Morgan's information. According to Dorsey's information, this result would be accurate only if the lower "b" were a somen (1884a, p. 91). However, this is a peculiarity of the Omaha.

4. [In the interest of brevity in the following, genealogical specifications will normally be indicated by the initial letters of each word, for example MB is to be read "mother's brother." Sister is represented by Z; PF is "parent's father" or "grandfather," PM is "parent's mother" or "grandmother," CC is "child's child" or "grandchild;" "m.s." is "male speaking," "f.s." is "female speaking."--R.H.B.]

5. Morgan's tables are supported here by the reports of others. According to Marshall (1873, 76 ff.) for the Toda FB = F (with a qualifier for elder or younger), FBS = B.

6. On the other hand MF, who is called grandfather, cannot also be called uncle.

7. This does not completely accord with Dorsey. According to his table, MMB = grandfather, and consistent with this, his agnatic descendants are called grandfather. Morgan's evidence however would be right for MMZSSS. In any case MMZ = grandmother; but her descendants do not (as remarked above) continue to bear the same designation; rather her son is uncle, his son and grandson are also called uncle. Morgan, table II, no. 194, is also not completely correct. According to this, MMBSDDD is niece, in fact, since MMBSDD = M, as daughter of this mother she is equivalent to Z; her daughter, however, is equivalent to niece. The correct equation should be MMBSDDDD = niece. But in these remote relations, the precise terms doubtless are not always retained.

8. If in figure I, Ego were a woman, she would be (as MBZ) = M of "b," and the latter is her daughter; the same is given by Dorsey.

9. Here both "m" and her brother "a" are intended as full siblings (i.e., as linked through the mother too).

10. Chuchuchowae, Morgan neglects to note this meaning (table II, nos. 260, 262). The same expression is also given (nos. 264-65) for HBW, WBW, and also (no. 261) for HZ. The expression seems to mean "whoever has a claim on me," thus "spouse," which, however, is not suited for the cases mentioned.

11. Why is the WB and WZH among the Creek called "my little separator" (unksaepuche--Morgan, table II, nos. 257, 258)? Does this indicate the avunculate right of this brother-in-law, which separates the husband from his children?

12. However, the designation developed above (sec. V) of FZH = MB among the Omaha is not precluded. This is shown by Morgan (II, no. 88), where for the Omaha and other tribes of their group, the equation with uncle (among the Omaha, inegi) is given and only among three tribes (nos. 22-24) of the Omaha group is the equation with brother-in-law presented.

13. We find isolated reports, however, among the Cherokee that a man marries his WM (Adair, p. 190), and the same is reported of the Creek (C. Swan, p. 273). But these seem to have been only occasional cases; at least, we do not encounter the corresponding equation W = WM.

14. Morgan's tables are also supported and expanded here through the reports of others. According to Marshall's report (1873, 76 ff.) among the Toda, FZ (mami) = mother-in-law.

15. Morgan's translation error is also found in table II, nos. 78 and 170, cited by Bernhöft.

16. Disregarding a few modifications. Although among the Choctaw tribes BS (f.s.) = grandson, this has, as explained above (sec. IV) another meaning.

17. The equation FZ = grandmother or mother among the tribes of the Choctaw group has another meaning (sec. IV).

18. For the Choctaw group the previous note also holds true here.

19. On the other hand, II, no. 102, for tribes 8 ff., is based on a translation error: hewaeteh among the Wyandot is not son, but nephew, as is correctly indicated in table II, nos. 128 and 170 (cf. no. 45). Similarly leyäah (II, 128, for tribe 7) is incorrectly rendered nephew instead of son.

20. Langsdorff (2; 58). Elsewhere there are only isolated reports of the presence of sibling marriage, for example in New England in the royal family (Waitz, 3; 106).

21. So much for the kinship terminologies of the North American tribes. Given the available material, I will venture no judgment concerning the South American tribes. However, von den Steinen's new work on the Bakairi language (1892, 14 ff.) shows the following equations: F = FB (tsoɑo, a term of endearment), M = MZ (ise); B = male cousin (parigo, elder, kxono, younger), Z = female cousin (xoru), B = BS. On the other hand, among the Carava of Brazil, none of the equations are found: F = waha, FB = waɔana, M = nadi, MZ = waɜa ɜira, MB = wanarura, father-in-law = wara debu, FZ = wahaura, mother-in-law = wariore ɜehar. Compare Ehrenreich (1894, 31).

22. One must consider here that the husband no longer has relations with a pregnant wife, and thus easily comes to desire another (Lafitau, 1:559 ff.; Lahontan, 2:137 ff.).

23. That the levirate right is also due the substitute brother is easily understood, since he enters the family with the brother.

24. It has been demonstrated for the Chin of Burma (Kohler 1886, 187) and the Malay (Kohler 1893, 324, which also covers the later development). Mucke (p. 224), because he does not see the connection between group marriage and cousin marriage, which is self-evident for anyone with an exact knowledge of Morgan's tables, accuses me of using cheap expressions without any real content. To this I answer that I will not direct a scientific polemic against such expressions.

25. Among them polyandry seems in general frequently to be-come alternating marriage (Kohler 1887c, 208).

26. Gason (1895, p. 169) says, "same names are given to both first and second cousins as brothers and sisters."

27. The same is found among American Indians (see Kohler 1897).

28. Taplin gives gelanowe; this includes a suffix (nowe, "my") and means "my brother."

Bibliography

Adair, James. The History of the American Indians....London:

    Dilly, 1775.

Alford, B. "Concerning the Manners & Customs, the Supersti-

    tions, etc., of the Indians of Oregon." In Information

    Respecting the History . . . of the Indian Tribes of

    the United States, Henry Rowe Schoolcraft, vol. 5.

    Philadelphia: Lippincott, Grambo, 1855.

Anonymous. Relation de ce qui s'est passé du plus remarquable

    aux missions des pères de la compagnie de Jésus, en la

    Nouvelle France, ès années 1676 & 1677. Albany, New

    York: Weed, Parsons & Co., 1854.

Anonymous. Relation de la mission du Missisipi du Séminaire

    de Québec en 1700. New York: Shea, 1861.

Bachofen, J. J. Antiquarische Briefe vornehmlich zur Kennt-

    niss der ältesten Verwandschaftsbegriffe. Vol. 2.

    Strassburg: Trubners Buchhandlung, 1886.

Badlam, Alexander. The Wonders of Alaska. San Francisco:

    The Bancroft Company, 1890.

Bancroft, Hubert Howe. The Works of Hubert Howe Bancroft:

The Native Races. Vol. 1: Wild Tribes. San Francisco: Bancroft & Co., 1883.

Bartram, William. Reisen durch Nord- und Süd-Karolina,
Georgien, Ost- und West-Florida, etc. Translated by
E. A. W. Zimmerman. Berlin: Vossische Buchhandlung,
1793 [original English edition, 1791].

Beauchamp, W. M. "Permanency of Iroquois Clans and Sachem-
ship." The American Antiquarian and Oriental Journal
8 (1886): 82-91.

Bernhöft, Franz. Verwandschaftsnamen und Eheformen der nord-
amerikanischen Volksstämme: Ein Beitrag zur Vorgeschichte
der Ehe. Rostock: Universitäts-Buchdruckerei, 1888.

------. "Altindische Familienorganisation." Zeitschrift
für vergleichende Rechtswissenschaft 9 (1891): 1-45.

Bessels, Emil. "Einige Worte über die Inuit (Eskimo) des
Smith-Sundes, nebst Bemerkungen über Inuit-Schädel."
Archiv für Anthropologie 8 (1875): 107-22.

------. "The Northernmost Inhabitants of the Earth." American Naturalist 18 (1884): 861-82.

Boas, Franz. "Notes on the Ethnology of British Columbia."
Proceedings of the American Philosophical Society 24
(1887 a): 422-28.

------. "Zur Ethnologie Britisch-Kolumbiens." Dr. A.
Petermanns Mitteilungen aus Justus Perthes' Geograph-
ischer Anstalt 33 (1887 b): 129-33.

------. The Central Eskimo. Sixth Annual Report of the
Bureau of Ethnology. Washington: Government Printing
Office, 1888.

------. "Die Entwicklung der Geheimbünde der Kwakiutl-
Indianer." In Festschrift für Adolf Bastian. Berlin:
Reimer, 1896.

Bonney, Frederic. "On some Customs of the Aborigines of the
River Darling, New South Wales." Journal of the Anthropological Institute of Great Britain and Ireland 13
(1884): 122-37.

Boscana, G. "Chinigchinich: A Historical Account of the
Indians at the Missionary Establishment of St. Juan
Capistrano, Alto California." In Life in California,
edited by Alfred Robinson. New York: Wiley & Putnam,
1846.

Bourke, John G. "Notes upon the Gentile Organization of the
Apaches of Arizona." The Journal of American Folk-lore
3 (1890): 111-26.

Bradbury, John. Travels in the Interior of America . . . .
Liverpool: Sherwood, Neely & Jones, 1817.

Buch, Max. Die Wotjäken: Eine ethnologische Studie. Helsingfors: Druckerei der Finnischen Litteratur-Gesell-
schaft, 1882.

Carver, Jonathan. Three Years Travels through the Interior
Parts of North-America, etc. Walpole, New Hampshire:
Thomas, 1813 [first edition, 1778].

Catlin, George. Illustrations of the Manners, Customs, and
Conditions of the North American Indians. 9th ed., 2
vols. London: Bohn, 1857.

Champlain, Samuel de. Voyages du Sieur de Champlain, ou
Journal ès découvertes de la Nouvelle France. 2 vols.

Imprimé aux frais du gouvernement, 1830.

Colden, Cadwallader. The History of the Five Indian Nations
    of Canada, etc. 2 vols. London: Lockyer Daves, etc.,
    1747.

Crauford, Lindsay. "Victoria River Downs Station, Northern
    Territory, South Australia." Journal of the Anthropo-
    logical Institute of Great Britain and Ireland 24
    (1895): 180-85.

Curr, Edward M. The Australian Race: Its Origin, Languages,
    Customs, Place of Landing in Australia and the Routes
    by which it Spread itself over that Continent. 4 vols.
    Melbourne: John Ferres; London: Trubner and Co., 1886-
    87.

Dall, William H. Alaska and its Resources. Boston: Lee and
    Shepard, 1870.

------. Tribes of the Extreme Northwest. Contribution to
    North American Ethnology, vol. 1. Washington: Govern-
    ment Printing Office, 1877.

Dawson, George M. "Lebensweise und Künste der Kwakiul."
    Das Ausland 61 (1888): 926-30.

Deans, James. "Totem Posts at the World's Fair." American
    Antiquarian 15 (1893): 281-86.

Department of the Interior, Census Office. Report on Indians
    Taxed and Indians not Taxed in the United States:
    Eleventh Census, 1890. Washington: Government Print-
    ing Office, 1894.

Domenech, E. H. D. Voyage pittoresque dans les grands
    déserts du Nouveau Monde. Paris: Morizot, 1862.

Dorman, Rushton M. The Origin of Primitive Superstitions
    and their Development into the Worship of Spirits and
    the Doctrine of Spiritual Agency among the Aborigines
    of America. Philadelphia: Lippincott, 1881.

Dorsey, J. Owen. Omaha Sociology. Third Annual Report of
    the Bureau of Ethnology (1881-82). Washington: Govern-
    ment Printing Office, 1884 (a).

------. "An Account of the War Customs of the Osages." Am-
    erican Naturalist 18 (1884 b): 113-33.

DuBois, Jean Antoine. Moeurs, institutions et cérémonies
    des peuples de l'Inde. 2 vols. Paris: Imprimerie
    royale, 1825.

Dunn, John. History of the Oregon Territory and British
    North-American Fur Trade: with an Account of the Habits
    and Customs of the Principal Native Tribes of the
    Northern Continent. London: Edwards and Hughes, 1844.

Dwight, Timothy. Travels in New-England and New-York. New-
    Haven: Dwight, 1821-22.

Eastman, Mary. Dahcotah, or, Life and Legends of the Sioux
    around Fort Snelling. New York: Wiley, 1849.

Egede, Hans. Herrn Hans Egede, Missionärs und Bischofes in
    Grönland: Beschreibung und Natur-Geschichte von Grön-
    land. Translated by Joh. G. Krüntz. Berlin: Mylius,
    1763.

Ehrenreich, Paul. "Materialen zur Sprachenkunde Brasiliens."
    Zeitschrift für Ethnologie 26 (1894): 20-37, 49-60,
    115-37.

Erman, A. "Ethnographische Wahrnehmungen und Erfahrungen an

den Küsten des Berings-Meer." *Zeitschrift für Ethno-*

  logie 2 (1870-71): 2:295-327; 3:149-75, 205-19.

Ernst, A. "Die ethnographische Stellung der Guajiro-Indian-

  er." *Zeitschrift für Ethnologie* 19 (1887): 425-44.

Fison, Lorimer, and Howitt, A. W. *Kamilaroi and Kurnai:*

  Group-Marriage and Relationship, and Marriage by Elope-

  ment; the Kurnai Tribe. Melbourne: G. Robertson, 1880.

Foelsche, Paul. "On the Manners, Customs, etc., of some

  Tribes of the Aborigines, in the Neighborhood of Port

  Darwin & the West Coast of the Gulf of Carpentaria,

  North Australia." *Journal of the Anthropological In-*

  stitute of Great Britain and Ireland 24 (1895): 190-98.

Franklin, Sir John. *Narrative of a Journey to the Shores of*

  the Polar Sea . . . . 3d ed. London: Murray, 1824.

Frazer, Sir James George. *Totemism.* Edinburgh: Black, 1887.

Gason, Samuel. "The Manners & Customs of the Dieyerie Tribes

  of Australian Aborigines." In *The Native Tribes of*

  South Australia, edited by J. D. Woods. Adelaide:

  Wigg, 1879.

------. "Of the Tribes, Dieyerie, Auminie, Yandrawontha,

  Yaraevuarka, Pilladapa." *Journal of the Anthropological*

  Institute of Great Britain and Ireland 24 (1895): 167-

  76.

Gibbs, George. *Tribes of Western Washington and Northwestern*

  Oregon. Contributions to North American Ethnology,

  vol. 1. Washington: Government Printing Office, 1877.

Gillings, J. "On the Veddahs of Bintenne." *Journal of the*

  Ceylon Branch of the Royal Asiatic Society 2 (1853): 83.

Hale, Horatio Emmons, ed. The Iroquois Book of Rites. Philadelphia: Brinton, 1883.

Hall, Charles Francis. Life with the Esquimaux. 2 vols.
London: Low, Son, and Murston, 1864.

Heckewelder, John G. E. Nachricht von der Geschichte, den
Sitten und Gebräuchen der Indianischen Völkerschaften,
welche ehemals Pennsylvanien und die benachbarten
Staaten bewohnten. Translated by Fr. Hesse. Göttin-
gen: Vandenhoeck & Ruprecht, 1821 [original English
edition, 1819].

Hennepin, Louis. Description de la Louisiane, nouvellement
découverte au sud'ouest de la Nouvelle France . . . .
Paris: A. Auroy, 1688 [first edition, 1684].

Hildebrand, Richard. Über das Problem einer allgemeinen
Entwicklungsgeschichte des Rechts und der Sitte.
Graz: Leuschner & Lubensky, 1894.

Hoffman, W. J. The Midewiwin or "Grand Medicine Society" of
the Ojibwa. Seventh Annual Report of the United
States Bureau of American Ethnology. Washington:
Government Printing Office, 1885-86.

Holmberg, H. J. Ethnographische Skizzen über die Völker
des russischen Amerika. 2 vols. Helsingfors: Friis,
1855-63.

Hunter, John Dunn. Manners and Customs of several Indian
Tribes Located West of the Mississippi . . . .
Philadelphia: Marwell, 1823.

Jackson, Sheldon. "Alaska and its Inhabitants." American
Antiquarian 2 (1879): 105-16.

Jolly, Julius. "Recht und Sitte (einschliesslich der ein-
    heimischen Litteratur)." In Grundriss der indo-
    arischen Philologie und Altertumskunde, vol. 2,
    edited by G. Bühler. Strassburg: Trübner, 1896.

Jones, Charles Colcock. Antiquities of the Southern Indians,
    particularly the Georgia Tribes. New York: Appleton,
    1873.

Jones, Peter. History of the Ojebway Indians: with special
    Reference to their Conversion to Christianity. London:
    Bennett, 1861.

Kate, H. F. C. ten. Reizen en Onderzoekingen in Noord-
    Amerika. Leiden: Brill, 1885 (a).

------. "Die Komantschen." Das Ausland 58 (1885 b): 846-49,
    875-79.

------. "Unter den Apachen." Das Ausland 59 (1886): 152-56,
    171-76, 184-87.

Kirkpatrick, C. S. "Polyandry in the Panjâb." The Indian
    Antiquary 7 (1878): 86-87.

Klutschak, Heinrich W. Als Eskimo unter den Eskimos. Wien:
    A. Hartleben, 1881.

Kohl, Johann Georg. Kitschi-Gami: oder, Erzählungen vom
    Obern See; Ein Beitrag zur Characteristik der Ameri-
    kanischen Indianer. Bremen: Schünemann, 1859.

Kohler, Josef. "Review of Karl Schmidt, Ius Primae Noctis."
    Zeitschrift für vergleichende Rechtswissenschaft 4
    (1883): 279-87.

------. "Das Recht der Chins." Zeitschrift für vergleich-
    ende Rechtswissenschaft 6 (1886): 186-98.

------. "Ueber das Recht der Australneger." Zeitschrift

für vergleichende Rechtswissenschaft 7 (1887 a): 321-

68.

------. "Ueber das Recht der Goajiroindianer." Zeitschrift

für vergleichende Rechtswissenschaft 7 (1887 b): 381-

84.

------. Die Gewohnheitsrechte des Pendschabs." Zeitschrift

für vergleichende Rechtswissenschaft 7 (1887 c): 161-

239.

------. Rechtsvergleichende Studien über islamitisches Recht,

das Recht der Berbern, das chinesische Recht und das

Recht auf Ceylon. Berlin: Heymann, 1889 (a).

------. "Indische Gewohnheitsrechte (1. Bihar, 2. Rajputen,

3. Jainas, 4. Dekkan, 5. Orissa)." Zeitschrift für

vergleichende Rechtswissenschaft 8 (1889 b): 84-147,

262-73.

------. "Frauenkauf und Eigentumsgemeinschaft bei den Es-

kimo Grönlands." Zeitschrift für vergleichende

Rechtswissenschaft 8 (1889 c): 86.

------. "Ueber die Gewohnheitsrechte von Bengalen." Zeit-

schrift für vergleichende Rechtswissenschaft 9 (1891):

321-90.

------. "Die Gewohnheitsrechte der Provenz Bombay." Zeit-

schrift für vergleichende Rechtswissenschaft 10 (1892):

64-142, 161-88.

------. "Ueber das Mutterrecht und Vaterrecht bei malavischen

Stämmen." Das Ausland 66 (1893): 321-25.

------. "Zur Rechtsphilosophie und vergleichenden Rechts-

wissenschaft." Juristisches Litteraturblatt 7 (1895
a): 193-201.

------. Der Ursprung der Melusinensage: Eine ethnologische
Untersuchung. Leipzig: Verlag von Eduard Pfeiffer,
1895 (b).

------. "Ueber das Negerrecht, namentlich in Kamerun."
Zeitschrift für vergleichende Rechtswissenschaft 11
(1895 c): 413-75.

------. "Die Rechte der Urvölker Nordamerikas (nördlich von
Mexiko)." Zeitschrift für vergleichende Rechtswissenschaft 11 (1897 a): 354-416.

------. Zur Urgeschichte der Ehe: Totemismus, Gruppenehe,
Mutterrecht." Zeitschrift für vergleichende Rechtswissenschaft 12 (1897 b): 187-353 [published separate-
ly, Stuttgart: Enke].

Kotzebue, Otto von. Neue Reise um die Welt . . . . Weimar:
Hoffman, 1830.

Krause, Aurel. Die Tlinkit-Indianer. Jena: Costenolde, 1885.

Kubary, Johann. "Die Bewohner der Mortlock-Inseln (Karolinen,
nördlicher Grosser Ocean)." Mittheilungen der Geo-
graphischen Gesellschaft in Hamburg 2 (1878-79): 224-97.

------. "Stammesverhältnisse der Mortloch-Insulaner." Das
Ausland 53 (1880): 524-29.

Lafitau, Joseph François. Moeurs des sauvages americuains,
comparées aux moeurs des premiers temps. 2 vols.
Paris: Saugrain, 1724.

Lahontan, Louis Armand Baron de. Nouveaux voyages . . .
dans l'Americue Septentrionale . . . . 2 vols. Le

Haye: Les Frères l'Honoré.

Langsdorff, Georg Heinrich. Bemerkungen auf einer Reise um
   die Welt . . . . 2 vols. Frankfurt am Mayn: Wilmans,
   1812.

Lawson, John. A new Voyage to Carolina. A New Collection
   of Voyages and Travels, vol. 1, edited by John Stevens.
   London: Knapton, 1711 [first published 1709].

Lewis, Meriwether. History of the Expedition under the
   Command of Lewis and Clark, edited by Elliott Coues.
   4 vols., New York: Harper, 1893]first published 1814].

Long, Stephen H. Narrative of an Expedition to the Source
   of St. Peter's River, etc. 2 vols. Philadelphia:
   Carey & Lea, 1824.

Loskiel, George Henry. Geschichte der Mission der Evangel-
   ischen Brüder unter den Indianern. Leipzig: Kummer,
   1789.

Lyon, G. F. The Private Journal of Captain G. F. Lyon.
   London: Murray, 1824.

Macfie, Matthew. Vancouver Island and British Columbia:
   Their History, Resources, and Prospects. London:
   Longman, Green, etc., 1865.

Mackenzie, Sir Alexander. Voyages from Montreal, on the
   River St. Laurence, through the Continent of North
   America, to the Frozen and Pacific Oceans. London:
   Cadell & Davies, 1801.

Margry, Pierre. Mémoires et documents pour servir à
   l'histoire des origines françaises des pays d'outre-
   mer. 6 vols. Paris: Maisonneuve, 1879-88.

Marquette, Jacques. Récit des voyages et des découvertes
    des P. Jacques Marquette, de la Compagnie de Jésus en
    l'année 1673, et aux suivantes . . . . Historical
    Collections of Louisiana, pt. 4, 1852.

Marshall, William Elliot. A Phrenologist amongst the Todas,
    or, The Study of a Primitive Tribe in South India.
    London: Longman, Green, 1873.

Matthews, M. C. "On the Manners, Customs, Religion, Super-
    stitutions, etc., of the Australian Natives." Journal
    of the Anthropological Institute of Great Britain and
    Ireland 24 (1895): 186-90.

Matthews, Washington. "The Gentile System of the Navajo
    Indians." Journal of American Folk-lore 3 (1890): 89-
    110.

Mayne, John Dawson. A Treatise on Hindu Law and Usage.
    Madras: Higginbotham, 1878.

Mayne, R. C. Four Years in British Columbia and Vancouver
    Island: An Account of their Forests, Rivers, Coasts,
    Gold Fields and Resources for Colonisation. London:
    John Murray, 1862.

Möllhausen, Baldwin. Wanderungen durch die Prärien und
    Wüsten des westlichen Nordamerika . . . . 2d ed.
    Leipzig: Mendelssohn, 1860.

Morgan, Louis Henry. League of the Ho-dé-no-sau-nee, or
    Iroquois. Rochester: Sage, 1851.

------. Systems of Consanguinity and Affinity of the Human
    Family. Smithsonian Contributions to Knowledge, vol.
    17. Washington: Smithsonian Institution, 1870.

------. Ancient Society. New York: Holt, 1877.

------. A Study of the Houses of the American Aborigines.
    First Annual Report of the Archaeological Institute
    of America, 1880.

------. Houses and House-Life of the American Aborigines.
    Contributions to North American Ethnology, vol. 4.
    Washington: Government Printing Office, 1881.

Mucke, Johann Richard. Horde und Familie in ihrer urgeschicht-
    lichen Entwicklung: Eine neue Theorie auf statistischer
    Grundlage. Stuttgart: Enke, 1895.

Murdoch, John. Ethnological Results of the Point Barrow
    Expedition. Ninth Annual Report of the United States
    Bureau of American Ethnology. Washington: Government
    Printing Office, 1892.

Nansen, Fridtjof. Eskimoliv. Kristiania: Aschehoug, 1891.

Nordenskiöld, Nils, and Baron, A. E. Grönland: Seine Eis-
    wüsten im Innern und seine Ostküste. Leipzig: 1886.

Nuttall, Thomas. A Journal of Travels into the Arkansa
    Territory. Philadelphia: Palmer, 1829.

Parkman, Francis. The Jesuits in North America in the
    Seventeenth Century. 11th ed. Boston: Little, Brown
    and Company, 1884.

Peet, Stephen D. "Houses and House-Life among the Prehisto-
    ric Races." American Antiquarian and Oriental Journal
    10 (1999): 333-57.

Pinart, Alph. "Notes sur les Koloches." Bulletins de la
    Société d'Anthropologie de Paris 7 (1872): 788-811.

Poole, Francis. Queen Charlotte Islands: A Narrative of

Discovery and Adventure in the North Pacific, edited
by John W. Lyndon. London: Hurst and Blackett, 1872.

Powell, J. W. *Wyandot Government: A Short Study of Tribal
Society.* First Annual Report of the Bureau of Ameri-
can Ethnology (1879-80). Washington: Government
Printing Office, 1881.

------. *Indian Linguistic Families of America North of
Mexico.* Seventh Annual Report of the United States
Bureau of American Ethnology. Washington: Government
Printing Office, 1885-86.

Powers, Stephen. *Tribes of California.* Contributions to
North American Ethnology, vol. 3. Washington: Government Printing Office, 1877.

Prescott, P. "Contributions to the History, Customs &
Opinions of the Dacota Tribe." In *Information Respecting the History . . . of the Indian Tribes of the
United States*, edited by Henry Rowe Schoolcraft, vols.
2, 3, 4. Philadelphia: Lippincott, Grambo, 1852-54.

Rauber, August Antinous. *Urgeschichte des Menschen: Ein
Handbuch für Studierende.* 2 vols. Leipzig, 1884.

Richardson, Sir John. *Arctic Searching Expedition . . . .*
London: Longman, Green, etc., 1851.

Rink, Hinrich Johannes. *Tales and Traditions of the Eskimo:
With a Sketch of their Habits, Religion, Language and
other Peculiarities*, edited by Robert Brown. Edinburgh: Blackwood, 1875.

Ritter, H. "Land und Leute im russischen Amerika." *Zeitschrift für allgemeine Erdkunde* 13 (1862): 241-70.

Ross, Sir John. Narrative of a Second Voyage in Search of
    a North-west Passage, and of a Residence in the Arctic
    Regions . . . . Philadelphia and Baltimore: Carey &
    Hart, 1835.

Sagard-Théodat, Gabriel. Le grand voyage du pays des Hurons
    . . . , edited by Emile Chevalier. Paris: Tross, 1865
    [first published 1632].

Sarasin, Paul, and Sarasin, Fritz. Die Weddas von Ceylon
    und die sie umgebenden Völkerschaften: Ein Versuch,
    die in der Phylogenie des Menschen ruhenden Räthsel
    der Lösung näher zu bringen. Ergebnisse naturwissen-
    schaftlicher Forschungen auf Ceylon in den Jahren
    1884-86, vol. 3. Wiesbaden: Kreidel's Verlag, 1893.

Schmidt, Karl. Jus Prinae Noctis: Eine geschichtliche
    Untersuchung. Freiburg in Breisgau: Herder'sche Ver-
    lagshandlung, 1881.

Schoolcraft, Henry Rowe. Notes on the Iroquois, or, Con-
    tributions to American History, Antiquities and Gen-
    eral Ethnology. Albany: Pease & Co., 1847.

------. Information Respecting the History, Conditions and
    Prospects of the Indian Tribes of the United States.
    6 vols. Philadelphia: Lippincott, Grambo, 1851-57.

Schürmann, C. W. "The Aboriginal Tribes of Port Lincoln in
    South Australia." In The Native Tribes of South
    Australia, edited by J. D. Woods. Adelaide: Wigg,
    1879.

Stationmaster, Powell's Creek Telegraph Station. "On the
    Habits, etc., of the Aborigines in District of

Powell's Creek, Northern Territory of South Australia."
Journal of the Anthropological Institute of Great
Britain and Ireland 24 (1895): 176-80.

Steinen, Karl von den. Die Bakai'ré-Sprache. Leipzig:
Koehler's Antiquarium, 1892.

Steinmetz, Rudolf S. Endokannibalismus. Vienna: Anthro-
pologische Gesellschaft, 1896.

Strachey, William. The Histoire of Travaile into Virginia
Britannia . . ., edited by R. H. Major. London:
Hakluyt Society, 1849.

Stulpnagel, C. R. "Polyandry in the Himalayas." The Indian Antiquary 7 (1878): 132-35.

Swan, C. "Position and State of Manners and Arts of the
Creek or Muscogee Nation." In Information Respecting
the History . . . of the Indian Tribes of the United
States, edited by Henry Rowe Schoolcraft, vol. 5,
Philadelphia: Lippincott, Grambo, 1855.

Swan, James G. The Indians of Cape Flattery. Smithsonian
Contributions to Knowledge, vol. 16. Washington:
Smithsonian Institution, 1870.

------. The Haidah Indians of Queen Charlotte's Islands,
British Columbia. Smithsonian Contributions to Knowledge, vol. 21. Washington: Smithsonian Institution,
1874.

Tanner, John. A Narrative of the Captivity and Adventures
of John Tanner, edited by Edwin James. New York:
Carvill, 1830.

Taplin, George. "The Narrinveri: An Account of the Tribes

of South Australian Aborigines." In The Native Tribes
of South Australia, edited by J. D. Woods. Adelaide:
Wigg, 1879.

Tylor, Edward B. "The Matriarchal Family System." The
Nineteenth Century 40 (1896): 81-96.

Venegas, Miguel. Noticia de la California, y de su conquista
temporal, y espiritual hasta el tiempo presente. 3
vols. Madrid: Fernandez, 1757.

Virchow, Rudolf. Über die Weddas von Ceylon und ihre
Beziehung zu den Nachbarstämmen. Berlin: Aus den Ab-
handlungen der Königlichen Akademie der Wissenschaften,
1881.

Waitz, Theodor. Anthropologie der Naturvölker, vol. 3.
Leipzig: Fleischer, 1862.

Watson, John Forbes, and Kaye, John William, eds. The
People of India. 8 vols. London: Indian Museum,
1868-75.

Westermarck, Edvard Alexander. The History of Human Marriage.
London: Macmillan and Co., 1891.

Wied-Neuwied, Maximilian Prinz von und zu. Reise in das
innere Nord-Amerika. 2 vols. Coblenz: Hoelscher,
1839-41.

Willshire, W. H. "On the Manners, Customs, Religion,
Superstition, etc., of the Natives of Central Aus-
tralia." Journal of the Anthropological Institute of
Great Britain and Ireland 24 (1895): 183-85.

Woods, J. D., ed. The Native Tribes of South Australia.
Adelaide: Wigg, 1879.

Wrangell, Contre-Admiral von. Statistische und ethno-
     graphische Nachrichten über die Russischen Besitzungen
     an der Nordwestküste von Amerika, edited by K. E. von
     Baer. Beiträge zur Kenntniss des Russischen Reiches
     und der angrenzenden Länder Asiens, edited by K. E.
     von Baer and Graf von Helmersen, vol. 1. St. Peters-
     burg: Verlag der Kaiserlichen Akademie der Wissen-
     schaften, 1839.

Yarrow, H. C. A Further Contribution to the Study of the
     Mortuary Customs of the North American Indians. First
     Annual Report of the Bureau of Ethnology. Washington:
     Government Printing Office, 1879-80.

Index

Lane, Robert and Barbara,
258
Langsdorff, Georg H., 206,
270
Lao-tzu, 5, 20
Lasson, Adolf, 244
Lawson, John, 133, 196, 205,
210, 264
Leach, Edmund R., 37, 251,
261
Lévi-Strauss, Claude, 1, 2,
23, 57-61, 235, 244,
245, 250, 258, 259
Lewis, M., 205, 208, 216,
264
Liebknecht, Karl, 239
Long, John, 22, 245
Long, Stephen H., 112, 135,
206, 207
Loskiel, George H., 108,
133, 207, 215, 264
Lounsbury, Floyd, 65-68,
260, 261
Lowie, Robert, 53-55, 256,
260
Lubbock, Sir John, 26, 246

McKinley, Robert, 58,
60-64, 259, 260
McLennan, John F., 20, 22,
23, 25, 26, 30, 32, 36,
37, 245, 246, 248, 251
Macfie, Matthew, 113, 117
Maine, Sir Henry S., 30,
248
Malinowski, Bronislaw, 37
Mann, Thomas, 8
Margry, Pierre, 215
Marquette, Jacques, 120, 264
Marshall, William E., 212,
213, 219, 267, 269
Mathew, John, 28, 29, 247
Matthews, M. C., 112, 133,
221, 222
Mayne, J. D., 213, 219
Mayne, R. C., 113, 117, 121,
133, 216
Mencken, H. L., 239
Moore, Sally F., 250, 258
Morgan, Lewis Henry, 20,
23-26, 28-30, 32, 36-39,
46, 47, 51, 53, 56,
73-75, 88, 91, 93,
106-9, 111, 112, 116,
117, 119, 133-35, 138,
140, 143, 145-50, 152,

153, 155, 157, 161,
164, 165, 169, 172,
176, 178, 180-83,
185-87, 192, 196-98,
200, 202, 204, 205,
214-16, 234, 245, 246,
255, 256, 262, 263,
265-69, 271
Mucke, Johann R., 69, 75,
91-103, 191, 262, 271
Murdock, George P., 36, 57,
251
Murdock, John, 211, 218, 258

Nansen, Fridtjof, 208, 209,
211, 218
Needham, Rodney, 2, 37, 54,
57, 235, 243, 244,
246-52, 256-58
Nietzsche, Friedrich W., 5,
15, 20
Nind, Scott, 22, 27, 245, 246
Nordenskiöld, Nils, 208, 218
Nuttal, Thomas, 204

Osterrieth, Albert, 8, 11, 12,
237-41

Parkman, Francis, 105, 106,
118, 133, 209, 210,
262, 264
Peet, Stephen D., 216
Petrarch, Francesco, 4, 5
Pinart, Alph., 114
Plato, 9
Poole, Francis, 211
Post, Albert H., 19, 91
Pound, Roscoe, 236
Powell, J. W., 106, 116, 133,
135, 157, 174, 199, 207,
209, 215, 216, 262
Powers, Stephen, 118, 121,
135, 136, 196, 210, 212
Prescott, P., 217

Rabel, E., 12, 236, 238, 241
Radcliffe-Brown, A. R., 55-57,
236, 251, 257, 258
Rauber, August A., 80
Ridley, William, 27
Rink, Hinrich J., 134, 218
Ritter, H., 113, 211
Rivers, W. H. R., 57, 258
Rivière, Peter, 248
Robertson Smith, W., 22
Ross, Sir John, 206